MARTIN LUTHER

THOMAS M. LINDSAY

CHRISTIAN FOCUS

Thomas M. Lindsay was born in 1843 in Lanarkshire, Scotland. He was educated at the Universities of Glasgow and Edinburgh. In 1872 he became Professor of Church History in the Free Church College, Glasgow, where he was later to become Principal. Lindsay was highly regarded as an historian of the Reformation period and he wrote a two-volume *History of the Reformation in Europe*. He died in 1914.

This volume was originally published in 1900 under the title *Luther and the German Reformation*. Only a small amount of editing has been done, and the reader should bear this in mind when the author refers to current events.

This edition published in 1996 by Christian Focus Publications, Geanies House, Fearn, Ross-shire IV20 ITW, Great Britain

© Christian Focus Publications

ISBN 1-85792-261-1

Cover design by Donna Macleod

PREFACE

Although Luther's life has been written scores of times, it has always seemed to me that there is room for another – for one which will be careful to set Luther in the environment of the common social life of his time. For it is often forgotten that the sixteenth century, in which he was the most outstanding figure, saw the beginnings of our present social life in almost everything, from our way of looking at politics and our modes of trade to our underclothing. To show what that life was, and to show Luther in it, would, it seems to me, bring him nearer us than has yet been done.

I do not for a moment pretend that this little book is even a sketch of the Reformer's life written in this way. That needed far more space than was permitted. Yet I have had the thought before me in writing, and for that reason have been careful to make as much use as possible of contemporary evidence.

The book has not been weighted with continual references to authorities. Instead of that a list of a large number of works consulted has been placed in the appendix, and their position there is, I trust, sufficient acknowledgment of the debt owed to them. One set of authorities I have been obliged to omit from this list – the numerous letters, records of conversations, extracts from diaries, all belonging to the times of Luther, which have been printed during the last twenty-five years in such journals as the *Studien und Kritiken*, the *Zeitschrift für die historische Theologie*, etc. The last edition of Köstlin's *Martin Luther: sein Leben und seine Schriften*, with its admirable notes and references, deserves a special mention. No one can write about Luther without acknowledging the debt he owes to it.

Thomas M Lindsay
Glasgow
13th April 1900

CONTENTS

INTRODUCTION

CHAPTER 1

LUTHER'S CHILDHOOD AND EDUCATION, 1483-1505

CHAPTER 2

THE YEARS OF PREPARATION, 1505-1517

INTRODUCTION

The epoch in European History which is called the Reformation may be looked at from many different points of view, but when Luther is taken as the central figure, one – *the religious* – must dominate all the others, and the various intricate intermingled movements must be regarded as the environment of this one central impulse. We are compelled to look on it as the time of a great revival of heart religion – perhaps the greatest which the world has ever seen: whether its magnitude be measured by intensity of religious conviction, by clearness of consecrated vision into those intellectual meanings of spiritual facts, and into those laws of spiritual events which we call dogmatic theology; or by its almost unique effects in fields remote from religious and ecclesiastical life, in the narrower meaning of these words. But this great revival was set in a picturesque framework of human impulses – political, intellectual, moral, social, and economic – such as the world has seldom seen before or since. History, with its warp and woof of 'When' and 'Where', of Time and Place, so wove and interwove all these impulses together that it is both possible and legitimate to describe the Reformation from many different standpoints, all of which are true.

Professor Leopold von Ranke may be taken as the most illustrious example of historians who have taught us to regard the Reformation as a great political force working political transformations not yet ended. It overthrew completely Medievalism, and started the modern conditions of political life on their career. It destroyed the medieval idea of a Christendom made visibly one by a supreme civil governor who ruled over the bodies of all men, by a supreme ecclesiastical chief who ruled their souls, and by a dominant scholastic which kept their minds in due submission, and 'red the marches' between sanctified wisdom and unholy lore. The two and a half centuries before the Reformation are full of revolts against this Medievalism. They saw the birth of modern European nations with conflicting interests, and the strong feelings of independent national life overthrew the medieval ideas of government, both secular and ecclesiastical. The authority of emperor and pope had been defied by almost every European nation long before the times of our epoch; but the failure of Charles V to restore the medieval empire in Germany may be taken as the date at which the old ideas of government passed away for ever.

The Reformation may be regarded as an intellectual movement, and then Erasmus will be its central figure. The siege and pillage of Constantinople by the Ottoman Turks in 1453 had dispersed the scholars of that rich and cultured city over Western Europe. Manuscripts and objects of art, hastily secured by trembling fugitives, sufficed to stock the rest of Christendom, and western nations again began to study the authors of a forgotten classical antiquity. A whole world of new thoughts in poetry, philosophy and statesmanship opened on the vision of the men of the dawn of the Reformation period. In the earlier days of the first Renascence, the 'New Learning' had been confined to a few daring thinkers, but the invention of printing, almost contemporaneous with the second Renascence, made the 'New Learning' common property, and the new thoughts acted on men in masses, and began to move the multitude. The old barriers raised by medieval scholasticism were broken down, and men were brought to see that there was more in religion than the medieval Church had taught, more in social life than the empire had promised, and that knowledge was a manifold unknown to the schoolmen. All this is true, and the Reformation may be studied, though scarcely explained, from this point of view.

Others again point out that the Reformation epoch was 'the modern birth-time of the individual soul' – the beginning of that assertion of the supreme right of individual revolt against every custom, law, or theory which would subordinate the man to the caste or class – a revolt which finally flamed out in the French Revolution. The Swiss peasantry began it when they made pikes by tying their scythes on their alpen-stocks, and, standing shoulder to shoulder at Morgarten and Sempach, broke the fiercest charges of medieval knighthood. They proved that, man for man, the peasant was as good as the noble, and individual manhood, asserted in this rude and bodily fashion, soon began to express itself mentally and morally. The invention of gunpowder and firearms completed what the pike had begun, and medieval knighthood perished when the princes battered down with cannon the strong new fortifications of Landstuhl, and Francis von Sickingen, 'the last of the knights' was slain when in fancied security. This intense individuality was fed by the events of the time. The invention of the mariner's compass, the discovery of America by Columbus, and of the sea route to the East by Vasco de Gama, not only revolutionised trade and commerce, they also fired the imaginations of men. The prevailing character of the thoughts and speech of the period show that men felt that they were on the eve of great events, that it was a time of universal expectation and of widespread individual assertion.

It is not the less true that the epoch was a time of economic revolution which bore heavily on the poorer classes, and scourged them into revolt. Below the whole medieval system lay the idea that land was the only economic basis of wealth; and in the earlier Middle Ages, where each little district produced almost all required for its own wants, and where the economic function of the towns was to be corporations of artisans, exchanging the fruits of their industry for the surplus of farm produce which the peasants brought to their market-places, this was undoubtedly the case. But the increasing commerce of the towns gradually introduced another source of wealth, and this commerce made great strides after the Crusades had opened up the East to European traders. The gradual result of this was to make the lesser nobles and the citizens implacable enemies. The nobles waylaid and pillaged the merchant trains, and the cities formed offensive and defensive leagues, and persuaded the larger territorial magnates to combine with them to secure the peace of the country and keep the roads safe. The combination of princes and cities against the lesser nobility drove the nobles into a position utterly repugnant to their pride. Already thrust from the position of defenders of society by the introduction of infantry and artillery as the most important factors in warfare, they saw themselves distanced by the burghers in the means of living ostentatiously; and while they despised the 'pepper-sacks', as they called the merchants, they felt themselves degraded unless they could vie with them in dress and adornment at the occasions of public display so dear to the medieval mind. Their only mode of direct revenge, to attack the merchant trains of goods or to make their 'horses bite off the purses of travellers', had been made somewhat dangerous by the combinations of princes and towns, and the only remaining thing for them to do was to squeeze their unfortunate peasants. For the peasant was the pariah of medieval society. He stood apart from the noble, burgher, and ecclesiastical power. He was the unprotected class whom all might spoil and whom all did oppress. He had memories transmitted from generation to generation of common lands, of free village communities, and of the inalienable rights of the tillers of the soil; but the introduction of Roman law, primarily and chiefly by ecclesiastical proprietors, which did not recognise these old rights, and looked upon the peasants as serfs, deprived them of the law's protection, and left them no power of resistance save revolt or flight to the towns, where they swelled the class of poorer citizens who remained outside the guild privileges.

The higher commercial opportunities offered by the opening of a sea passage to the East Indies by the discoveries of Vasco de Gama led to a disintegration of the Medieval Town Corporations; for the wealthier merchants formed themselves into trading companies outside the old guilds, and amassed great wealth. A war of classes ensued: the trading companies and capitalists against the guilds, the poorer classes against the wealthier, the peasants against the nobles, and the nobles against the towns and the princes.

This seething discontent was stirred to its depths by sudden and mysterious rises in prices, affecting first the articles of foreign produce, to which all the wealthier classes were greatly addicted, and at last the ordinary necessaries of life. The cause, it is now believed, was not the debasing of the coinage, for that affected a narrow circle only, nor was it the importation of the precious metals from America, for that came later, but the larger output of the mines at home. Whatever the cause, the thing was an irritating mystery, and each class in society was disposed to blame the others for the evil.

We have thus, at the beginning of the epoch, a restless and disturbed state of society, caused by mysterious economic causes which no one understood, but which drove wedges into the old social structure, bereaving it of all power of cohesion.

It was into this mass of seething social discontent that the spark of religious protest fell – the one thing wanted to fire the train and kindle the social conflagration.

With all these sides of the Reformation epoch we have to do only casually. They are the environment of the religious movement of which we must speak when we take Luther as the central figure of the time. Still, we must remember that they are all there; and we should greatly mistake the period to be studied if we thought that the religious protest was everything. All these various movements combine to make the period what it was; and if the religious impulse gave life to the political agitation, moral depth to the intellectual and social impulses, and gave to the economic protests a character that is more medieval than modern, we must remember that these various currents lent their strength to the religious movement and gave it an impetus and an importance which it would not otherwise have had. The Peasants' War as it is called, was the parting of the ways; up to 1525 the Lutheran Reformation absorbed all the various streams of dissatisfaction; after that the revolution and the Reformation pursue separate paths, and the revolution gathered round it the more radical elements of the religious revolt, which are summed up under the word *Anabaptism* – a name which included a great variety of conflicting opinions. Luther had some real connection with all these sides of the great movement of his days.

He had the fullest sympathy with the patriotic aspiration of

Germany for the Germans – it is the central thought in his *Address to the Nobility of the German Nation*; but although disclaiming any place as a politician, he soon came to see that the times were not ripe for a national centralisation, and that centralisation under the rule of the great territorial magnates gave the only hope of the fulfilment of national aspirations.

He never classed himself among the Humanists, but he had very great sympathy with many sides of the Humanist movement; he made full use of the learned labours of Erasmus, and was recognised as a leader by most of the German Humanists; but his absorbing aim was the reformation of the ecclesiastical and religious life, and that to an extent deprecated by some of the more distinguished Humanist leaders.

No man was a more distinguished exponent of the rights of the individual human soul; he stood at Worms another 'Athanasius contra mundum'; but this inalienable right was for him the incapacity to believe incredibilities, to adopt solemn shams, or to live under the rule of religious falsehoods.

He was a peasant's son, and voiced over and over again the wrongs of the class from which he had sprung; but he was 'modern' enough to see that there are two ways by which wrongs can be set right – the way of war and the way of peace – and that the way of peace is the only sure path in the long-run. He held by this firmly, and risked his life among the infuriated peasants as readily as when he stood before the Emperor and the Diet at Worms.

He was a religious reformer first and foremost, and was content to be that and nothing else, and yet his large spiritual personality shared in all the movements and aspirations of his time. Hence it is that among his contemporaries men of such different circles of thought as the Elector Frederic and Franz von Sickingen, Ulric von Hutten and Philip Melanchthon, Hans Sachs and Reuchlin, Albert Durer and Lucas Cranach, believed him to be the greatest man in Germany, and that we, living so many centuries later, may fitly take him as the representative man of his epoch.

CHAPTER 1

LUTHER'S CHILDHOOD AND EDUCATION

1. Birth – Parents

The little town of Eisleben, with its narrow streets and high-roofed, red-tiled houses, climbs slowly up the side of one of the great billowy plains which are the feature of this centre of the German Fatherland. All round it lie signs of the copper and silver mines – tall chimneys, heaps of refuse, and great holes and rifts in the sides of the slopes. The miners throng the town, a short, sturdy race, with curious rolling gait. At one end of a narrow street, 'at a meeting of three streets, with a little bit of garden beside it, as became the place they say it was – an *inn* – stands the house where Luther was born. Over the door is a head of him in stone, with

'Christi Wort ist Luther's Lehr,
Drum vergeht sie nimmermehr'

('Christ's own word is Luther's lore,
So it lives for evermore')

carved round it. You enter the first room to the left, and stand where he was born. It is a largish room – day and night room it was, one would think, in the inn-time. You can fancy the quiet thankful mother, with the grave face, high cheekbones, and full mouth, lying there and listening, as she told Melanchthon she did, while the clock strikes twelve, when all was over, and laying the very hour up, with many other things about this babe, in her heart with faith and prayer. You can fancy the firmly-set undersized man, with the piercing eyes and fine, decided lips, sitting by the fire, vowing that if head can plan and hands can labour, this lad of his shall be spared the grinding toil he has known, shall enjoy the splendid advantages he has missed, shall be a great man and a scholar. Next morning you see Frau Wirthin and him going up the narrow 'Gasse' to St Peter's, much enjoined and directed by the anxious Margarethe, carrying the little stranger to get his name and blessing from the saint of the day, Martinus.'[1]

Hans and Margarethe Luther had come from Mohra (Muirtown), a little peasant township lying in the north-west corner of the Thüringen Wald, and a few miles to the south of Eisenach.

This was the original home of the Luther family; old records tell us that a very large number of the inhabitants bore that name; there are still several families of Luthers in the village, and the distinctive Luther features are still observable. Luther himself now stands in bronze in the village square, near the ancient well, opening the Bible to his fellow-villagers. On the front is carved 'Unserm Luther in seinem Stammort.' The old traditional family house stands opposite, doubtless much patched during the centuries, but with the old walls green with rose-bushes and other climbing plants.

It was the custom in these old days among the Thuringian peasants that only one son, and that generally the youngest, remained to inherit the family house and croft. The others went out into the world furnished with something from the family saving-box. The mining industry, away northwards in the Mansfeld region, attracted these Mohra peasants, and Hans and Margarethe Luther only followed a common custom when they left the old village and sought a new abiding place for the family that was to come among the mines of Eisleben and Mansfeld. This was why the mother-pangs came on Margarethe Luther on that bleak 10th of November in 1483, so far away from kith and kin.

Six months after the birth of his eldest son, Hans Luther settled in the village of Mansfeld, a miner and then a smelter of copper ore. The Counts of Mansfeld, who owned all the region, and who had many years before started the mining industry, had the habit of building small furnaces for smelting the ore, and of letting them out

---

[1] *Letters from the Land of Luther*, by Robert Barbour.

on lease to miners who desired to better their condition, and who were trustworthy persons. Hans Luther soon leased one and then three of these furnaces. He early won the respect of his neighbours, for he became in 1491 one of the four members of the village council.

The family life, however, in the earlier years was one of grinding poverty, and Luther himself often recalls the struggles of father and mother. Of his mother he says that he has often seen her carrying the wood for the family fire, gathered in the pine forest, on her own shoulders. It was a hard struggle to find food and clothing for the seven children, to provide for the education of the eldest, to pay the yearly rent of the furnace, to lay by in the family strong-box the money to be afterwards spent on the 'plenishing' when the young burghers, Kaufmann, Polner, and Mackenrod carried off the three daughters to new homes.

Luther's home-life should be lingered over, for it was the making of him, and the ideal he had before him in his famous days had its birth in the family house at Mansfeld. The old home can still be seen, with its double square windows, its solid substantial walls, and, inside, its window seats, where Mother Margarethe could watch her seven young ones going to school or playing in the street.

Father and mother were both spare, short, and dark-complexioned (*braunlicht*), says the Swiss Kessler; the father of good plain peasant stock. 'I am a peasant's son,' said Luther; 'my father, grandfather, and great-grandfather were all genuine peasants.' The mother, Margarethe Ziegler, came of the burgher class, for Hans Luther had married above his rank. Luther always mentions his father with great reverence; he recalls how he had pinched himself in his poverty to give him an education; how he owed it all to him, both birth and upbringing. The old man used to thank God that He had made him tough in body and in soul; a man of clear understanding, and not afraid to contradict – two qualities which the Augustinian monks observed in the son when they sent him up to Rome on the business of the Order – mostly silent, but with a gift of pregnant, pithy expression, a gift which the son inherited. He was a man of quiet, deep piety, but one who thought that God could be best served in the common citizen's life, and who heartily despised monks, men 'full of cant and hypocrisy,' he said. He had a strong sense of parental rights, and was a hard disciplinarian.

Luther was specially his mother's child. Spalatin has recorded that when he saw her first he was struck with the strong likeness of son to mother in face and build of body. He got from her, besides his mysticism, those strange streaks of superstition which characterised him, the vein of poetry which ran through him, his wit, his love of hymns and of proverbial sayings. Melanchthon was devoted to the mother, and we can fancy the two talking about the famous son when the friend, in quest of biographical notes, spent some days in the old family house at Mansfeld. She could tell him the day on which Martin was born, and the hour, for she remembered lying in bed and counting the minutes till the clock struck twelve, but she could not be sure of the year, and the biographer had to content himself with brother James' statement that the family had always believed that Martin was born in 1483. Melanchthon calls her a model of all womanly worth, and says that she was noted for chastity, reverence for God, and prayer. The parents taught their children the Ten Commandments, the Creed, and the Lord's Prayer – the teaching which Luther afterwards made possible for all German children by his Catechism. They taught them that pardon comes from the free grace of God. The truth which Luther afterwards preached to all men he learned in the home circle at Mansfeld, adding nothing essential. This evangelical faith and teaching was set – and quite naturally it seemed then – in the framework of the usages of the medieval Church. St George was the patron saint of the Mansfeld miners, and St Anna was their beloved protectress. Her name was on the church bells, and every pull at the ropes in the belfry was an invocation.

It is in such families we are to see the roots of the great Reformation which was on the eve of coming. The spiritual forebears of the Reformation leaders are not to be sought in dubious Waldenses or in still more questionable Albigenses, but in pious Christians like

Hans and Margarethe Luther, who taught the boy within the family circle the evangelical truths he was afterwards to thunder forth from the Wittenburg pulpit. For if we look into the matter, the Reformation did not bring to light many truths which were absolutely unknown in the medieval Church. The spiritual life of the medieval Christian was fed on the same divine thoughts which are the basis of Reformation theology. They can scarcely be found, however, in the volumes of medieval theologians. They are embedded in the hymns and in the prayers of the Church of the Middle Ages, sometimes in the sermons of her great revivalist preachers, always in the quiet parental instruction in pious homes. These truths are all there, as poetic thoughts, earnest supplication and confession, fervent exhortation, or motherly teaching. When the medieval Christian knelt in prayer, stood to sing his Redeemer's praises, spoke as a dying man to dying men, or as a mother to the children about her knees, the words and thoughts that came were what Luther and Zwingli and Calvin wove into Reformation creeds and expanded in Reformation sermons. This Reformation which Luther led was the outcome of the old family piety which had flowered during all the previous centuries, heedless of the fact that it had much in it which had little in common with the ecclesiastical system and professional theology which it accepted without question. The Mansfeld home made Luther what he became, its teaching was the seed of his theology; and from the thousands of homes like his the great Reformation sprang.

2. Peasant Life

Luther came from the peasants of Germany. The German peasant life in the end of the fifteenth and beginning of the sixteenth centuries surrounded Luther in his childhood. Few have cared to study it. Yet from rescued collections of laws governing the peasant communes (the *Weisthümer*), from stray folk-songs and *Fassnachtspiele*, from a few references in chroniclers, and from the old engravings of the time, we can, in part at least, reconstruct the old peasant life and its surroundings. Only it must be remembered that the life differed, not only in different parts of Germany, but in the same districts and decades under different proprietors; for the German peasant was so dependent on his over-lord that the character of the proprietor counted for much in the condition of the people.

The larger hamlets were usually surrounded by a stout fence, made with strong stakes and interlaced branches, and having gates; and within this stood, almost always among the houses, a small church, a public-house, a house or a room where the village council met and where justice was dispensed, and near it always the 'stocks' and sometimes a gallows. The houses were wooden frames, filled in with sun-dried bricks; cattle, fodder, and the family were sheltered under the one large roof. The timber for building and repairs was got from the forest under regulations set down in the *Weisthümer*, and the peasants had leave to collect the fallen branches for firewood, the women collecting and carrying and the men cutting and stacking under the eaves. All breaches of the forest laws were severely punished; so were the moving of landmarks – for wood and soil were precious. Most houses had small gardens, in which grew cabbages, lettuces, parsley and peas, poppies and hemp, apples, cherries and plums, as well as other things whose medieval German names are not translatable by me.

There might have been a rude plenty in their lives had it not been for the endless exactions of many of their lords and the continual robberies to which they were exposed from bands of sturdy rogues which swarmed through the country, and from companies of soldiers who thought nothing of carrying off the peasant's cows, slaying his swine, and even firing his house. They had their diversions, none too seemly. They clung to the festivals of the Church as holidays, which they spent eating and drinking at the public-house, and dancing in front of it. Hans Sachs makes us see the scene. The girls and the pipers waiting at the dancing-place, and the men and lads in the public-house, eating calf's head, tripe, liver, black puddings and roast pork, and drinking sour milk and the country wine, till some sank under their benches, and there was such a jostling, scratching, shoving, bawling, and singing that not a word could be heard. Then three young men came to the dancing-place; his sweetheart had a garland ready for one of them, and the dancing began; other couples joined, and at last sixteen pairs of feet were in motion. Rough jests, gestures, and caresses went round. The men whirled their partners off their feet, and spun them round and round, or seized them by the waist, and tossed them as high as they could; while they themselves leapt and threw out their feet, till Hans Sachs thought they would all fall down. The scenes were even coarser at the night-dances, which often followed the labours and jokes of the spinning house. For it was the custom in most German villages that the young women resorted to a large room in the mill or in the village public-house, and brought their wool, their distaffs and spindles, some of them old heirlooms and richly ornamented, to spin all evening. The lads came too, for the ostensible purpose of picking the fluff off the lasses' clothes, or holding the small beaker of water into which they dipped their fingers as they spun. On festival evenings, and especially at carnival time, the lads treated their sweethearts to a late supper and dance, and went home with them, carrying their distaffs and spindles. All the old German love folk-songs are full of allusions to this peasant courtship.

Such were the toilsome, lewd, grimy surroundings of that peasant life out of which Luther came; and they must be taken into account when we read of the harsh training and severe family life of which Luther and some other reformers who came from the peasant class had painful recollections. Pious parents of this class – and there must have been thousands of them – felt that they could scarcely be too severe in order to keep their children unstained by the evil life abounding all round them. The more deeply one studies the social life of the times, and especially of that stratum of the people whence Luther sprang, the more one can see how very much Luther owed to the wise severity of his parents. It must be remembered also that those peasant people were grossly superstitious, and that many of their most reprehensible social usages were the inheritance of the old pagan times, many a trace of which remained uneffaced by the teachings of the medieval Church. The peasants came to the little village churches on the forenoons of the Sundays and festival days, but their everyday worship consisted of small offerings to kobolds and sprites of all kinds – each variety excelling the others in the power of working mischief on poultry, swine, cattle, crops, and the bodies of men and women, and therefore needing to be propitiated. For the position of the Christian Church in medieval Germany was, as some one has said, not unlike that of settlers in a virgin country. Little clearances had been made and homesteads built, but the great, dark, unsubdued forest, full of ferocious beasts and creeping things, remained enclosing and threatening.

3. Education – Schools – University

Young Martin Luther was sent to school at Mansfeld; for Mansfeld, small mining town as it was, had its school. Germany in the fifteenth and the beginning of the sixteenth centuries was well provided with schools of a kind. Most of the small parish priests belonged to the peasant class, and the singing in the service in the parish churches had to be done by the village boys; and as the services were in Latin, education was needed for priests and choristers. Everywhere over Europe the 'song-schools' for the boys of the parish choir had become schools for the children of the village or small town.

The education given was not very good, and the method of imparting it still worse. The children were taught to read and to write and to do a little ciphering; and they were also drilled in the Latin declensions and conjugations. From the old engravings of Burgmaier and others we can see what the schools were like. A small bare room, with a large box-like desk, in which the master sat, with birch in one hand and the other upon a book; the children sitting below him on the floor, and holding out their hands when they thought that they could answer his questions. Books were scarce; the master himself well furnished if he had an old copy of

Donatus' Grammar and a Terence, or a bit of Cicero; the younger scholars had small blackboards on which they learned to make letters and sentences; the older ones carried an inkhorn, a long case for pens, and a satchel. The schoolmasters were a poor set of creatures, and their scholars experienced more of the pains than of the pleasures of learning. Luther said that his master treated the boys as the public executioner did thieves; he himself was flogged fifteen times one morning because he could not repeat declensions which he had never been taught. John Butzbach says that his school-master was continually flogging the boys, and that when one was being scourged, the others had to stand round and sing a hymn.

The country schools did not satisfy the craving for education which displayed itself all over Europe in those days. It laid hold on the burgher class especially; and the townspeople of many a German city founded superior high schools, and paid scholars out of the city revenues to be teachers and rectors. Many of the German towns entered into a generous rivalry in the matter of education, and had several high schools. Breslau, that 'paradise of students' as it was called, had no less than seven. Such towns attracted students from great distances, and the town's authorities built student hostels, where the strangers found shelter and sometimes firing, but seldom food. The townspeople in many cases added a students' hospital for those who fell sick. All these possibilities of learning attracted great numbers of boys and young men from all parts of Germany and Switzerland, and added a new class to the vagrants who thronged the roads of Germany during the later Middle Ages. The wandering student was a feature – and not always a reputable one – during the epoch. Children of ten and eleven years of age left their country villages in charge of an older student, and set off to join some famous high school; but these older students were often nothing but vagrants, with just enough of learning to impose on the simple peasantry, from whom they took gifts for charms against toothache or other troubles, or begged or stole. The small unfortunates entrusted to their charge were treated in the cruellest fashion, and often died by the roadside. We have two or three autobiographies written by 'wandering students' of which the most interesting is that of Thomas Platter, from which Freytag has made long extracts; another is by Johann Butzbach; both cover the period of Luther's student time.

Thomas Platter was born in the Valais in Switzerland. He wished to go to school and college in order to become a priest. When he was in doubt what to do, a cousin of his, who had been at Ulm and Munich, returned to spend a few days in his native valley, and offered to take charge of Platter. The child had not gone far when he discovered that cousin Paulus was a merciless tyrant, who had got possession of the boy to make him beg for him on the road and in the towns. He treated him very cruelly. When the poor boy could not keep up with the older lads – for the two were soon joined by other *bacchantes* with their *scutones* (for so the older and the younger scholars were called) – 'my cousin Paulus came behind me with a rod, or little stick, and switched me on my bare legs, for I had no stockings and very bad shoes.' Platter wandered over a great part of Germany with this ruffian, and could not escape from his clutches, although he tried hard to get away more than once. He was a small boy, with a fair, pitiful face, and made a capital beggar, bringing in more food than the others did, and was thus a valuable property. The elders made the small boys steal fowls and all kinds of vegetables. They did not care to carry cooking utensils with them on their journeys, and stole an iron pot for their evening meal. When they camped, the older students generally sought out some quiet spot near a small stream; the big fellows lopped off branches, made a hut, and kindled a fire. The fowls brought in by the youngsters were plucked, and their legs, heads, and giblets were thrown into the pot with shred vegetables, and the flesh was roasted on wooden spits. They supped the stew with the spoons they carried in their belts, and they ate the roast when it became brown, along with sliced turnips.

Platter spent a long time in Breslau; but his tyrant did not allow him to study much, if at all. He tells us that Breslau was divided into seven parishes, each with its high school, and that each scholar

could beg only within the parish of the school to which he belonged; if an unfortunate youth got beyond the bounds of his school
parish, he found himself among enemies, who, crying 'ad idem, ad
idem' rushed at him, flinging stones and beating him. He spent
most of the morning in begging for food, and the people were very
kind to him, he says, 'because he was so small and was a Swiss;
for the Breslauers were very fond of the Swiss'; and he often
brought to his *bacchant* enough for six meals. In the evenings he
went round the public-houses and begged and sang for beer, and
they gave him so much that the poor boy was often the worse for
it. He fell ill at Breslau, and was taken to the students' hospital,
where he had a good doctor, and was well nursed in a good bed,
but the vermin were so many and so large that he wished he were
out of it.

The wandering student occurs frequently in the *Fastnachtspiele*,
or popular comedies of the carnival time, and he is always a beggar, and generally a rogue. It is not to be wondered at that Luther,
with his memory full of those wandering students, denounced the
system in which men spent twenty, even forty, years in student
life, and in the end knew neither Latin nor German, 'to say nothing
of the shameful and vicious life by which our worthy youth have
been so miserably corrupted.'

Luther's parents looked after him too well to allow him to go
off with one of the wandering *bacchants*; but as they were not
fortunate enough to live in a town which possessed a high school,
they selected Magdeburg, perhaps because it contained an institution founded by the disciples of Gerard Groot, the great Flemish
educationalist, in whose schools so many of the great men of the
fifteenth century were trained. We know little or nothing about his
life there. He fell ill of fever, and was at death's door. He saw two
things which made his whole religious sensibilities tingle, and which
he never forgot – one, a prince of Anhalt, who for his soul's safety
had become a barefooted friar, carried the begging sack on his bent
shoulders through the town, and was worn to skin and bones by
his fastings, scourgings and prayers; and the other, an altar-piece in

a church, the picture of a ship, 'wherein was no layman, not even a king nor a prince; there were none but the pope, with his cardinal and bishops, at the prow, with the Holy Ghost hovering over them, the priests and the monks with their oars by the sides; and thus they went sailing heavenward. The laymen were swimming along in the water around the ship. Some of them were drowning, some were drawing themselves up to the ship by ropes which the monks, moved by pity and making over their own good works, cast out to them, to keep them from drowning, and to enable them to cleave to the vessel and go with it to heaven. There was no cardinal nor bishop nor monk nor priest in the water, but laymen only.' Those two visions sank deeply into his heart. That is about all we know of Luther at Magdeburg.

The following year the boy was sent to Eisenach to the high school in the parish of St George. His fever at Magdeburg had doubtless alarmed the mother, and as she had relations in Eisenach, which lay near the Luther home of Möhra, she thought her delicate lad would be better looked after. We do not hear that Luther lived with any of these relations. He probably got a share of a room at the scholars' hostel, and, like other poor students, he sang in the streets, begging for bread. Luther tells us about it in his 'Sermon on the Duty of Sending Children to School.' 'Do not,' he says, 'despise the boys who beg from door to door, saying, "A little bread for the love of God"; and when groups of poor people sing before your house, think that ye hear great princes and lords. I myself have been such a beggar pupil, and have sung for bread before houses, especially in the dear town of Eisenach, though afterwards my beloved father supported me at the University of Erfurt, with all love and self-sacrifice, and by the sweat of his brow helped me to the position which I now occupy. Still for a time I was a "poverty student," and I have risen by the pen to a position which I would not exchange for that of the Sultan of Turkey, taking his wealth and giving up my learning.'

The little town of Eisenach lies in a valley, surrounded then, as now, with rich woods, and above the closely packed peaked-roofed houses rises the hill, crowned by the Wartburg, where St Elizabeth of Hungary, the holy Landgravine of Thuringen, spent the happier part of her life, and where Luther, three hundred years afterwards, was to be sent for safety. The boys of the high school, the small Luther among them, sang in the choir of St George's Church, and a great part of the interior remains still as it was in his days. It was in Eisenach that, according to Mathesius, the poor boy, begging and singing, attracted the attention of a lady of gentle birth, and that she and her husband took him into their house and made him one of the family. Historians make out that she was Frau Cotta, and belonged to a noble burgher family. Luther never names her; but he refers often to his dear *wirthin* in Eisenach, and he more than once quotes sayings of hers. Once, in his *Commentary on the Book of Proverbs*, xxx.10, he quotes her, saying, 'There is nothing on earth more lovely than the love of husband and wife when it is in the fear of the Lord.' The entrance into this family must have opened a new world to Luther. It was a richer life than was possible in his hard peasant home, and full of fine human feelings. It was probably the best part of his education in Eisenach. Yet the master of the St George's high school was a distinguished man. He was that Trebonius who never entered his classroom without bowing to his pupils, unkempt lads as most of them must have been, because he used to say, 'Future burgomasters, chancellors, doctors, and magistrates are among those boys.'

We have some few indications of the lad's quiet, pious tendencies while at Eisenach. The whole religious feeling of the town was under the spell of the holy Elizabeth; the place contained no less than nine monasteries and nunneries, many of them dating back to the times of the pious Landgravine, and some of them devoted to that practical charity which was her ruling characteristic.

Who knows what thoughts went through the mind of the boy as he gazed on the picture, over the altar in St George's Church, of the holy Landgravine who had given up family life and children to earn a medieval saintship, and saw the setting sun blazon her good deeds painted on the glass windows? Was it not enough to lead him, with his poetic imagination and his brooding mysticism and melancholy, away from the hard homely piety of his peasant parents, and from the more cultured family religion of his new friends in Eisenach, to that convent life for which Elizabeth had, three hundred years before, given up so much? We can fancy him, with that reverence for noble womanhood which has always lain deep in the heart of the best type of German boy and man, seeing in the holy Elizabeth a glorified Mother Luther and Frau Cotta. But if such thoughts came, they were only precious secrets, not to be revealed to anyone; and, so far as his outside life was concerned, he was still the obedient son, advancing in school and college towards the trained lawyer which his father destined him to become.

When school-days were over, Luther was sent by his father to the University of Erfurt. A measure of prosperity was crowning the hard labours of Hans and Margarethe Luther, and they could now pay for their boy's support when he was away from home. Luther quitted the ranks of the 'poor students,' and was able to give his whole time to his studies.

The old tile-roofed town has not altered much since Luther came to it in the summer of 1501, and entered his name in the university album in letters which can still be read, 'Martinus Ludher ex Mansfelt'; the Gera still crosses and recrosses the streets, and goes round the old fortifications; and there is still the careful cultivation which won the old name, 'The Kitchen Garden Town'.

The university was one of the oldest in Germany, and, when Luther entered it, the most renowned. 'He who would study well must go to Erfurt,' was a common saying. The great man of the place was Johan Trudwetter, the 'Erfurt Doctor,' whose fame and genius, all good Germans thought, had made Erfurt as well known as Paris. The teaching and course of study was thoroughly medieval, but on what was esteemed to be the advanced side of medieval thought. The faculty of philosophy prepared the way for the study of law and theology; it began with logic, and went through dialectic, rhetoric and music, to physics, astronomy, etc. The commentators followed belonged to the Nominalist School, and Luther learned there to call William of Occam his 'dear master'. Humanism had found entrance before Luther matriculated, and lectures on the purely classical authors had become part of the faculty of philosophy. The new Humanism did not attack the older course of study, openly at least, at Erfurt. The young Humanists affected to be poets, wrote Latin verses sometimes in praise of their older colleagues, and were content to veil their eclectic theosophy from their gaze. Their leaders, Mutianus and Crotus, delighted to reveal to a band of admiring, half-terrified juveniles that there was but one God and one Goddess, taking the various names Jupiter, Mars, Jesus, and Juno, Diana, Mary; but those things were not supposed to go further than the walls of the room. In short, the Humanists affected to make a select and secret society, writing Latin verses to each other, and corresponding after the manner of the ancients. Spalatin, afterwards court preacher to the Elector of Saxony, and one of Luther's warmest friends, belonged to this select circle.

As for Luther himself, we have no very clear account of what he did and how he fared in the university town. We have to piece together a picture of his student-life from references in correspondence, recollections of his fellow-students, and scattered sayings of his own in after-life. They all reveal a self-contained young man, resolved to profit to the uttermost by the advantages of the place for acquiring knowledge, and so to justify the self-sacrifices of his parents. He worked hard at the prescribed studies, and though he did not care much for the medieval course, he was quick to see what was its real use. '*Dialectic* speaks simply, straightforward, and plainly, as when I say, "Give me something to drink." But *rhetoric* adorns the matter, saying, "Give me of the acceptable juice in the cellar, which finely froths and makes people merry." *Dialectic* declares a thing distinctly and significantly in brief words. *Rhetoric* counsels and advises, persuades and dissuades; she has her place and fountainhead, whence a thing is taken; as this is good, honest, profitable, easy, necessary, etc. These two arts St Paul briefly taught when he says, "That he may be able by sound doctrine, both to exhort and to convince gainsayers."'

He took much more delight in the classical studies, but not in the genuine Humanist fashion. He cared much more for the thoughts than for the language, and delighted in the glimpses of the new world which the classical writers revealed to him. But when he found that those studies were drawing him away from his prescribed tasks, he had sufficient mastery over his desires to curb his classical tastes. He had a very modest estimate of his powers as a Latinist. He called himself a 'peasant Corydon,' and thought that his speech was too rough for him to excel as a fine writer; and it is almost amusing to note how careful he is to try, not always successfully, to write a finer latinity than usual when he corresponds with his Humanist friends. Upon the whole, one gets the idea of a very level-headed man, with a strong sense of the practical side of his studies, respected by his professors, and refusing to be carried away into any excess of Humanism on the one hand, or of sensuality on the other. He did not look back with any great delight to his student-days at Erfurt; perhaps he thought that he had been forced to spend too much time on useless studies; perhaps he was undergoing, almost unconsciously, the inward struggles which were soon to become only too apparent to himself.

The singular thing is that we know very little about the inner religious life of Luther during those student-years. No great man has ever made himself so well known as Luther afterwards did. His correspondence, his sermons, his commentaries, and all his books reveal the man himself, and are full of little autobiographical details; but all that comes after the great conflict had been fought and won. His inner life during his student-days is a sealed book for us. There was unrest, there was an inward war – there must have been; but it is revealed in one or two exclamations only, and we can scarcely be sure that those discover it. It would almost appear that during the later years of his stay at the university, Luther was leading a double life. In the one he was the bright, hard-working, practical student, taking his various degrees in an unexpectedly short time – his bachelor's degree in October 1502 and his master's in 1505, when he stood second among seventeen successful candidates. Melanchthon tells us that his conspicuous ability had become the wonder of the whole university. The other life was that inward hidden struggle which he seems to have been only half-conscious of, and to which he can scarcely be said to have referred to in after-life.

He had finished, and with almost unique distinction, his Arts course, and was about to begin the study of law, when he suddenly plunged into the Erfurt Convent. So sudden and unexpected was the plunge that his friends felt bound to account for it somehow; and their interjectional explanations have been woven into later legends. There seems to be little doubt that he had a severe illness at the close of the philosophy course; and this, it is said, brought him to the decision. An old tradition, which there is no reason to disbelieve, states that on July 2, 1505, fourteen days before he entered the convent, he was returning from a visit to his parents, and had already reached the village of Stotterheim, close to Erfurt, when he suddenly found himself in a great thunderstorm, and that in fear he cried out, 'Help me, St Anna, and I will become a monk'; and this, it is said, was the crisis. His friend Crotus has declared that he believed that Luther was as suddenly called to enter the convent as Saul was called on the Damascus road. There is also the statement he made to his father, that he was called by a voice from heaven; the assertion of Mathesius and Melanchthon that he had suddenly lost by death a dear friend; and the fact that he entered the convent on St Alexius day. A later tradition has woven all these separate things into the well-known story of the journey with Alexius, the thunderstorm, Alexius struck dead by lightning, the voice which sounded in Luther's ears, 'What shall it profit a man if he gain the whole world and lose his own soul?' But this is later tradition. We have no certain account of the conflict of soul which ended in the sudden resolve (Luther himself tells us that it was sudden) to save his soul within the quiet of the cloister walls.

CHAPTER 2

THE YEARS F PREPARATION

1. In the Convent

Luther had entered the convent. He had floated down the stream of school-day and student life, feeling, almost imperceptibly, eddies and currents, and now they had swept him to the sea, and there was no jumping ashore. He had gone to the convent of the Augustinian monks. The prior had put the usual question, 'What seekest thou, my son?' and Luther had made the well-known answer, 'I seek the mercy of God and your fellowship.' He had been received; he had donned the novice's garb; and for one whole year – a year to be spent in learning what lay before him as a monk – he was invisible to the world beyond the convent gate. The grief in the old home at Mansfeld can scarcely be described. Was it for this that Margarethe had borne the mother-pangs so far away from all kith and kin, and had bent her poor back to gather and carry sticks for the cottage fire? Was it for this that the father had pinched and saved, and denied himself and his all manner of small comforts, that his boy should become a great lawyer and be the making of them all? To become a monk, to add one to the overflowing crowd of 'rogues and hypocrites', as the sturdy old peasant called them?

Meanwhile the young novice was learning how to become a monk. He was to live under rules and usages which regulated every hour of his life – rules which exhausted the whole religious life in certain definite and prescribed forms. He had to spend so many hours of the day and the night in hearing the chanting of the services, in prayers recited standing, in hearing masses said, in fasting. He had to learn the minutiae of all these services – how he was to stand or sit or kneel, how he was to move his feet and his hands and his head in the different parts of the service. When he had been thus drilled for a year he was supposed to be fit for reception into the Order. The day came at last. The church of the Augustinians was crowded with townspeople and students from the university. After the usual services the novice Martin, kneeling down before the prior, Wienand of Diedenhofen, made the irrevocable vow: 'I, Brother Martin, do make profession and promise obedience unto Almighty God, unto Mary the Virgin, and unto thee, my brother, Prior of this cloister, in the name and stead of the General Prior of the Eremites of St Augustine until death.' He was robed in the black frock and hood of his Order, the long white scapulary or scarf was thrown over him, and hung down before and behind, a lighted taper was placed in his hands, to signify the newly-enlightened conscience; the prior whispered the prayer over him kneeling, the choir sang the 'Veni Creator Spiritus'; he was led up the altar steps, the monks welcomed him with the kiss of peace, and in their midst he slowly marched behind the screen – no longer a man in the world, but a monk in the cloister. Many an old student friend, and some of his former professors, watched the black-robed figure slowly disappear behind the convent door and went home to curse the monks who had robbed the university of its most distinguished student, and the world of one who was expected to play a great part in it.

What made him do it? What made so many noble men and women, all down the stream of medieval history, think that it was not possible to serve God to the uttermost except inside the walls of a convent, unless they abandoned family, friends, and life for others and among others in the world which Christ came to save?

To answer this question involves the history of the practical piety of the pre-medieval and medieval Church, the history of the old penitential services, the history and growth of asceticism, and many kindred subjects. The more one studies the whole subject, the more the conviction comes that there was scarcely one single act in the long interwoven series but had in its due time and place some salutary use, and which was not the genuine outcome of an honest human soul striving to humble itself before God in an agony of genuine sense of sin. The evil came when spontaneous acts of repentance and honest endeavour after new obedience became stereotyped customs, then prescribed regulations, and lost all the bloom of fresh and spontaneous action. But however the delusion arose, that the best way to serve God was to abandon home and family and the world for which Christ died, Luther had it. Two pictures had taken hold of his childish mind at Magdeburg: the one was the sight of the young prince of Anhalt, who, to save his soul, had become a bare-footed friar, and the other, the altar-piece in a church at Magdeburg (page 26). Pictures like these might well efface the pious teaching of father and mother; and when intense conviction of sin came, and the consequent dissatisfaction with his surroundings, we easily conceive how the young man surrendered himself to the thought that he had to get rid of everything to which he was accustomed ere he could be in a position to find the salvation he longed for. At all events he went into the convent in good faith, and for years, till he was in the midst of the controversy about Indulgences, he was thoroughly persuaded that he had done the only thing he could do, and was perfectly sure of his vocation to be a monk. He threw himself with ardour into the new conventual life; he went through all the observances he had been taught with careful assiduity. He practised obedience, he fasted, he prayed, he kept his body under with scourging and want of sleep. He once at least spent three whole days without eating or drinking; he was once missed from the services, and was found fainting on the floor of his cell. 'If ever a monk could win heaven by monkery, I must have reached it,' said Luther long afterwards. Yet he felt no nearer God; he had no sense of pardon, no feeling of the upspringing of a new spiritual life.

The prior of the Augustinians, John Staupitz, was a wise and large-hearted man. He had the root of evangelical faith in him, just as Luther's father and mother had. In after years he sympathised with most of Luther's doctrines, and yet he never left the Roman Catholic Church. Such a man was resolved to make the best of the monastic life which he shared, and to do the best for the monks under his charge. He insisted that every monk who was fit for it should read theology, and every convent was provided with a Latin Bible, which the monks were instructed to study. Luther tells us how the monks showed him the great Bible, bound in red leather, and how the first thing he read was the story of Hannah and Samuel, and how it made him think of his mother and himself. He was set to study the scholastic theology; he tells us how he read and read till he could repeat from memory the great folios of William of Occam; how he pored over the works of John Gerson and Bonaventura and Dionysius. He spoke slightingly of these studies in after years. Yet he knew that the study did him good, though not in the way he most longed for. 'I still keep those books which tormented me,' he said. 'Scotus wrote very well on the Master of the Sentences, and diligently essayed to teach upon these matters. Occam was an able and sensible man.' Occam made him know the fallibility of popes, and Gerson showed him the ecclesiastical value of General Councils.

The study of the Bible did not bring him much consolation at first. In the mood of mind in which he was, the passages which spoke of the jealous and righteous God, the God who punishes sin, burned themselves into him. The slightest unconscious deviation from the minutest conventual regulation of posture or position of hands or feet was a sin which tortured him. Staupitz told him almost roughly once to cease confessing till he had some real sin to confess. An aged monk asked him to recite the Creed, and made him stop when he came to the clause, 'I believe in the forgiveness of sin.' 'Do you believe that?' he said. 'Then put the word "my" in; say "I believe in the forgiveness of *my* sins."' Pardon comes in the appropriation of the promise. That comforted the storm-tossed soul, but only for a moment. Then came the thought; pardon follows contrition, confession and penance; how can I know that my contrition has gone deep enough? How can I be sure that my confession has included every sinful thought, word and deed? Then followed again the old weary round of torturing self-examination.

It was the thought of the 'righteousness of God' which troubled him most, and seemed a very wall raised to prevent his approaching God. At last his spiritual advisers, and especially Staupitz, began to see more clearly what his real difficulties were, and tried to explain to him that the righteousness of God for everyone who trusts in Christ is *on the sinner's side*, and not against him. This sent Luther to the Bible again with new hopes. He began the study of the Epistle to the Romans over again. But let us tell the story in his own words:

'I sought day and night to make out the meaning of Paul; and at last I came to apprehend it thus: Through the gospel is revealed the righteousness which availeth with God – a righteousness by which God, in His mercy and compassion, justifieth us; as it is written, "The just shall live by faith." Straightway I felt as if I were born anew. It was as if I had found the door of Paradise thrown wide open. Now I saw the Scriptures altogether in a new light – I ran through their whole contents as far as my memory would serve, and compared them, and found that this righteousness was really that by which God makes us righteous, because everything else in Scripture agreed thereunto so well. The expression "the righteousness of God," which I so much hated before, now became dear and precious – my darling and comforting word. That passage of Paul was to me the true door of Paradise.'

So Luther found the peace he had so long sought in the old, old way, which is always new – by simply taking God at His word, by trusting in His promise. He had not needed to come to the convent to find his new life; but his going there had not hindered him from finding it. There were the promises of God, and there was a man trusting them; and all that righteousness, justice and almighty power were now behind him and beneath him, binding him to God, not barring him out from Him.

But it is not to be thought that this new and blessed change made Luther then and there a reformer of abuses in the ecclesiastical life. He was still a monk, and believed in his monastic vocation.

He was still a faithful son of the medieval Church, with its pope and cardinals, its bishops and monks, its masses, its pilgrimages and its indulgences. All these external things remained unchanged. The thing that was changed was the relation in which one human soul stood to his God. His conversion (if one likes to call it by that name), his vision and appropriation of the pardoning grace of God revealed in Jesus Christ, and the assurance he had of that, was simply one fundamental fact on which he, a single human soul, could take his stand as on a foundation of rock. He could now enjoy his monastic life and all the duties which it gave him to do; there was something real in them and in the religion which they expressed. The very fact that his salvation had come to him within the convent only made him the surer that he had done right in taking the monastic vows, and he felt convinced that now even his father would approve of what he had done.

2. In the Convent – Ordained

Meanwhile he was to be ordained, and an ordination then as now, was a sort of gala occasion; old friends assembled, and it was customary that the father of the candidate brought some small money gift to the son. Old Hans Luther came, with no great good-will, only he did not wish to shame his oldest son. He brought a company of Mansfeld friends, who rode to the convent door 'on twenty horses'. He handed over the usual present of twenty gulden, and sat at the ordination dinner. This did not suffice for the ardent young priest; he had to justify himself for leaving the life his father had marked out for him, and he longed to hear that his father accepted the justification.

He began (he has told us the story himself): 'Dear father, why have you been so set against me, so wrathful; why is it that you are still perhaps unwilling to see me a monk? It is such a peaceful, pleasant, and godly life.'

The old man glanced round the table, at which sat professors, masters, as well as monks, and said: 'Did you never hear that a son must obey his parents? and you learned men, have you never read in the Holy Scriptures that a man should honour his father and his mother?' No arguments from the company about the beauties of the monastic life were of any avail; and when at last Luther insisted that he had only followed the divine call, the sturdy old peasant replied: 'God grant that it may not prove a delusion of the devil.' No man would convince him that the monk's life was better or more godly than the life lived amid wife and children by the fireside, and in the world of everyday work.

Luther did not believe him at the time; but the days came when his father's words seemed to be the text for many a fiery oration against monkery. He delighted to dedicate his tract *On the Monastic Vow* to his father. The dedication said: 'You were right, dear father, after all.' But that was in the future.

Luther was now a priest; and he, who took everything belonging to the spiritual world with such earnestness, was oppressed beyond measure when he thought of what he was called upon to do. For it was now his office to perform the sacrifice of the Mass; it was in his power, he thought, in virtue of his ordination, to bring the Lord Jesus Christ down from heaven to earth. He, by his prayer of consecration, could change bread and wine in such a way that they were no longer what they seemed to be, but the actual body of Christ which had hung on the Cross, and the actual blood which had gushed forth at the thrust of the Roman soldier's spear; and with the body and blood he could bring the human soul of the Saviour, that soul which had exclaimed, 'My God, My God, why hast Thou forsaken Me!' and with the human soul that ineffable and eternal Godhead which in virtue of the Incarnation dwelt for evermore within. He trembled before this holy mystery, as he conceived it to be. He quaked with fear when he was called on to say Mass; he shuddered at the carelessness of his fellow-priests, at the light way in which they spoke of this awful mystery, of this miraculous power placed in the hands of weak men by God. In these early days, after his conversion, he had no doubt about the Romanist doctrine of Transubstantiation; he accepted it and trembled.

He had to hear confession and to pronounce absolution. But here he was on more familiar ground. His own experience had taught him that man could never forgive sin; that God alone could do that; that the priest's function was much more human. He could be the spiritual guide of those who came to confess; he could warn against false grounds of confidence; he could declare that God pardoned all who truly confessed and were sorry for their sins. Yet he never in these early days proposed to do away with the confessional or to reform its practice. He simply set the evangelical truth in the framework of medieval practice, like a soul in a somewhat ungainly body. The practice of confession was for him what it was in our old Columban Church – a 'soul-friendship' – wherein one brother could help another out of his Christian experience; and the absolution was simply the privilege of proclaiming the fact that God had pardoned the humble and trusting penitent. He still prescribed penances, for he thought that commanded in the Bible. Where the Greek word which we translate 'repent' occurred, the Vulgate or Latin Bible, which Luther had, read 'do penance'. Years afterwards Melanchthon showed him that the real scriptural word meant 'change your mind'.

3. At Wittenberg

All the while Luther was beginning to show himself a good man of business, with an eye for the heart of things. He became the confidant of the heads of his community, and was entrusted with many delicate commissions, and sent on some embassies on behalf of his Order. In 1508 he was called to a wider sphere of work.

Frederic the Elector of Saxony had long meditated on having a university within his dominions, and in 1502 had begun one in the town of Wittenberg. Staupitz and Dr Pollich, who accompanied the Elector on his pilgrimage to the Holy Land, were his two chief advisers. There was not much money to spare at the Electoral Court, and everything was done in the most frugal German fashion. The money got from the sale of indulgences years before – money which the Elector would not allow to leave the country –

served to make a beginning. Some parishes were united to the Castle Church – the Church of All Saints its ecclesiastical name – and the tithes furnished the stipends of the professors, who were to be prebendaries of the Church. Staupitz suggested that the professors in theology and philosophy might be furnished by the Augustinian Order, and as monks they did not need salary.

The town of Wittenberg was of some official importance in Electoral Saxony; but it was small (only 356 rateable houses in 1513) and mean-looking; the houses were old and poor-looking structures of wood; the surrounding country stony, with stretches of barren heath; the people rough and boorish, much inclined to beer-drinking.[1] It must have been a strange little place, full of contrasts; the Elector's palace, the great Castle Church, full of the relics which the Elector had brought home from the Holy Land; the new Augustinian Cloister, and one or two more fine buildings; and then the wretched little houses of wood, plastered with mud and thatched with straw, while the broad rushing Elbe flowed past between its banks of heath. This was to be the cradle of the German Reformation, and thither came Luther in 1508, transferred from Erfurt to be Professor of Philosophy in the small university.

Staupitz had early recognised the power lying latent in the young monk. It had been Luther's duty, since his ordination, to take his turn of preaching to his fellow-monks. At Wittenberg his earliest sermons were delivered in an old chapel, thirty feet long and twenty wide, of wood plastered with clay, which stood near the new cloister, and which had been given to the monks to be a convent chapel. It was there that Luther began his evangelical sermons, delivered at first to a handful of monks and professors. 'That monk has deep eyes and wonderful fancies,' said Dr Pollich, who was amongst his earliest hearers.

In 1511 his work at Wittenberg was interrupted by a command to go to Rome on the business of his Order. Staupitz, who was at the head of a number of reformed convents of the Augustinian Order, wished to bring several other Augustinian convents under

---

[1] There were no fewer than 170 brewing houses.

the same regulations, and indeed had been authorised by the Pope to do so. Some of these unreformed convents had protested and appealed to Rome, and Staupitz wished Luther and a fellow-monk, John of Mechlen, to represent him before the papal court. Thus Luther, who had seen monastic life from the inside, was destined to make a personal acquaintance with Rome itself.

He started with ten gold florins in his purse. The journey was to be made on foot; food and lodging were to be got in friendly monasteries. The two Augustinians went by Switzerland. Luther admired the fertile valley of the Po, lying between the Alps and the Apennines; he praised the patient agriculture of the Italians, the vines, the olives, the oranges, and the figs. He says nothing of the Art collections of Florence, but he praises the wonderful hospitals which the benevolence of the people had erected for the suffering sick, and in which honourable ladies waited on the poor. He contrasted the sobriety of the Italians with the drunkenness of the Germans; and he thankfully acknowledged the wonderful hospitality extended to the two stranger German monks. But the luxury of the larger monasteries pained him; the monks feasted on fast days in a way that Germans would not have done on festivals; the people were dishonest and crafty, and seemed to care little for spiritual things. This journey was for Luther and his companion a pilgrimage also. They meant to visit all the holy places, and pay due reverence to the shrines of the martyrs. They approached the imperial city with the liveliest expectation. When they first came in sight of its walls, Luther raised his hands in an ecstasy, exclaiming, 'I greet thee, thou Holy Rome!' He felt like a Jewish pilgrim at the first glimpse of Jerusalem.

His official business did not cost very much time; the dispute seems to have been amicably settled by a compromise. His business done, he set himself to see the city with the devotion of a pilgrim and with the thoroughness of a German. He visited all the oldest churches, swallowed wholesale, he says, all the legends his guides repeated to him; studied the ruins of ancient Rome; marvelled at the Colosseum and at the Baths of Diocletian. Only once did his evangelical faith rebel against all this superstition. There was and is in Rome a great staircase, its steps worn with the pressure of thousands of pilgrims – the Holy Staircase, which was said to have once formed part of Pilate's house. An indulgence from penance for a thousand years is promised to those pilgrims who climb it on their knees. Luther began the ascent, repeating the usual prayers, but when he got half-way up, he remembered the text 'The just shall live by his faith'; he rose from his knees, stood for a moment erect, and then slowly walked down again.

But if Luther was still unemancipated from medieval superstitions, his sturdy German piety and his plain Christian morality turned his reverence for Rome into loathing. The city, which he had greeted as holy, was a sink of iniquity; its very priests were openly infidel, and scoffed at the services they performed; the papal courtiers were men of the most shameless lives; he was accustomed to repeat the Italian proverb, 'If there is a hell, Rome is built over it.' It was much for him in after days that he had seen Rome for that month which he had spent in the papal capital.

4. In the Convent – Professor and Doctor of Theology

Luther was back at Wittenberg in the early summer of 1512. His professorial duties seem to have been laid aside for some months, and he was busily engaged on various duties connected with the convent. The vicar-general, Dr Staupitz, had, however, designed him for higher work.

Luther had taken the opportunity while at Rome to learn something of Hebrew from a Jewish Rabbi, and to get lessons in Greek from a refugee from Constantinople, and Staupitz wished him to become Doctor in Theology and the chief theological professor at Wittenberg. Luther long resisted, and yielded not to persuasion but to commands. Very unhappy about it all, he was sent to the Erfurt convent to prepare for graduation. Had he premonitions, dim or clear, of what lay before him, when he so strenuously resisted the persuasions of his superior? Had his studies in medieval theology, and his new found liberty in expounding the Scriptures, taught him that there was a long fierce fight before him? He must have had some misgivings; but the future was as dark to him as it is to all of us. 'No good work comes about by our own wisdom; it begins in dire necessity; I was forced into mine; but had I known then what I know now, ten wild horses would not have drawn me into it.' That is what Luther said about this very introduction to theological teaching.

To become a doctor of theology in these days involved a lengthy ceremony. It began with a thesis proposed by the graduate-to-be – a proposition whose truth he was to defend against all-comers. Next day at early morning the bells of the churches were set a-ringing as on a great festival. The university authorities, with students and strangers and townsmen, marched through the streets, the newly created doctor in their midst. In the hall the candidate delivered a short address; he took the Wittenberg University vow, 'I swear to defend evangelical truth vigorously' (*viriliter*); the doctor's cap was placed on his head; and the great gold ring, with its silver boss carved with three intertwined circles symbolising the mysteries of theology, was placed on his finger. He was now Dr Martin Luther, sworn to defend the truth of the gospel as God made that known to him. Three days later, he became a member of the Senate of the university, and some weeks after, Staupitz, who had now seen his favourite in what he believed to be his true position, resigned his chair, and Luther took his place as regent of the university. He had already become sub-prior of his convent, and the Elector, who had heard him preach sometimes in the little chapel, had defrayed the expenses of his graduation.

Then began that wonderful series of expositions which gradually drew to the small, poor and remote University of Wittenberg students from all parts of Germany, and then from all parts of Europe.

He began with the Psalms, which he used to call the Bible within the Bible. There is preserved in the Wolfenbüttel Library two fragments of these early lectures of Luther. His text was the Latin Version, and his notes from which he delivered the lectures are written on the wide margins and between the lines of print. He selected the Epistle to the Romans for his New Testament subject, and this led him to dwell on the thought of justification. Then came lectures on the Epistle to the Galatians. These lectures were like a revelation of the Bible to the Wittenberg students; the townspeople heard about them, and grave burghers enrolled themselves as students in order to listen to the new and living explanations of the Word of God.

To have the scene before us, we must imagine the professor sitting at his desk with his book and his notes, the students on hard benches or on the floor without books, writing both text and comment on sheets of paper, or following all and storing all up in their memories and transcribing when they got home to their lodgings. The multiplication of books and the cheapening of paper has made a wonderful revolution. Luther used a Latin Bible. He had begun to study both Hebrew and Greek in the Erfurt monastery, and he had improved his visit to Rome by trying to learn something more about these biblical languages; but with all this he knew that he was weak in languages, and there was little Greek or Hebrew known in the Wittenberg University until three years later, when Melanchthon was brought from Erfurt. Luther had few commentaries to assist him. He did not trust very much to medieval explanations of the sacred text, but he did not disdain any help that he got from De Lyra and others.

All these early years of his professorial work he was studying hard. Augustine was his favourite theologian, and he prized him not so much for his formal theology as for his deep acquaintance with the human heart. He must have been reading the sermons of John Tauler, the great German mystic, about this time; and a little later he became acquainted with a little book called *The German Theology*, the work of an unknown mystic of the earlier part of the fifteenth century. Luther tells us that he learned more about heart religion from this little book than from anything else save the Bible. He published a portion of it in the end of 1516 in order to show people how they ought to pray; and in 1518 he published the whole book, with a preface explaining his indebtedness to it. All his former doubts and fears had fled. His Christianity was now of the most joyous kind. 'Taste and see how good the Lord is' is the burden of many a private letter.

In these earlier years of his professoriate he undertook the duties of preacher in the town church of Wittenberg. He did so apparently because the pastor was unable to do his work from ill-health; indeed, he seems to have gradually slid into this position. In the convent chapel he had preached to persons who could perhaps appreciate learned discourses, but he had now to do with the common rude man, with 'raw Saxons' as he said, and he knew that the first merit in a sermon is that it can be understood. The people had no Bibles, but most of them knew the Lord's Prayer and the Ten Commandments. 'The common people heard him gladly.' He spoke in plain nervous German. He gathered collections of German proverbs and country sayings, and used them as illustrations. He noted that our Lord used the homeliest illustrations, talking of tilling the ground, of mustard seed, of sparrows and sheep and fish; and he went and did likewise. It is impossible to misunderstand Luther's sermons. Above all, he had a way of making the Bible living, of showing that it was full of histories of men and women who had lived and talked and eaten and slept and married and given in marriage.

All this was new. No matter what the text was, the sermon was sure to come round in the end to that doctrine of grace which he had first learned by the hearing of the ear at his mother's knees, then cast behind him in his student days, and finally got hold of again after sore conflict in Erfurt monastery – the doctrine of the radical distinction between the law and the gospel – the doctrine that the divine righteousness is not mere punitive justice, but saving merit made over once for all to every believer in Christ – the doctrine that faith is not belief in propositions, but a trust in, and a personal fellowship with, a crucified Lord.

The town's church where those sermons were preached is a great roomy building with two towers, standing near the market-place in Wittenberg. The old pulpit lies in fragments in the Luther House; but the font, a heptagon with the apostles engraved on the faces, a beautiful work in bronze by that exquisite artist Peter Vischer of Nürnberg, remains where it stood when Luther bent over it to sprinkle little children in the name of the Father, the Son and the Holy Ghost. As you stand there it is not difficult to recall the church filled with an eager audience, to see the wan wild face with the high cheek-bones and traces of the convent fasts and struggles and the deep-set gleaming eyes, and to hear the clear musical voice launching forth proverb-like sentences in the vigorous mother tongue – for Luther's words were 'half-battles'.

In 1516 he had additional duties laid upon him; he was made a superintendent of a circle of eleven Augustinian convents, among them his old convent at Erfurt. He had to make regular visitations, to preach to the monks, to discuss with them theological difficulties, to explain the rules of the Order, to discipline erring brethren, and to give solemn decisions on dozens of trifling questions, such as: 'On what occasions certain brethren were to wear their white scapularies'; 'who ought to clean out certain fish ponds', and 'who ought to carry the fish from the ponds to the monastery?' He tells us all about this in his correspondence, and has a glance at everything humorous which passes. Here is how he relates how full of work he is (he is writing to John Lange, prior of Erfurt): 'I have need of two secretaries, and do almost nothing all day long but write letters; ...I am convent preacher; reader at meals; I am required to preach every day in the parish church; I am director of studies; ...I am vicar of the Order, i.e. prior eleven times over; I have to superintend the Leitzkau fish pond; I have charge of our people of Herzberg at Torgau; I lecture on St Paul, and collate the Psalms.' Besides all this, he was already watching John Tetzel, still at a distance from Wittenberg, and his Indulgence-selling. Yet he can find time for letters like the following: 'Learn, dear brother, Christ and Him crucified; learn to sing to Him, and doubting thyself to say to Him: "Thou, Lord Jesus, art my righteousness while I am Thy sin; what is mine Thou hast taken upon Thyself, and what is Thine Thou hast given to me." Beware of aspiring to such purity that thou shalt no longer seem to thyself a sinner; for Christ does not dwell except in sinners... For if by our labours and afflictions we could attain peace of conscience, why did He die? Therefore, only in Him, by a believing self-despair both of thyself and of thy works, wilt thou find peace.'

In 1516 the plague came to Wittenberg. Most of the inhabitants who could do so fled from the town, and his Erfurt brethren asked Luther to come there for a time. Here is part of his answer: 'Why should I flee? I hope the world would not collapse if Brother Martin fell. If the pestilence spreads I will indeed disperse the monks throughout the land. As for me, I have been placed here. My obedience as a monk does not suffer me to fly; since what that obedience once required it demands still. Not that I do not fear death (I am not the Apostle Paul, but only the lecturer on the Apostle Paul), but I hope the Lord will deliver me from my fear.'

Luther could scarcely expect to avoid all opposition to his new mode of teaching; but he did not fear it. He was a teacher of theology, and he could not avoid knowing that he taught somewhat differently from most teachers. He comforted himself with the thought that while others were doctors of theology he always claimed to be a doctor of the Holy Scripture, and that it was therefore his business to expound the Scriptures above all other portions of theological study. His whole life and work rested on one fundamental thought, that God of His own free grace pardoned sin for the sake of our Lord Jesus Christ, and that no man, however saintly, could work out his own salvation. Every hope that man had rested on that. The thought was his foundation of rock. This and the theology based on it he believed to be scriptural, and the only scriptural theology. It was the doctrine which the great Augustine had taught; and Luther called it Augustinian, not Lutheran.

But it was not the theology taught in the common theological classes at Erfurt or Leipzig. There, professors lectured on and expounded the Sentences of Peter of Lombardy and of his manifold commentators – the books which had tormented Luther while he was at Erfurt. He not merely felt that this theology was useless, he distrusted it altogether. He found that it was more pagan than Christian; that it was based much more upon the great pagan philosopher Aristotle than on the Epistles of St Paul. Yet it was sanctioned by the authority of the weightiest names of the medieval Church. A collision was inevitable at some time or other. Luther did not shirk it; he rather invited it. Privately and publicly, it may even be said formally and officially, he insisted that the sole test of theological verity was the Holy Scripture, and that if this were acknowledged as it ought to be, the Augustinian theology would everywhere displace the scholastic.

This was the condition of affairs at Wittenberg when Luther became involved in the controversy about Indulgences.

CHAPTER 3

INDULGENCE CONTROVERSY

1. The Indulgence

Luther began his work of reformation in an attack on what was called an Indulgence proclaimed by Pope Leo X, farmed by Albert, archbishop of Mainz, whose commissary was John Tetzel, a notorious Dominican monk. So far as the common people were concerned, this Indulgence meant that on the payment of certain specified sums of money, spiritual privileges, including the forgiveness of sins, could be obtained by the purchasers. The Pope proclaimed this Indulgence to be a great boon, and as such the majority of the common people received it. They were encouraged to look upon it in this light by most of the clergy, and by all who wished to stand well with the higher ecclesiastical powers.

Of course, many people thought ill of these Indulgences. Most secular princes felt that their poor territories were being drained of money to enrich the papal court, grave burghers saw that all manner of evil living followed the trail of the Indulgence-seller, and good parish priests felt the same. Pope Julius had proclaimed an Indulgence in 1501, and the Elector Frederic had not allowed the money raised in his dominions to leave the country. It had been levied for the ostensible purpose of assisting to pay for a war against the Turks and in defence of Christendom; and Frederic declared that he meant to keep the money until the war began. He actually used it to found the University of Wittenberg. John Wessel had openly protested against that earlier Indulgence, and had died in the prison of a Dominican monastery in consequence. Those earlier objectors had never reached the heart of the matter, the con-

science of the people had never been touched, and upon the whole
the multitude were ready to accept the Indulgence for the boon
which the Pope declared it to be.

The money raised was to be devoted to the building of St Peter's Church in Rome, and to serve the pious purpose, so the Pope
said, of raising a worthy tomb over the bones of the great apostle,
which were asserted to have been laid in a Roman grave. People
were a little sceptical about the destination of the money; but the
buyers had their Indulgence tickets, and it did not matter much to
them what became of the funds after the money had left their
pockets. So the Indulgence-seller had generally a brilliant welcome
when he entered a German town. Myconius, who at the time was
a schoolboy of thirteen, and was one of the crowd at Annaberg in
East Saxony, tells us that when 'the Commissary or Indulgence-
seller approached a town, the Bull (announcing the Indulgence)
was carried before him on a cloth of velvet or gold, and all the
priests and monks, the council, the schoolmasters and the scholars, all the men and women went out to meet him with banners
and candles and songs, forming a grand procession; then, all the
bells ringing and all the organs playing, they accompanied him to
the principal church; a red cross was set up in the midst of the
church, and the Pope's banner was displayed; in short, one might
think they were receiving God Himself.'

Albert of Brandenberg, who had been archbishop of Magdeburg
and was then archbishop of Mainz, thought that he could gain
some advantage out of all this enthusiasm for the Indulgence. He
was a comparatively young man, fond of display, a patron of learning, affecting Humanist sympathies, and full of expensive tastes
for pictures, cameos, etc. He had spent large sums of money in
order to gain his dignities, and had promised his clergy that he
would himself pay for his second archiepiscopal *pallium*. He was
deeply in debt to the great Augsburg banking house, the Fuggers,
and in desperate straits for money. He persuaded the Pope to allow
him to farm the Indulgence for the greater part of Germany, and
hired John Tetzel, who had previously acted as the papal under-

commissary, to be his commissary. The archbishop himself drew up, to attract buyers, a statement of the benefits coming to all who purchased Indulgences, and Tetzel used this statement as a text on which he could enlarge.

The Indulgence, according to the archbishop, possessed the following inestimable efficacies:

it ensured to those who bought the tickets complete forgiveness of sins, participation in the grace of God, and freedom from purgatory;

it gave them a ticket or letter, stamped with the Pope's seal, which allowed them to select a confessor, whom they pleased, who would absolve them from all crimes and punishments, and would permit them to exchange any vows they had taken upon themselves for some other more agreeable good works;

it made them sharers in all the good works of the universal Church, in all the benefits of prayers, pilgrimages and other ecclesiastical good works performed by all the members of the whole Church;

it provided a full remission of sins to all departed persons then in purgatory.

Tetzel went far beyond the letter of his instructions. He shouted, 'The soul flies out of purgatory as soon as the money rattles in the box'; 'the red cross of the Indulgence is of equal power with the cross of Christ'; 'the "Papal Letters" have such power that they would absolve a man who had violated the Mother of God.' But his blasphemies did not display more sordid money-getting than did the papal Commission itself. It declared that certain sins were outside the power of the Indulgence to remove. They were as follows:

'Except the crimes of conspiracy against the person of the supreme Pontiff, of the murder of bishops, or of other superior prelates, and the laying violent hands upon them or other prelates, the forging of apostolic letters, or conveying of arms and other prohibited things into heathen countries, and the *sentences and censures incurred on occasion of the importation of the alums of apostolic Tolfa from heathen countries contrary to the apostolic prohibition.'*

The meaning of the word italicised is that all persons who imported alum into Christendom were guilty of an unpardonable sin; and although no reason is given it is not far to seek.

A certain Giovanni di Castro discovered alum stone in the mountains of Tolfa, not far from Civita Vecchia, and within the papal dominions. This was a mine of wealth for the Holy See. Di Castro made sure of his discovery by calcining the stone. He then appeared before the Pope and said: 'I announce to you a victory over the Turk. He draws yearly from the Christians above 300,000 pieces of gold, paid to him for the alum with which we dye wool of various colours, because none is found here, but a little at Ischia... I have found seven hills so abundant in it that they might supply seven worlds. If you will send for workmen and cause furnaces to be made and the stones to be calcined, you may furnish alum to all Europe, and that again which the Turk used to acquire by this article will be thrown into your hands.' The Holy See made haste to work its newly found treasures, and in order to secure the whole profit to itself, it made it a sin to import any alum into Europe. The money to be obtained from the Indulgence was not to be allowed to interfere with the papal revenue from its alum mines; and so the importation of alum was declared to be a sin unpardonable by any Indulgence.

Myconius tells us how Tetzel's sermons and the conversations of the monks about the Indulgence, made him believe in the efficacy of the pardon tickets. He had come from a pious home. His parents had taught him the Ten Commandments, the Creed, and the Lord's Prayer. His father had often expounded them to him, and he had told him over and over again that he must continually pray to God to pardon his sins, that God alone could pardon, and that He grants pardon to those who sincerely seek it and that of His *free* grace. But when the boy (he was only thirteen years of age) heard the monks insist that Tetzel was right, and that pardon could be reached through the 'papal letters' that were being sold, he thought that his father must have been wrong, and he was anxious to get an Indulgence ticket for himself. He could not believe, however, that God's pardon could be bought for money. That part of his father's teaching stuck fast to him. One day he chanced to hear that the pardon tickets could be got by the poor for nothing; he saw a proclamation, and observed that this was really written on it – *pauperibus dentur grati*. Boylike he thought that this reconciled his father's teaching and that of the priests, and he resolved he would do his best to get one of the precious tickets. One day (it was Whitsuntide, 1516) Tetzel announced that the sales were getting fewer, and that he would be compelled to take down the red cross and 'close the door of heaven'; he advised everyone to buy at once, for if they omitted the chance now given them to secure the 'papal letter', no priest could absolve them for certain sins; he concluded by saying that during the few remaining days of sale the prices would be reduced. Myconius tells us that he could not believe that the 'papal letter' would do him any good unless he got it for nothing. Then and not till then it really represented to him the *free* grace of God; and he recounts the strenuous endeavours he made to get an Indulgence ticket without paying for it. The priests, who acted as Tetzel's salesmen, were so wearied out with his importunities, that they offered to give him the money in order to buy the ticket in the usual way, so as not to create an inconvenient precedent. Tetzel shouted at him more than once that he could not get the ticket. The priests, however, more anxious than the commissary to keep faith, at last let him have what he had so earnestly desired, and on his own terms. His story brings the scenes surrounding the Indulgence-selling very vividly before us.

Tetzel, early in 1516, had been selling his Indulgences in the Meissen district, not very far from Wittenberg, and Luther had watched his progress and his practices. He preached at least one sermon on the subject; and both sermon and private correspondence reveal a very perturbed mind. The strongest thing that he said was that the Indulgence was a very mischievous instrument in the hands of avarice. Meanwhile Tetzel, going from place to place in the end of 1516 and in the earlier months of 1517, was approaching Wittenberg. People went from Wittenberg to Jüterbog and Zerbst and other places where Tetzel had 'set up the red cross' and opened a sale of Indulgences. Some of Luther's own people, parishioners of his, men and women who came regularly to him for confession, had bought the 'papal letters', had shown them to him, and had demanded priestly absolution in due form without either confession of sin or showing any signs of real sorrow. He could and did refuse to acknowledge their 'letters'; they had complained to Tetzel, and the commissary had uttered threats. Luther found himself wading in deep waters. The Indulgence, he knew, was doing great harm to poor souls; he got the letter of instructions given to Tetzel by his employer, the archbishop, and his heart waxed wroth against it. But still at the basis of the Indulgence, bad as it was, there lay the great truth, Luther thought, that it is the business of the Church to declare the free and sovereign grace of God. Besides, even in the form which the Indulgence took, as a theory at least, it belonged to a class of things and institutions from which many pious souls found help to holy living, and it was rooted in doctrines in which Luther, if he did not earnestly believe, was at least prepared to acquiesce.

A large number of the pious associations of the later Middle Ages were founded on ideas which lay at the basis of the practice of giving Indulgences. However near to their Lord, God's Word, the Sacraments and prayer brought faithful Christian men and women, the machinery of the Catholic Church, which lay all around them and in which they had a place, was accepted by them as unquestionably and quietly as a law of nature. This machinery included among other things the countless treasure of good works, prayers, fastings, mortifications of all kinds, which holy men and women of old had done, and which were available for others if the Pope could be persuaded to transfer them. When men and women united in a pious confraternity, the Pope, it was believed could transfer to the community a surplus of prayers and masses and other ecclesiastical good deeds, and this became for pious living what a good bank account is to a man starting in business.

Freytag gives us, as an example of this, an account of *St Ursula's Schifflein* or the *Brotherhood of the Eleven Thousand Virgins*, a pious association, which had Frederic, the Elector of Saxony, for one of its founders and directors. It was really a brotherhood of poor and pious people who wished to assist each other by mutual prayer, and had a charter from the Pope highly approving of its objects. To encourage them the Pope made over to them by statute a collection of spiritual treasures which are as carefully enumerated as the assets of a business firm – 6,455 Masses, 3,500 Psalters (i.e. repetitions of the 150 Psalms), 200,000 Rosaries (i.e. repetitions of the prayers which went to make a complete rosary), 200,000 *Te Deums*, 1,600 *Glorias in Excelsis*, 11,000 prayers for the Patroness, St Ursula, 630 times 11,000 Paternosters and Ave Marias. The whole redeeming power of these good works was handed over by the Pope for the spiritual benefit of the members of the brotherhood. A layman was entitled to become a brother if he could show that he had repeated in his lifetime 11,000 Paternosters, and it was pointed out that this condition was not a very hard one, because the 11,000 could be accomplished in a year at the rate of 32 per day.

Many such brotherhoods bought their spiritual treasures from the Pope with money, and sold them in the shape of entrance fees, etc, to the members. There was neither buying nor selling about *St Ursula's Schifflein*, which was a genuine attempt to encourage a prayerful life by means of mutual example and encouragement. The machinery of the Church, however, secured *this* encouragement, that, if by any accident members failed in praying as they had promised, they had always this spiritual treasure to count upon. There is no list of members of this association, so far as I know, in existence: but, if there were, it is most probable that it would include some of Luther's strongest admirers in the town of Wittenberg. What difference in principle could be found between the Pope transferring a mass of spiritual benefits to a pious brotherhood, and his handing over an indefinite amount to Archbishop Albert to dispose of as he thought fit, through Tetzel or otherwise?

The theory of Indulgence could also be justified from another side. From the earliest times the Church of Christ, while proclaiming the free pardoning grace of God revealed in the Person and Work of Christ, had always insisted that the pardon was for those who were truly penitent, and who had a real resolve to try at least to live the life of new obedience to which Christ has called His people. When penitents professed sorrow for sins, they were required to show their sorrow in some open sign of repentance. The Church from a very early period preferred that these signs of sorrow should take the form of prayers or gifts of charity or some form of practical benevolence such as the manumission of slaves. Suggestions of this kind are apt to become prescriptions, and ecclesiastical prescriptions tend to become stereotyped and conventional. When the ecclesiastical *praxis* of sorrow, confession, and pardon became fixed in the so-called 'sacrament of penance', there were already attached to it stereotyped signs of sorrow required by the Church, and these were called *satisfaction* and latterly *penance*. In the ordinary practice of the Church they were required before pardon could be pronounced by the mouth of the priest in absolution; and although they had an evangelical origin, and could always be explained with an evangelical meaning, the common effect they produced was to obscure the freely given pardon of God. Indulgence could be explained and justified on the ground that the Church was able to dispense with those signs of sorrow which were her own prescription; and it was possible to say that there was a right use of Indulgence when the Church proclaimed pardon apart from the signs of sorrow, for that was a manifestation that, after all, pardon did not depend on the due manifestation of prescribed signs of contrition, but on the free grace of God.

To attack the Indulgence was to make an assault upon part at least of the machinery of the great medieval Church, and Luther believed with his whole heart that he was a devout and obedient son of that Church. Besides, he had a profound contempt for men who believe that they are born to set the world right. He compared them to a player at ninepins who thinks that he cannot fail to knock down twelve when there are only nine pins standing. 'I am but a young doctor,' he said, in reply to some exhortation to stand forward, 'fresh from the foundry, hot and happy in the Word of God.' Tetzel was no business of his; and yet his poor people, souls whom God had given *him* in charge – ! At length, after much hesitation and deep distress of mind, he felt compelled to interfere, and, as was usual when his mind was made up, he went unflinchingly to the root of the matter in the most direct and dauntless fashion.

It was characteristic of the man that he resolved to bear the whole responsibility by himself. He wrote to the three persons most concerned – to the archbishop of Mainz, who farmed the Indulgence, and according to whose instructions the 'papal letters' were sold; to Tetzel, the archbishop's commissary, who had charge of the sales; and to the man who was his own ecclesiastical superior, Bishop Scultetus, who was set over the church in which Luther preached and the university in which he taught. He seems, however, to have taken care that none of these persons could interfere with him, for his letter to the archbishop is dated on the eve of the day on which he acted. All his personal friends were kept in complete ignorance of what he was about to do. He did this, he afterwards declared, that no-one, and especially not the Elector, might be involved by his action.

He took the best way of publishing his opinions widely that occurred to him. The Castle Church at Wittenberg had always been closely connected with the university, and the doors of the church had, since the foundation of the university, been used by its officials as a university board on which to publish important documents. The day of the year which drew the largest concourse of strangers to the church was the first of November, All Saints' Day. It was the anniversary of the foundation and consecration of the church, and was also commemorated by a prolonged series of services. In accordance with a common custom, the Pope had solemnly promised an Indulgence of some kind to all who took part in the yearly commemorative services. There could be no more convenient time or place. At noon on the day in question Luther nailed his Ninety-five Theses to the door of the church. It was a strictly academic proceeding. A doctor in theology offered a 'Disputation', for so he called it, 'for the purpose of explaining the efficacy of the Indulgence.' The explanation had ninety-five heads, all of which 'Doctor Martin Luther, theologian', was prepared to make good against all comers. The strict academic etiquette was thoroughly preserved, and the document was of course written in Latin.

The 'document' differed from most academic disputations in this that everyone wished to read it. Luther had made a duplicate in German. Copies in the two languages were sent to the University Printing-Press, which could not throw them off fast enough to keep pace with the demands which came from all parts of Germany. The theses had the effect of a torch thrown among dry fuel. The first to protest was Tetzel, who wrote counter-theses, which the students burnt. Other protests followed; but the great mass of pious German people saw in these theses what they had always believed.

2. The Effect of the Theses

The question arises: Did Luther in these famous Theses break away from the thought and feeling of the medieval Church, or did he only give expression to its deepest and most devout thoughts on sin and on pardon? It has always appeared to me, with reverence be it spoken, that the relation of the Reformation theology, and therefore of Luther, to the teaching of the medieval Church can be compared with the relation between the teaching of our Lord and the Mosaic Law. He came to fulfil it, and not to destroy it. He showed the real moral depths in it. He stripped it of the temporal and accidental elements which had gathered round it. He fulfilled it by making visible what it really was. So Luther's teaching fulfils the best instruction of the medieval Church and carries on its noblest work. For when we think of it, there is scarcely a thought of Luther's that is not to be found in the hymns, prayers, and most evangelical preaching of the Middle Ages. The difference between Reformation and medieval theology is that the former solves an antinomy which the latter contains; for we may say with Dr Wace that medieval theology had resulted in a 'dead-lock', and that Luther solved the antinomy and dissolved the dead-lock.

The task to which the medieval Church had to set itself was to tame, civilise, and evangelise the fierce Teutonic tribes which had submerged the ancient world. It set itself to that task with an energy and a self-devotion seldom equalled and never surpassed. We are apt to forget in our criticisms of that medieval Church the conditions amid which it fulfilled its mission. A Boniface or an Augustine spoke to men as savage and bloodthirsty as Chaka's Zulu warriors, and who had scarcely more developed morals. They spoke as a wise and advanced civilisation speaks to savages; as heavenly wisdom speaks to sinful folly. The necessity of speaking from above, and the humble acquiescence of those spoken to, easily grows into infallible utterance on the one side and a belief that implicit obedience is the proper attitude of mind on the other.

Can we measure the action and reaction of teachers and taught, or say how much the barbarian readiness to receive the vulgarly supernatural is responsible for magical theories of the sacraments and of the expiative power of self-torture? Have we marked how many tribal customs worked their way into the canon law, say of marriage? But when all criticisms are made, the medieval Church was a stern school of religious and moral discipline. It preached the 'divine righteousness and its inexorable demands'. It taught, and elevated its convert nations by teaching, that sin is sin altogether apart from extenuating circumstances, by placing before them ideals of saintly and ineffable purity. Says Dr Wace:

'The glorious cathedrals which arose in the best period of the Middle Ages are but the visible types of those splendid structures of ideal virtues which a monk like St Bernard, or a schoolman like St Thomas Aquinas, piled up by laborious thought and painful asceticism. Such men felt themselves at all times surrounded by a spiritual world at once more glorious in its beauty and more awful in its terrors than either the pleasures or the miseries of this world could adequately represent. The great poet of the Middle Ages affords perhaps the most vivid representation of their character in this respect. The horrible images of the *Inferno*, the keen sufferings of purification in the *Purgatorio*, form the terrible foreground behind which the *Paradiso* rises. Those visions of terror and dread and suffering had stamped themselves on the imagination of the medieval world, and lay at the root of the power with which the Church overshadowed it. In their origin they embodied a profound and noble truth. It was a high and divine conception that the moral and spiritual world with which we are encompassed has greater heights and lower depths than are generally apprehended in the visible experience of this life; and Dante has been felt to be in a unique degree the poet of righteousness.'

The mission of the medieval Church was to be a stern preacher of righteousness, and Luther was a true child of that Church. Its message had been received by him, and had sunk into his soul. He was such a true son of his Church that he felt more deeply than most the point where the message, of its formal theology at least, failed. It contrasted the divine righteousness and man's sin and weakness. It insisted on the inexorable demands of the law of God, while it uttered despairingly that man could never fulfil them. It brought the human soul to a dead-lock. The man who could show some way of extrication which would not abate one jot the demands of the law of God, nor lower the standard of divine righteousness, was no rebel against his Church, but rather the exponent of its deepest teaching. He solved the antinomy by showing that, as it had been caused by setting over against each other the righteousness of God and the sin of man, and keeping the two sides distinct and separate, and that God must be brought over to man's side, so that His righteousness could become man's; or, in other words, that there must be a direct and intimate fellowship between man and God. But all fellowship implies trust; and trust, the personal trust of man in a personal God, gives him that fellowship with God through which the things which belong to God can be-

come his. Without this personal trust all divine things, the Incarnation, the Passion, the Word, the Sacraments, however true as matters of fact, are outside the man, and cannot be truly possessed.
But when man trusts in God, and when the fellowship which trust
always creates is established, then they can always be shared in by
the man who trusts. This is what is meant by saying that the 'just
shall live by *faith*'.

It was from this view of a personal relation between God and
man, created by a personal trust in the fatherly promises of God,
that Luther had learned to regard all things which concerned God
and His faithful people, and this had its effect on the way in which
he looked at contrition and at pardon for sin. The sorrow for sin
which must be experienced by the man who feels himself to be in
fellowship with God through his sense of trust cannot be removed
by any sentence of absolution, but must continue lifelong, for it is
fed by the very love to God which the fellowship, with its sense of
abiding unworthiness, evokes. The constraint to obedience based
on fear of punishment gives place to the higher and stronger mo-
tive of a glad response to the wishes of One who is loved. For
Justification by Faith does not mean that one trusts in God and gets
off; but that one trusts in God and goes on through life, drawn,
instead of driven, into all holy living. It also follows that the man
who desires and enjoys fellowship with God must think much more
of God's personal forgiveness than of the mere remission of the
consequences of sin; the loss of the former strikes at the sense of
fellowship itself, while the sense of fellowship renders the latter
bearable even when most burdensome, for it teaches man to accept all manner of trials and adversities, all God's judgments and
discipline, in perfect peace of soul, because none of them can really separate him from his God.

In all this Luther felt himself to be, and was the exponent of the
deepest and truest religious teaching of the medieval Church, and
the heir to all that preaching of righteousness which makes Dante's
great poem appear to be the soul of the Middle Ages. He solved
the antinomy of the Church's teaching without letting go either of

the truths represented. But what Dr Wace and others, who have pointed out this clearly, have failed to recognise is, that Luther's solution was familiar to the simple piety, although unknown to the academic theology of the Middle Ages; and that Luther taught little more than he and Myconius and thousands of others had been taught at their mothers' knees, for the theology of the heart is always far in advance of that of the schools.

The opponents of Luther, on the other hand, could not represent the deepest thoughts of medieval theology. When face to face with the dead-lock indicated above, they could not avoid tampering with the requirements of divine righteousness in order to assist human weakness. They distinguished between the commandments of the divine law and the counsels of perfection; they invented a dispensing authority which could modify the requirements of divine justice; they proceeded step by step, in half-acknowledged ways, to get rid of the severity of those rules of moral life and those ideals of moral purity which it was the duty of the Church to sustain in all their force, until at last they had lowered themselves to the depth of degradation which the Indulgence, as worked by Tetzel, exhibited.

When we turn to the Ninety-five Theses of Luther we can notice at least three main thoughts. He draws a strong distinction between what belongs absolutely to God and what he admits may be within the power of the Pope, or what is ecclesiastical machinery. The personal forgiveness of sin, with Luther is the one thing of overwhelming moment, is in the hands of God, and of God alone. But all those external and conventional signs of sorrow which have been ordered by the Church are in the hands of the Pope, to be dispensed with if he orders it. 'Every Christian, who feels true compunction, has, of right, plenary remission of pain and guilt, even without letters of pardon.' 'We must beware of those who say that these pardons from the Pope are that inestimable gift of God by which man is reconciled to God.' 'The Pope has neither the will nor the power to remit any penalties, except those which he has imposed by his own authority or by that of the canons.' He rings the changes on this main theme. He denounces, in quoting, all the assertions of Tetzel which go to obscure the difference, such as that the red cross of the Indulgence has equal power with the Cross of Christ. He insists that the law of the Christian life must be a continuous repentance, and that this evangelical repentance is something quite different from the confession and satisfaction which are performed under the ministry of priests. He proclaims that ecclesiastical good works, which can be remitted by the Pope, are by no means so valuable as those spontaneous offerings of charity which show the heartfelt thanks and humility of the soul whom God has pardoned.

The Theses are not a reasoned treatise; they are the work of a man who wishes to drive his meaning into the minds of his readers by repeated blows. They are ninety-five sledge-hammer strokes delivered at the grossest ecclesiastical abuse of the age. They are written in such plain, nervous language, that no-one could fail to understand what they meant, although it might not be so easy to comprehend all that they implied.

The theses made a great impression far and wide. The speed with which they got into circulation was, for the age, unprecedented. They were read and known over the great part of Germany within a fortnight after they were published; and Myconius tells us that they had gone far beyond Germany in four weeks. They were discussed privately by people of all ranks and classes. This was no doubt due, as Luther said, to the dislike that so many people had for the Indulgence. But the boldness of the thoughts, and the clear, trenchant language, which Luther knew so well how to use, had their effect. So effective were they that the sales of 'Papal Letters' declined rapidly, to the great disgust of Archbishop Albert and his commissary Tetzel. But Luther was disappointed that no-one came forward to dispute the questions he had raised; and he was hurt that his friends were very silent about the matter. The common opinion among those most friendly was that while he had spoken what was true, he had done a very rash thing, and that he could not fail to suffer for it. Luther's bishop told him that he found nothing heretical in his theses, but advised him to be content with what he had done, and publish nothing further upon the matter.

On the other hand, Archbishop Albert was as much dissatisfied with the part he was forced to play. He wished to begin an ecclesiastical process against Luther at once, but was dissuaded from doing so by his advisers, and had to content himself with writing to the Pope. Tetzel, with his usual audacity, wrote and published counter-theses, and another Dominican monk, Conrad Wimpina, did the same. These controversialists contented themselves, however, with sheltering themselves behind the omnipotence of the Pope in all matters belonging to faith and morals; they did not enter into the deep moral and theological questions raised by Luther. The students of Wittenberg, who were enthusiastically on the side of Luther, succeeded in buying and stealing some eight hundred copies of Tetzel's counter-theses, and burning them in the market-place of that town. This act of violence did not do the cause of their hero any good. Luther, debarred by his bishop from publicly answering his opponents, contented himself with quietly preaching sermons in which he explained the moral questions involved in the sinner's relations to God and the pardon and free grace offered in the gospel.

In April 1518 the Augustinian monks held their usual chapter or General Assembly at Heidelberg, and Luther went there in spite of many warnings from his friends that it was dangerous for him to leave Wittenberg. The Elector Frederic, although he did not approve of Luther's views on the Indulgence question, evidently did what he could to secure the safety of one whom he declared to be a 'pious man'. At these general chapters of the Augustinian Order a large amount of time was spent on theological discussions, and Luther had the consolation, hitherto denied him, of defending his theses publicly in the presence of theological opponents; and in spite of the fact that he found much more opposition than he had expected, he returned to his work at Wittenberg very much strengthened and comforted in mind.

Meanwhile one theologian John Eck, formerly a personal friend of Luther's, a theological professor in Ingolstadt, had been care-fully studying the theses, and with increasing dislike. Eck was by far the ablest opponent of Luther that Germany produced: a clear-signed and learned man, and a forcible and ready debater. He saw that the theses were based on principles which would justify the opinions of John Huss, or, as they were commonly called, 'the Bohemian Heresy', and that if carried out they would destroy the whole medieval conception of the supernatural powers of the clergy, and the dominion over the laity which the gifts supposed to be bestowed in ordination gave them. He made his first attack on Luther in a book of annotations on the theses, which he called *Obelisks*; and from this time forward two men, both sons of peas-ants, stood forward as the champions, the one of the Romish hier-archy and the other of evangelical liberty.

3. Luther and Leo X

When Luther came back from Heidelberg, he prepared for final pub-lication an elaborate defence of his Theses. He called it *Resolutiones*, and it is perhaps the most carefully prepared of all Luther's writ-ings. It was rewritten several times, and long meditated over. It was dedicated to the Bishop of Brandenberg; it was also sent to the Pope, accompanied by a letter to His Holiness, in which Luther, in the strongest language, professed himself to be a loyal and obedient son of the Church and of the Pope; he went so far as to say that he would 'recognise in the Pope's voice the voice of Christ'; and that he had the greatest confidence in the Pope's personal character. In the *Resolutiones* he went over the ground taken in the theses, and explained at length the relation of the priest to the sinner in priestly absolution, what he meant by the absolute authority of Scripture, and what he understood by the 'power of the keys'.

Pope Leo X was not a man to take any doctrinal matters very seriously. His one intention was to enjoy the papacy. He was rather anxious about the state of Germany, for the aged Emperor, Maximilian, was anxious to have his grandson nominated to be his successor; and the election of such a powerful prince to the impe-

rial throne did not promise an easy pontificate. He had heard a
good deal about Luther before the monk addressed him, and he
had written confidentially to the general of the Augustinians that he
was to do his best to keep things quiet, and calm down any excitement that had arisen. There was, however, at Rome, and in a place
of authority, a very violent opponent of Luther. This was Silvester
Mazzolini, called Prierias, from his birthplace, Prierio. He was a
Dominican, was papal censor for the Roman Province, and an
Inquisitor. He had written against the theses, and urged the Pope to
do something, and that speedily, to end the heresy, for so he thought
it, of the German monk. The Pope consented, and on the 7th of
April, Luther received a summons to present himself at Rome within
sixteen days. The sudden summons to appear before the Inquisito-
rial office at Rome could be represented as an insult to the University of Wittenberg, of which Luther was the official head. To obey
the summons was to invite destruction. Luther wrote to Spalatin,
and suggested that the German princes ought to defend the rights
of German universities attacked in his person. Spalatin wrote to
the Elector and to Emperor, both of whom were at Augsburg at the
Diet. They were willing enough to insist on a trial on German soil.
Frederic was anxious to maintain the dignity of his university, and
had a high regard for Luther, although he did not yet share his
opinions. The Emperor's keen political vision discerned a useful
although obscure ally in the young German theologian. He wished
to secure Frederic's interest for his proposal to have his grandson
nominated to be his successor, and he had long meditated on the
need for notable reforms in the Church. 'Luther is sure to begin a
game with the priests,' he said to Pfeffinger, Frederic's secretary;
'the Elector should take good care of that monk, for he will be of
use to us some day.' The Pope was urged to grant a trial on German soil, and as he was no less anxious than the Emperor to secure
to his side the support of Frederic, he at once consented. It was
accordingly arranged that instead of going to Rome, Luther should
present himself before the papal legate at Augsburg.

Luther at once set out in obedience to the mandate, although some faint-hearted friends tried to hold him back. The Elector gave him twenty gulden for the expenses of the journey, and when he reached Augsburg provided him with a jurist who could advise him on points of law. Travelling on foot, he got to Augsburg on the 8th of October 1518, and after some days' waiting, had an audience of the legate, the Cardinal Cajetan. Luther found the Cardinal willing to discuss the questions raised by the theses, and learned that there were two points to which he specially objected: first, that Luther denied, by implication at least, the existence of a 'treasury of merits', which could be dispensed by the Pope to the faithful, as in the Indulgence; and secondly, that he seemed to hold that the sacraments were not efficacious apart from faith in the receiver. He indicated that if Luther would unconditionally recant those two propositions, the rest might be condoned. Indeed, Luther received the impression that if he would admit the existence of the 'treasury of merits' and assent to the use made of it in the Indulgences, nothing further would be said; 'for I saw,' said Luther, 'that it was money, and not doctrine, that they cared for at Rome.' Luther would have yielded almost anything, except the truth that the just shall live by his faith; a truth on which these two propositions were founded which the legate required him to recant. On this he could not yield, and the legate dismissed him with threats. His friends at Augsburg were so alarmed for his safety that they smuggled him out of the city, and he went off riding on such a sorry horse that it would have been much less fatiguing to have walked.

The legate, highly indignant at Luther's refusal to recant, wrote to the Elector warning him against sheltering a heretic, to which Frederic replied that he could not deem a man to be a heretic whom no theologian in Germany had hitherto succeeded in showing to be in the wrong.

Before leaving Augsburg, Luther had prepared a protest against the legate's decision, and had appended an appeal to a General Council. It is probable that he had been thinking about this before he left Wittenberg; for it is recorded that he had said that the papists believed that the Church was in the Pope and the representation in the Cardinals, while he thought that the Church was in Christ and the representation in a General Council. At all events this appeal was a masterstroke of policy. For one thing, it made use of a well-known and legitimate weapon of defence against papal tyranny. No one could accuse the great University of Paris of heresy, and yet not more than six months earlier (in March 1518) its theologians had appealed to a General Council against a decision of the Pope, which they believed was an infringement of the ecclesiastical liberties of the Church of France. It enabled the Elector and the Emperor to protect the reformer until his appeal had been heard and decided upon. It was besides an offer to the Emperor and the German princes of the most effectual means of wringing from the papal court ecclesiastical reforms for which all Germany was crying out.

In Luther's hands, however, old weapons acquired new powers, and this was soon to be apparent with regard to the time-honoured appeal to a General Council. For as the effect of the appeal came to be recognised, Luther published the three great Creeds of Western Christendom – the Apostles', the Nicene, and the Athanasian – as his Confession of Faith; and in his preface he said:

> 'I have caused these three Creeds of Confessions to be published together in German, Confessions which have hitherto been held throughout the whole Church; and by these publications I testify once for all that I adhere to the true Church of Christ, which up till now has maintained these Confessions, but not to that false, pretentious Church, which is the worst enemy of the true Church, and which has surreptitiously introduced much idolatry alongside of those beautiful Confessions.'

The result of the publication of the appeal and of the Creeds was that people were able to see that even Western Christendom was wider than the papacy, that it had a Creed which tested orthodoxy, and that it had a Court of Appeal which preserved its discipline, and that one might be an orthodox Catholic Christian, although the Pope and the papal Curia had thrust him from their communion. The publication of the Creeds in German was much later than the first issuing of the appeal; but it is well to see now all that Luther had in his mind when on his return to Wittenberg from Augsburg he carefully redrafted and published this appeal to a General Council.

The political condition of affairs in Germany was too delicate and the need for conciliating the political support of the Elector Frederic was too important, for the Pope to proceed rashly in the condemnation of Luther, which had been pronounced at Augsburg by the papal legate. With its habitual caution, the papal court resolved to refrain from hasty action. The Pope determined to send a special delegate to Germany to find out and report upon the condition of matters there. He selected his chamberlain, Charles von Miltitz, belonging to a noble Saxon family, members of which were in the service of the Elector, a man whom the Elector had used as his agent at the Court of Rome. No selection could be more acceptable to Frederic. The Pope did more to gain over Luther's protector. It was well known that Frederic was a devout man in the common medieval sense of the term; he had made a pilgrimage to Palestine, and had brought home a great store of relics, all of which are fully set forth in Lucas Cranach's book – *Wittemberger Heiligenthums Buch von 1509*; those relics were shown to the faithful on high festivals, and Frederic had procured from the Pope an Indulgence for the pilgrims who came to see and adore. He thought himself entitled to receive that mark of the Pope's friendship which was called the 'Golden Rose', and had privately asked for it through Miltitz himself. The 'Golden Rose' was now sent with a gracious letter.[1]

Miltitz was armed with several letters from the Pope to Frederic, in which Luther was called a 'child of the Devil', to the Saxon Councillor Pfeffinger, and to other magnates in Germany. He had

[1]The 'Golden Rose' is an artificial rose made in filigree work of gold. About two ounces weight of gold is employed for the purpose. On the first Sunday in Lent the Golden Rose was solemnly blessed by the Pope. After service, when the Pope left the church with his clergy, he carried the Rose in his hand. It was afterwards sent to the sovereign or prince on whom the Pope wished to bestow a special mark of personal friendship. It is now usually sent to ladies. The Queen of Spain got it to console her for the troubles inflicted in the war with the United States; and the mother of baby Boris to comfort her when, in spite of all her exertions, the baby was baptized according to the rites of the Greek Church.

full powers to do the best he could to calm things down, and was only fettered by the instructions to conclude nothing without taking the legate along with him.

Miltitz set to work very cautiously. He was not able to confer with the legate, who had gone to Austria, nor could he persuade Tetzel to come to meet him. The Indulgence-preacher declared that he dared not travel, being in fear of his life, so much had Luther stirred the authorities against him, not only in all parts of Germany, but also in Hungary, Bohemia and Poland. Miltitz soon discovered that any high-handed proceedings against Luther would bring about an explosion of wrath in Germany. Nearly half the men he met with were on Luther's side. He therefore resolved to meet Luther in as friendly a way as possible, and had interviews with him in Spalatin's presence at Altenberg. There Luther was persuaded to write a conciliatory letter to the Pope, and pledged himself to keep silence on religious matters in dispute, *provided his opponents did the same*; and Miltitz prevailed upon the Pope to write to Luther, and address him as his 'dear son'. Miltitz then went to Tetzel, and having discovered the character of the man, he got the Dominican authorities to confine the former commissary for Indulgences to the monastery of his Order in Leipzig. The poor man died not long afterwards in disgrace, abandoned by his party. It was characteristic of Luther that when he heard of Tetzel's disgrace and illness he sent him a comforting letter.

Luther had promised to keep silent until the matters in dispute had been referred for investigation to two honoured German prelates, the Archbishop of Trier (Treves) and the Bishop of Würzburg, but only on condition that his opponents refrained from attacking him. He faithfully adhered to the pact. But his opponents refused to let him alone; and he was practically forced by Dr Eck to take part in the great theological discussion at Leipzig.

4. The Leipzig Disputation and its Results

The Leipzig Disputation, as it is called, is one of the most important episodes in the history of the Reformation. It brought the two German champions face to face. Eck so forced the discussion that it became plain that Luther's Augustinian theology led him much further than he had at first believed, and really involved much more than a protest against some prominent abuses in the medieval Church.

It is needless to enter into the details of the negotiation which led up to this famous Disputation. Duke George of Saxony, afterwards one of Luther's bitterest enemies, was keen to have such an important Disputation held in the presence of his university. Matters were so arranged by his opponents that Luther was forced to vindicate his own honour – bitterly attacked by Dr John Eck – and the reputation of the University of Wittenberg, by consenting to take part in the discussion.

Luther and Carlstadt left Wittenberg on the 24th of June 1520, in two common country carts, Carlstadt by himself in the first, and Luther with his friend Melanchthon, who since August 1518 had joined the teaching staff of Wittenberg, in the second. They were accompanied by the young Duke Barnim of Pomerania, who was the rector of their university, and by some of the Wittenberg lecturers, among whom were Nicholas Amsdorf and Johann Lange of Erfurt. About two hundred students, armed with spears and halberts, walked beside the carts, partly to honour and partly to protect their professors. The Wittenbergers had come among a people little friendly.

'In the hotels where the Wittenberg students lodged, the landlord kept a man standing with a halbert near the table to keep the peace while the Leipzig and the Wittenberg students disputed with each other. I have seen the same myself in the house of Herbipolis, a book-seller, where I went to dine... for there was at table a Magister Baumgarten... who was so hot against the Wittenbergers that the host Herbipolis had to restrain him with a halbert to make him keep the peace so long as the Wittenbergers were in the house and sat and ate at the table with him.'

Dr Eck had come to the town a few days previously, and went about with great ostentation. The 26th was spent in settling the terms of the debate, and the Disputation was begun with all fitting solemnities on the 27th of June. The university did not contain any room large enough to hold the company assembled to hear the discussion, and Duke George gave the use of the great hall in his castle of Pleisenburg, and had it appropriately furnished – two great chairs being placed for the disputants. But let Master Fröschel, who was present, speak:

> 'When we got to the church... they sang a Mass with twelve voices which had never been heard before. After Mass we went to the Castle, where we found a guard of burghers in their armour with their best weapons and their banners; they were ordered to be there twice a day, from seven to nine o'clock in the morning and from two to five o'clock in the afternoon, to keep the peace while the Disputation lasted. When we got to the Castle, Peter Mosellanus stepped forward and delivered a Latin oration, and then we all went to lunch. The Disputation was to begin at two o'clock in the afternoon, and there appeared George Rhau the precentor, with his choir and with the town pipers, and they began to sing and to blow the Veni Sancte Spiritus; thereafter the Disputation began, first Dr Carlstadt with Dr Eck.'

The disputation between Carlstadt and Eck lasted five days, and it was generally conceded that Eck had the best of the argument. Then came Luther's turn. He had been treated very discourteously during the days that had passed; when he went to church to worship, the priests took away the elements from the altars lest they should be polluted by the approach of a heretic. He was made to feel that he was an outcast, while his opponent was honoured in every way. At last, on the 4th of July, the two theologians, both peasants' sons, faced each other. Young Mosellanus has given us a striking picture of the two men. 'Martin is of medium height; his body is slender, emaciated by cares and study; one can count almost all the bones; he stands in the prime of his age; his voice sounds clear and distinct.' Mosellanus further tells us that Luther was remarkably courteous and friendly in his intercourse with all; however hard his enemies pressed him, he maintained his calmness and his good nature, though in debate he was somewhat bitter. It was cause of general remark that he carried a bunch of flowers in his hand, and often looked at it and smelt it, especially when the discussion got hot. To Mosellanus the whole aspect of the man, in the peculiarly trying circumstances in which he was placed, almost assured him that Luther could not be what he was without having the assurance of the presence of God with him.

Of Eck he says: 'He has a huge square body, a full strong voice coming from his chest, fit for a tragic actor or a town crier, and more harsh than distinct; his mouth, eyes, and whole aspect give one the idea of a butcher or a rude soldier rather than of a theologian.' Mosellanus also tells us that Eck gave one the idea of striving to overcome rather than to win victory for the truth, and that there was as much sophistry as good reasoning in his arguments. Besides, he was continually misquoting his opponent's words or trying to give them a meaning which they were not intended to convey. Eck evidently impressed him badly.

The debate, which had lasted five days, was confined almost exclusively to the questions relating to the supremacy of the Pope over the Catholic Church of Christ. When we compare the incidents of the discussion with Dr Eck's first attack on Luther in his *Obelisks*, it becomes evident that the intention of the papal champion was to force Luther to make admissions which would bear out Eck's accusation that Luther's theses on Indulgences were really an attack on those hierarchical and priestly conceptions of the Christian ministry, on which the external organisation of the medieval Church was based. In this he was eminently successful. He compelled Luther, step by step, to avow that the Church is not the hierarchy and those dependent on it, but the whole company of faithful believers ruled by ministers who are the 'servants' of the community. Eck had declared in his *Obelisks* that Luther's theses contained implicitly the 'Bohemian Heresy', and he tried to force this out at Leipzig. The exciting moment in the discussion came when this was made evident. 'One thing I must tell,' to quote our eye-witness, Master Fröschel, 'which I myself heard in the Disputation, and which took place in the presence of Duke George, who came often to the Disputation and listened most attentively; once Dr Martin spoke these words to Dr Eck when hard pressed about John Huss: "Dear Doctor, the Hussite opinions are not all wrong." Thereupon, said Duke George, so loudly that the whole audience heard, "God help us, the pestilence!" ("Das walt, die Sucht"), and he wagged his head and placed his arms akimbo. That I myself heard and saw, for I sat almost between his feet and those of Duke Barnim of Pomerania, who was then the Rector of Wittenberg.'

Poor Duke George! What would he have thought had it been told him that he would be chiefly known because of a saying of the pestilential Luther? 'Dare not go to Leipzig?' said Luther once. 'If I had business there I would go, though it rained Duke Georges nine days running!' He was a stately, magnificent man; the hand-somest, wealthiest and most learned of all the German princes. His contemporaries called him George the Rich, George the Learned (he had written a history of his father's exploits in Latin), and George the Bearded from his magnificent flowing beard. The old prints of the time let us see a stately gentleman, with aristocratic features and high forehead, his breast blazing with jewels where the beard allows them to be seen. He was always strong for the old religion, and wrote, schemed and conspired on its behalf. His life was full of troubles. Of his large family of ten children not a son remained to inherit his lands, and his brothers all took the Lutheran side. When he felt old and frail, near death, he wrote to his brother, the next heir, then very poor, that he would hand over everything to him at once – lands, palace and possessions – provided only he vowed to remain faithful to the old religion. The brother honour-ably declined. Then Duke George made a will that his successor in his dukedom must be a Roman Catholic, and asked his Estates to ratify it. The Estates respectfully refused. This second refusal proved too much for the old man. He took to bed, and never rose again. Carlyle tells a pathetic story of his end. 'A reverend Pater was endeavouring to strengthen him by assurances about his good works, about the favour of the saints and suchlike, when Dr Rothe, the Crypto-Protestant medical gentleman, ventured to suggest in the extreme moment, "Gracious Lord, you were often wont to say, 'Straightforward is the best runner!' Do that yourself; go straight to the blessed Saviour and Eternal Son of God, who bore our sins, and leave the dead saints alone!" "Ay then – Help me then," George groaned out in low sad murmur, "true Saviour, Jesus Christ; take pity on me, and save me by Thy bitter sorrows and death!" and yielded up his soul in this manner.'

Dr Eck was delighted at the success of his tactics, and he and his friends had no doubt whatever that he remained the victor in the controversy; while Luther, on the other hand, returned to Wittenberg, in great depression of spirit, to bury himself in his professorial and pastoral work there. He took care, however, to prepare the Disputation for publication, and to complete his argument on the position of the Pope in the Church. According to Eck and his friends, the battle had been won. Luther had been forced to declare himself, and that in such a way that there only remained room for a papal Bull declaring him an excommunicated heretic, and delivering him over to the civil authorities for punishment.

What Eck did not see was that some defeats are victories; and while he was congratulating himself that he had at last thrust Luther outside of the pale of the medieval Church, he did not perceive that this was exactly what would give Luther an immense accession of outside strength. He showed that Luther was an unyielding opponent of Rome, and almost all Germany was at that time looking for such a champion. Eck had effected what the clear-sighted politician Miltitz dreaded: that Luther should be forced into such a position that, whether he liked it or not, he would become the rallying centre for all those who were longing to see a 'Germany for the Germans'.

This Leipzig Disputation was therefore perhaps the most important episode in the whole course of Luther's career. It made him for a few years at least the 'man of Germany' with almost every German. Leipzig made Luther see clearly for the first time what lay in his opposition to the Indulgences; and it made others see it also. He and other men now saw that the principles laid

down in the theses struck at the whole round of medieval ecclesiastical life. The noblest teaching of the Middle Ages, which announced an awful divine righteousness with its inexorable demands,
made it impossible for any man or woman to live such a perfectly
pure and holy life in the sight of God, that he could accumulate a
store of merits so abundant that part could be handed over to less
impeccable mortals. This thought destroyed the basis on which
were founded the worship of saints, the reverence of relics, and
the religious uses of pilgrimages. On the other hand, the proclamation of the free pardoning grace of God made monastic life, with its
vigils, its fasts, its scourgings and mortification of all earthly and
family affections, a useless thing. All these things were apt to be
hindrances rather than helps to that true life of the soul which is
lived in communion with God, and which was produced by trust
on Him and on His promises. After this Leipzig Disputation Luther
found out his true religious position in a way that he had never
previously done. The effects were soon visible in the sermons and
tracts in German which his tireless pen produced, and which the
printing-press sent broadcast over Germany. This teaching found
its freest expression in the two treatises *On the Liberty of the Christian Man*, and *On the Babylonian Captivity of the Church of God*.

The Leipzig Disputation had besides given Luther, all unconsciously to himself, a position in the eyes of men who had cared
very little for his stand about Indulgences. The German patriot,
when he read the account of what took place at Leipzig, saw a
man defying Rome, and asserting in the face of that oldest of
despotisms the principles of individual and national liberty. To his
mind the one thing that prevented Germany from being a free and
united nation like England, France or even Spain, was the thraldom
in which the land was held by the Pope and the Roman Curia. The
German Emperor had to be crowned by the Roman pontiff, the
title of the king of the Germans was the king of the Romans; the
legates of the Pope and of the Curia took advantage of the divided
state of the country to set one province against another, and rule
over all by fermenting the quarrels which otherwise might easily

have been ended. The exactions of the Pope and the Curia impoverished the bishops, the nobles and the cities, and this impoverish-
ment reacted on the artisans and peasant classes and increased the
hardships of their lives. The one supreme duty of every patriotic
German – as men like Ulrich von Hutten thought – was to deliver
their country from the political degradation caused by its political
bondage to the Roman Curia. It is after the Leipzig Disputation
that we hear of Ulrich von Hutten and Franz von Sickingen in the
latter's castle of Ebernburg, spending some time every day after
dinner in reading over carefully and then discussing Luther's writings, till Sickingen could say, 'And does anyone dare try to under-
mine Luther's doctrines or think that he can if he tries?' Scenes
like this in the castle of Ebernburg were happening all over Germany, and Luther's correspondence grew to be burdensome in
consequence, and he was encouraged to take all Germany into his
confidence in his *Address to the Nobility of the German Nation*.
To such length had the attack on Indulgences led him.

The Leipzig Disputation taught Luther that both Church and
State needed a reformation, and that reform meant separation from
the Roman Curia as its first step. It became clear to him also that
such a reform and reconstruction could only be effected by a movement which combined the whole population of Germany, and that
it ought to be carried out, not by fire and sword, but by the spread
of the principles of genuine religion through the whole population.
His weapon was the printing-press, and few understand how
unweariedly and how uniquely Luther made use of it. One might
almost say that Luther was the man who started the trade in books
printed in German.

Dr Burkhardt, archivist at Weimar, has given us the following
remarkable facts.[1] He tells us that the number of books which
were issued from the printing-presses in the German language and
within Germany, from 1480 to 1490, did not exceed 40 a year; that
the numbers issued during the first ten years of the sixteenth cen-

---

[1]*Zeitsch. f. hist. Theol.* 1862, p 456; cf also Ranke, *Deutsche Geschichte im Zeitalter der
Reformation*, ii p 56, 6th ed.

tury were not greater; and then he gives the exact numbers for individual years. In the year 1513 the number of books in the German language issued from German presses was 35; in 1514 it was 47; in 1515, 46; in 1516, 55; and in 1517, 37. Then Luther's printed appeals to the German people began to appear in the shape of sermons, addresses, short tracts, etc, and the German publications of the year 1518 were 71, no less than 20 of which were from Luther's pen; in 1519 the total number of German published books was 111, of which 50 were Luther's; in 1520 the number of printed German books rose to 208, of which 133 were Luther's; while in 1523 the whole number of German books had risen to 498, of which no less than 183 were from Luther's pen.

These facts not merely show us the incredible and restless activity of the man, they also prove that almost all Germany was eager to read whatever he printed. Eye-witnesses describe how crowds waited at the doors of the printing-house when any specially important sermon or booklet was almost ready, to get the earliest copies; that men could not wait till they got home to read it; that readers were surrounded by eager crowds, who insisted on the booklets being read aloud to them in the streets and market-places.

Perhaps no one has ever had such a power over his contemporaries as Luther exercised. His writings were not merely printed books giving information; they came as the heart of a brother-man from the depths of his heart, speaking in ringing, inspiriting tones, and using language that all could understand. He seemed able to *say* what others were only thinking, and he dared to speak aloud what others only whispered to their own hearts. The accusation which Eck hurled against him that he was repeating the words of John Huss, a condemned and burned heretic, only seemed to give his utterances more power. These old words could not be hushed, it was seen; they had risen again from the dead, and therefore they were felt to be endowed with an eternal life. 'No one,' said Melanchthon, 'comes near Dr Luther, and indeed the heart of the whole nation hangs on him. Who stirs the heart of Germany – of nobles, peasants, princes, women, children – as he does with his noble, faithful words?'

CHAPTER 4

THE THREE GREAT REFORMATION TREATISES

1. 'Christian Liberty' and 'The Captivity of the Church'

In 1520 Luther published the three writings which contain the principles of his reformation. They appeared in the following order: *To the Christian Nobility of the German Nation, respecting the Reformation of the Christian Estate*, probably in the beginning of August; *The Babylonian Captivity of the Church*, probably before the end of September; and *Concerning Christian Liberty*, early in October. These three books are commonly called in Germany the 'Three Great Reformation Treatises', and the title befits them well. Luther wrote and published them after three years of controversy, following upon the publication of the Theses, had made his position perfectly clear to himself, and at a time when he knew that he had to expect nothing from Rome but a sentence of excommunication. However the details of his teaching may have afterwards changed, it remained in all essential positions unaltered from what we find it in these three books.[1]

The short tractate on 'Christian Liberty' had a somewhat pathetic history. The good Miltitz still hoped that the final breach between Luther and the papacy might be avoided; and he earnestly counselled Luther to write a friendly letter to the Pope, and send His Holiness a short, simple statement of what his inmost religious beliefs were. Luther did so; and this booklet was the result. It has for its preface the letter to Pope Leo, which concludes thus: 'I, in

---

[1]These three treatises, exhibiting the principles of the Lutheran Reformation, together with the theses against Indulgences and Luther's Short and Greater Catechisms, have been translated and published in English, with two explanatory Essays – one on the 'Primary Principles of Luther's Life and Teaching', by Prebendary Wace, and the other on the 'Political Course of the Reformation in Germany (1517-1546)', by Professor Bucheim, London: Hodder & Stoughton, 1896. I have taken the translation of the extracts quoted from this volume.

my poverty, have no other present to make you, nor do you need anything else than to be enriched by a spiritual gift. I commend myself to your paternity and blessedness, whom may the Lord Jesus preserve for ever. Amen.'

The short treatise is a brief statement, free from all theological subtleties, of the priesthood of all believers, which is the result of justification by faith. Luther begins by an antithesis: 'A Christian man is the most free lord of all, and subject to none; a Christian man is the most dutiful servant of all, and subject to everyone'; or, as St Paul puts it, 'Though I be free from all men yet have I made myself servant of all.' He expounds this by showing that no outward things have any influence in producing Christian righteousness or liberty; neither eating, drinking, or anything of the kind, neither hunger nor thirst, have to do with the liberty or the slavery of the soul. It does not profit the soul to wear sacred vestments or to dwell in sacred places, nor does it harm the soul to be clothed in worldly raiment, and to eat and drink in the ordinary fashion. The soul can do without everything except the Word of God, and this Word of God is the gospel of God concerning His Son, incarnate, suffering, risen, and glorified, through the Spirit the Sanctifier. 'To preach Christ is to feed the soul, to justify it, to set it free, to save it, if it believes the preaching; for faith alone and the efficacious use of the Word of God bring salvation.' It is faith that incorporates Christ with the believer, and in this way 'the soul, through faith alone, without works, is, from the Word of God, justified, sanctified, endued with truth, peace, liberty, and filled full with every good thing, and is truly made the child of God.' For faith brings the soul and the Word together, and the soul is acted upon by the Word, as iron exposed to fire glows like fire, because of its union with the fire. Faith honours and reveres Him in whom it trusts, and cleaves to His promises, never doubting but that He overrules all for the best. Faith unites the soul to Christ, so that 'Christ and the soul become one flesh'. 'Thus the believing soul, by the pledge of its faith in Christ, becomes free from all sin, fearless of death, safe from hell, and endowed with the eternal righteousness, life, and salvation of its husband Christ.' This gives the liberty of the Christian man; no dangers can really harm him, no sorrows utterly overwhelm him, for his is always accompanied by the Christ to whom he is united by faith.

'Here you will ask,' says Luther, '"If all who are in the Church are priests, by what character are those whom we now call priests to be distinguished from the laity?" I reply, By the use of these words, "priest", "clergy", "spiritual person", "ecclesiastic", an injustice has been done, since they have been transferred from the remaining body of Christians to those few who are now, by a hurtful custom, called ecclesiastics. For Holy Scripture makes no distinction between them, except that those who are now boastfully called Popes, bishops and lords, it calls ministers, servants and stewards, who are to serve the rest in the ministry of the Word, for teaching the faith of Christ and the liberty of believers. For though it is true that we are all equally priests, yet we cannot, nor ought we, if we could, all to minister and teach publicly.'

The first part of the treatise shows that everything which a Christian man has goes back in the end to his faith; if he has this he has all; if he has it not, nothing else suffices him. In the same way the second part shows that everything that a Christian man does must come from his faith. It may be necessary to fast and keep the body under; it will be necessary to make use of all the ceremonies of divine service which have been found effectual for the spiritual education of man. The thing to remember is that these are not good works in themselves or in the sense of making a man good; they are all rather the signs of his faith, and are to be done with joy, because they are done to the God to whom faith unites us.

This brief summary of what Luther called a 'summary of the Christian life' will give an idea of the little book which perhaps most clearly manifests that combination of revolutionary daring and wise conservatism which was the most outstanding feature in Luther's character. It maintains that ceremonies, or what may be called the whole machinery of the Church, are most valuable, and indeed indispensable, provided they are looked at from the right point of view, and are kept in their proper place; while, on the other hand, they may become harmful to, and indeed most destructive of, the true religious life, if they are considered in any other sense than as means to an end. It therefore follows that, if through human corruption and neglect of the plain precepts of the Word of God, those ceremonies instead of aiding the true growth of the soul are hindering it, they ought to be changed or done away with; and the fact that the soul of man, in the last resource, needs absolutely nothing but the Word of God dwelling in it, gives men courage and tranquillity in demanding their reformation. It is the assertion of this principle, at once simple and profound, which places Luther in the forefront of all reformers of religion, and which marks him off from all previous witnesses for the truth, however courageously they may have testified against the ecclesiastical abuses of their days. The principle itself is the doctrine of Justification by Faith stripped of theological accessories, and stated in the simple language of everyday life.

The immediate application of this principle which Luther made, to define by it the relative positions of the clergy and the laity, was so important that it may be called a second principle. It is the assertion of the spiritual priesthood of all believers. He declared that men and women living lives in the family, in the workshop, and in the civic world, held their position there, not by a kind of indirect permission wrung from God out of His compassion for human frailties, but by as direct a vocation as that which called men to what by a mistake had been deemed the only religious life. The principle of the spiritual priesthood of all believers was able to deliver the laity from the vague fear of the clergy which enthralled them, and was also a potent spur to incite them to undertake a reformation of the Church which was so sorely needed.

These principles Luther at once applied in his two longer treatises on the Church and on the Christian Estate or Commonwealth.

In the *Babylonian Captivity of the Church* Luther declares that everything must be brought to the one test of the authority of the Word of God. This shows us how Luther thought that his principle of Christian liberty is to be applied, and what limitations were to be placed on its exercise. The essence of the liberty of a Christian man is the faith which he possesses, and faith is not mere abstract sentiment, but a personal trust in a personal Saviour who has given promises to be trusted in and messages to be accepted. These promises and messages are given us in the Word of God, which is a tissue of promises and prayers, and thus exhibits the union and communion of the believing man and the Saviour God. The promises may be simple promises, or they may be promises wrapped in a visible sign, or they may be contained in pictures of the life of a believing man or nation in communion with God. However they are given, they are contained in the Word of God, which is therefore the rule both of the exercise and of the limitations of our Christian freedom. He applies this to a criticism of the elaborate sacramental system of the Roman Church, and the result of the application is to convince him that the Roman Curia has held the Church of God in bondage to human traditions and commandments of men, which run counter to the plain messages and promises of the Word of God. The ideas which guide him throughout the book are brought together at the close; and there we learn that while Luther considers it possible to apply the word 'sacrament' to all those things to which a divine promise has been made, such as prayer, the Word, the cross, yet it is best to limit the use of the word to those promises which have visibly and divinely appointed signs attached. The result is that there are only two sacraments – Baptism and the Lord's Supper, or the Bread as Luther calls it – and that the other so-called sacraments are but ceremonies of human institution, salutary or otherwise.

It is unnecessary to describe the contents of this book at any length, but it may be interesting to notice briefly what Luther has to say on the one topic of Christian marriage.

Nothing in the whole round of Romish interferences with scriptural commands and messages excited Luther's indignation like the way in which it had degraded the whole conception of Christian marriage.

'What shall we say of those impious human laws by which this divinely appointed manner of life has been entangled and tossed up and down? Good God! it is horrible to look upon the temerity of the tyrants of Rome, who thus, according to their caprices, at one time annul marriages and at another time enforce them. Is the human race given over to their caprice for nothing but to be mocked and abused in every way, and that these men may do what they please with it for the sake of their own fatal gains... And what do they sell? The shame of men and women, a merchandise worthy of these traffickers, who surpass all that is most sordid and most disgusting in their avarice and impiety.'

Luther points out that there is a clear and scriptural law on the degrees within which marriage is unlawful, and that no human regulations ought to forbid marriages outside these degrees or permit it within them. He declares himself in favour of the marriage of priests, and says that there is nothing in Scripture or in the usages of the early Church forbidding it. He says that personally he detests the thought of divorce, 'and even prefers bigamy to it'; but that it is clearly permitted by Christ in certain cases, and that the Roman Curia, now forbidding and now permitting, have defied all laws human and divine for the sake of money-making.

The justness of Luther's indignation at the scandals of the Roman Curia in relation to the Church's matrimonial legislation can only be appreciated by those who have studied the havoc it made in the family life of palace, castle and burgher's home in the fifteenth and sixteenth centuries.

2. The Reformation of the Christian Estate

In his address *To the Nobility of the German Nation, respecting the Reformation of the Christian Estate*, Luther applied the principles laid down in his treatise on *Christian Liberty* to the reformation of the political Commonwealth. No writing coming from Luther's pen produced such an instantaneous, widespread and powerful effect as this treatise did. It was issued from the printing-press some time in the beginning of August (the exact date is unknown), and before the 18th of the month four thousand copies were in circulation throughout Germany, and the presses could not print fast enough for the demand. Such a circulation was extraordinary for the times, and was quite unprecedented.

The treatise was a thoroughgoing antidote to the Bull of excommunication which was soon to be published in Germany. It was the political and social manifesto of the Reformation, and its effects were seen at the two Diets held at Nürnberg in 1522 and 1524, where its indictment of the Roman Curia was practically adopted by the Diet. It owed its power to the spiritual insight, the moral energy, and the tact which, in spite of occasional violence of language, it displayed throughout.

The spiritual insight is to be seen in the way in which it lays down the principle of the independence of the human soul of all merely human powers and arrangements, in which it insists on the equal spiritual rights and responsibilities of layman and cleric, and in which it asserts the true sanctity and spirituality of all natural relationships of family, home, trade and profession of noble, burgher, artisan and peasant.

The moral energy is displayed in the way in which one abuse after another is brought forward in swift irresistible succession, and the veil of legal chicanery is stripped from one monstrous exaction after another, and in the boldness with which the author points to plague-spots which were due to the vices of the people themselves.

Its wonderful tact is disclosed in the modest beginning: 'It is not out of mere arrogance and perversity that I, an individual poor man, have taken upon me to address your lordships.' It appears in the courteous address to the young Emperor, Charles V, from whom German patriots were expecting so much, and in whom they were soon to be sadly disappointed: 'God has given us a young and noble sovereign, and by this has roused great hopes in many hearts; now it is right that we too should do what we can, and make good use of time and grace.' It is seen in the deft omission from the title of all reference to the Holy Roman Empire and the delicate suggestion thereby of a 'Germany for the Germans'; in the appeal to the nobles who were, with the Emperor, the legal representatives of the German nation, and on whose shoulders the author lays the responsibilities for the good government of the realm; and in the use of the German language, which makes the address an appeal to the whole German people – nobles, burghers and peasants.

The great source of the clamant evils which oppress the German people is, according to Luther, the Pope and the Roman Curia, and the reason why the nation has been slow to deliver itself from the evils which overwhelm it is because its arch-enemy has entrenched itself behind a triple fortification believed to be impregnable. The first thing to do is to tear down these defences, which are: (1) that the Temporal Power has no jurisdiction over the Spiritual; (2) that they cannot be admonished from Scripture, since no one may interpret Scripture but the Pope; (3) that they cannot be called in question by a Council, because no man can call a Council but the Pope. These are their defences, and Luther proceeds to demolish them.

The Romanists assert that the Pope, bishops, priests and monks are the *spiritual estate*, while princes, lords, artificers and peasants are the *temporal estate*; but this is simply an hypocritical device. All Christians are of the spiritual estate, and there is no difference between them save that of office and of work given to do. Every man has work given him to do for the commonwealth, and he may be restrained and punished if he does not do it properly, whether he be Pope, bishop, priest, monk, tailor, mason or cobbler.

As for the statement that the Pope alone can interpret Scripture – if that were true, what is the need for the Holy Scriptures? 'Let us burn them, and content ourselves with the unlearned gentlemen at Rome, in whom the Holy Ghost dwells, who, however, can dwell in pious souls only. If I had not read it, I could never have believed that the devil should have put forth such follies at Rome and find a following.'

The third 'wall' falls of itself with the other two; for we are plainly taught in Scripture that if our brother offends we are to tell it to the Church, and if the Pope offends, as he often does, we can only obey the Word of God by calling a Council; and this the Emperors used to do.

Then comes the indictment. There is in Rome one who calls himself the Vicar of Christ, and who lives in a singular state of resemblance to our Lord and St Peter, His apostle; for this man wears a triple crown (a single one does not content him), and keeps up such a state that he requires a larger personal revenue than the Emperor.

He has surrounding him a number of men, called cardinals, whose only apparent use is that they serve to draw to themselves the revenues of the richest convents, fiefs, endowments and benefices, and spend the money thus got in keeping up the state of a wealthy sovereign in Rome. When it is impossible to seize upon the whole revenue of an ecclesiastical benefice, the Curia joins some ten or twenty together, and mulcts each in a good round annual sum for the benefit of a cardinal. Thus the priory of Würzburg gives one thousand gulden yearly, and Bamberg, Mainz, and Trier pay their quotas.

The papal court is enormous – three thousand papal secretaries and hangers-on innumerable, and all waiting for German benefices, whose duties they never fulfil, as wolves wait for a flock of sheep. In this way Germany pays to Rome a sum of three hundred thousand gulden annually – more than it pays to its own Emperor. 'Do we still wonder why princes, noblemen, cities, foundations, convents, and people grow poor? We should rather wonder that we have anything left to eat.'

Then look at the way in which Rome robs the German land. Long ago the Emperor permitted a Pope to take the half of the first year's income from every benefice – the annates – for the special purpose of providing money for a war against the Turk. This money was never spent for the purpose destined; yet it has actually been regularly paid for a hundred years, and the Pope regards it as a regular and legitimate tax, and employs it to pay posts and offices at Rome. 'Whenever there is any pretence of fighting the Turk, they send out commissions for collecting money, and often send out Indulgences under the same pretext... They think that we Germans will always remain such great and inveterate fools that we will go on giving money to satisfy their unspeakable greed, though we see plainly that neither *annates*, nor absolution money, nor any other thing – not one farthing – goes against the Turks, but all goes into their bottomless sack... and all this is done in the holy name of Christ and St Peter.'

He then enumerates the ways, many of them mere legal chicanery, by which the Pope gets the right to appoint to German benefices. He exposes the gross exactions connected with the bestowal of the pallium on German prelates; the trafficking in benefices, in all manner of exemptions and permissions to evade ecclesiastical laws and restrictions, the most shameless instances being those connected with marriage; and describes the Curial Court as a place 'where vows are annulled; where a monk gets leave to quit his Order; where priests can enter married life for money; where bastards can become legitimate; and dishonour and shame may arrive at high honours; all evil repute and disgrace is knighted and ennobled; where a marriage is suffered that is in a forbidden degree, or has some other defect... There is a buying and a selling, a changing, blustering and bargaining, cheating and lying, robbing and stealing, debauchery and villainy, and all kinds of contempt of God that Antichrist could not reign worse.'

Luther, lastly, proceeds to give some suggestion for amending matters – twenty-seven in number. The first eight and the seventeenth are such that if carried into effect they would have the effect of creating a German National Church with an ecclesiastical Council, to be the highest court of ecclesiastical appeal, and to represent the German Church as the Diet did the German State. Suggestions nine, ten, eleven, and twenty-six, aim at the complete abolition of the supremacy of the Pope over the State. In most of the others he deals with ecclesiastical abuses which do not spring from the supremacy and greed of Rome, but which are productive of much religious and social evil. Luther would check the multitude of pilgrimages, which he thinks do not tend to good morals, and lead men to pursue a life of wandering beggary. For the same reason he would limit or suppress the mendicant orders. 'It is of much more importance to consider what is necessary for the salvation of the common people, than what St Francis, or St Dominic, or St Augustine, or any other man, laid down, especially since things have not turned out as they expected.' He would bring some daylight into the convents both for men and women, and believes that everyone who wishes to leave the convent ought to be allowed to do so, since God will accept voluntary service only. He thinks that there are too many saints' days and ecclesiastical festivals, which are only seasons of gluttony, drunkenness and debauchery, and would retain the Sunday only. He also considers that it is time that the German Church came to some terms with the Bohemians, who, whatever their sins, did nothing so bad as deliberately break a solemnly given safe-conduct.

In one of his suggestions (fourteenth) he deals with the terribly sad condition of the German country parish priests, and he does this in a tender and sympathetic way. 'We see also how the priesthood is fallen, and how many a poor priest is encumbered with a woman and children, and burdened in his conscience, and no one does anything to help him, though he might very well be helped.' Luther's sympathy goes out to the man; ours goes forth more to the woman. The priest's concubine, the Pfaff's Frau, is the common butt of the medieval rustic poetry; and she is accused of all manner of things in the coarse wit of the times. 'I will not conceal,' says Luther, 'my honest counsel, nor withhold comfort from that unhappy crowd, who now live in trouble with wife and children, and remain in shame, with a heavy conscience, hearing their wife called a priest's harlot, and the children bastards... I say that these two (who are minded in their hearts to live together always in conjugal fidelity) are surely married before God.'

His remaining paragraphs treat briefly of social evils which cannot be called ecclesiastical. He refers to the rampant beggary which disgraces Germany and which comes both from the mendicant monks and from the numerous vagrants. He calculates how much a town of ordinary size actually taxes itself when it supports by casual almsgiving the troops of sturdy rogues who wander through it. His remedy for the disease is that each town should support its own poor in a charitable fashion. He has also some solemn words addressed to the luxury and the licensed immorality of the cities; and with these words of warning he closes the address.

This call to the Nobility of the German Nation appealed to all Germans, and produced a great effect on the very class to which it was directly addressed. Apart from its immediate effect on Luther's relation to his contemporaries, it ought to be remembered that it is really the first definite announcement that Germans ought to work together for a united Germany, and was the first practical step taken in the movement to create a German nationality which has made such an advance in our own generation, and whose end is not yet.

Meanwhile at Rome the Bull condemning Luther had been prepared, and was published there in the middle of the month of June. It seems to have been drafted by Eck, Cajetan and Prierias, and the workmanship was mainly Eck's. It is a very curious document. It begins pathetically: 'Arise, O Lord, plead Thine own cause; remember how the foolish man reproacheth Thee daily; the foxes are wasting Thy vineyard which Thou hast given to Thy Vicar Peter; the boar out of the wood doth waste it, and the wild beast of the field doth devour it.' St Peter is then invoked, and the Pope's distressful state at hearing the news of Luther's misdeeds is described at length. The Bull then cites forty-one propositions, said to be Luther's, and condemns them. It is worthy of notice that there is no condemnation of Luther's evangelical principles, but of the objections to Romish practices which flowed from these principles. All Luther's writings, whenever and wherever found, are ordered to be burnt. The Pope details his many 'fatherly dealings' with his rebellious son, and adds that even yet, if he will only recant, he is prepared to welcome him back to the fold; if he remains obstinate there is nothing before him but the fate of a heretic.

This Bull was published, by Eck and by the Roman legate Alexander, in some parts of Germany. When it reached Wittenberg both the Elector and the university took no notice of it, notwithstanding threats that the privileges of the university would be withdrawn. The Elector, some time later, asked Spalatin to find out what effect the Bull was having on the students and citizens, and the chaplain reported that there were nearly six hundred students in Melanchthon's classes and over four hundred in Luther's, while the crowds of people attending Luther's preaching were so great that the churches could scarcely contain them. The Bull had not caused the people of Wittenberg to shun Luther. The legate was determined to make a personal appeal to the Elector; he waylaid him at Cologne as he was returning from the coronation of the young Emperor, and demanded that he should publish the Bull in his dominions, publicly burn Luther's writings, and deliver up Luther himself to the Pope as a heretic. He added the curious threat that if this was not done, the Pope would withdraw the title of Holy Roman Empire from Germany and treat the land as Constantinople and the Eastern Empire had been treated. Upon this Frederic secretly consulted Erasmus. The cautious Dutchman told him 'that Luther had sinned in two points; he had touched the crown of the Pope and the bellies of the monks'; while in an interview with Spalatin the great humanist declared that the attacks upon Luther came from ignorance enraged at science and from tyrannical presumption. Thus fortified, the Elector replied to the legate that he had never made common cause with Luther, nor would he protect him if he attacked the Pope, but that as matters stood Luther must have a fair trial. His Elector therefore protected Luther, and the Reformer was able to go on preaching, teaching and writing in peace.

The Bull was proclaimed in some parts of Germany, and copies of Luther's writings were seized and burnt; but the curious *Documenta Lutherana*, published a few years ago by the Vatican, reveal that this was done with increasing difficulty, and that the excitement caused by burning Luther's books was so great that the legate sometimes trembled for his life.

Meanwhile Luther worked on indefatigably with his pen. Attacks on the Bull and its authors in Latin and in German flowed from the Wittenberg press, and among others an elaborate defence and explanation of the forty-one propositions cited in the Bull. Luther also solemnly renewed his appeal to a General Council, and published it in Latin and in German.

When tidings came to him that his writings had been burnt in several parts of Germany, he resolved on the momentous step of burning the Book of Decretals, that part of the Canon Law in which the papal supremacy is supported by many a fictitious document, and with them the Bull itself. So on the 10th of December, 1520 he posted a notice inviting the students of Wittenberg to witness the burning of the 'Antichristian Decretals' at nine o'clock in the morning. A great multitude of students, burghers and professors collected in the open space before the Elster Gate, where a great bonfire had been built. One of the masters kindled the pyre; Luther laid the Books of Decretals on the glowing mass, and they caught the flames; then in solemn silence Luther placed a copy of the Bull in the flames, saying in Latin: 'As thou hast wasted with anxiety the Holy One of God, so may the eternal flames waste thee' ('Quia tu conturbasti Sanctum Domini, ideoque te conturbernet ignis aeternus'). He waited until the flames had consumed the paper and then with his fellow-professors and other friends slowly re-entered the town and went back to the university.

The opportunity was too good a one to be lost by the students. The solemnity of the occasion at first impressed them, and some hundreds standing round the flames sang the 'Te Deum'. Then the spirit of mischief seized them, and they began to sing funeral dirges in honour of the burnt Decretals. Thereafter they got a large peasant cart, erected a pole in it, and hung on it a banner six feet long emblazoned with a copy of the Bull. They piled the cart with the works of Eck, Emser and other Romish controversialists, hauled it through the town and through the Elster Gate, and tumbling Bull and books on the still glowing embers of the bonfire, they burnt them together. Then sobered again they sang the 'Te Deum' and separated.

It is scarcely possible for us in the nineteenth century to understand the thrill that went through all Germany, and indeed all Europe, when the news sped that a poor monk had burnt the Pope's Bull. It was not the first time that a Bull had been burnt, but the burners had been great monarchs, with trained armies and a devoted people behind them, while in this case it was a monk with nothing but his manhood to back him. It meant that a new world had come into being, and that the individual human soul had found its own worth. It is as impossible to date epochs as it is to trace the real fountainhead of rivers. In the one case a guess is made and some event is fixed on as the beginning of the new period, and in the other some nameless rill is selected as the source. But it is easy to see the river when it begins to roll in volume of water, and to discern the epoch when some utterly unlooked-for event startles mankind. So this burning Pope Leo's Bull showed that modern history had begun.

An oak tree now stands between the Elster Gate and the Elbe River, planted long ago to mark the spot where the Bull was burnt.

CHAPTER 5

AT THE DIET OF WORMS

1. The Election of the Ruler of the Holy Roman Empire

While Luther and Eck were debating at Leipzig, the eyes of Europe were turned to another corner of Germany – to the venerable town of Frankfort-on-the-Maine – where, according to ancient custom, the Electors met to choose the ruler of the Holy Roman Empire. Old Kaiser Max had died very unexpectedly on the 12th of January 1519, and the intervening five months had been spent in ceaseless intrigues by the partisans of Francis I of France, and of Charles, the young King of Spain and grandson of the late Emperor. Francis was then at the height of his power and fame. His kingdom was the most compact in Europe, his home position secure, and his foreign policy had hitherto been successful. Charles was an unknown youth of nineteen, the fruit of an unhappy marriage, the child of poor Joanna of Spain, whose early melancholy had turned to incurable madness after the death of her husband, and whose gloomy temperament he seemed to have inherited. His political insight, his patient industry, his wide ambition were all to be developed in the future, and were still unknown. Perhaps the very brilliancy and powers of Francis were against him; the German princes did not want a masterful overlord, and the princes on the Rhine feared the absorption of their territories into France. Long before the day of election arrived the French party had melted away; everyone seemed ashamed to be thought to belong to it.

This did not mean that the Electors were satisfied with the other candidate. We can see from the matters discussed at the later Diets under Maximilian, and from the political literature of the time, that the German people were longing for some firm central power which could check the encroachments of the Roman Curia. Then there was a clamant need for a strong central Government to put down that curse of Germany, the right of 'Private War', practised not merely by the greater princes, but claimed by all the free nobles of the Empire; and for a central court of appeal strong enough to enforce its decisions, where all disputes could be settled by just arbitration. The cities, the traders, the peasants and all peace-loving citizens longed for something like this. It was universally felt also that it was high time that Germany should be considered as a nation with one national language, common national usages, and national laws which should preserve individual rights and liberties unknown to the Roman law which was superseding the old usages. This thought was especially dear to the leaders of the peasants, for the Roman law did not recognise the *free peasant at* all. There were also two strong under and counter currents which were to make themselves felt some years later, which represented the aristocratic and the democratic revolutionary spirit, and which, curiously enough, seemed to express themselves in the one political formula, 'God and the Emperor'.

It is needless to say that those revolutionary ideas did not find any sympathy within the electoral college, but they contributed to the feeling of the gravity of the situation, and made the Electors the more sensible that the ecclesiastical abuses and the disorders arising from private war should, if possible, be put an end to, and that it was their duty to select an Emperor who had a knowledge of German affairs and power to enforce reforms. Their first thought was to elect a purely German Emperor, and they turned instinctively to the Elector of Saxony, the most venerated prince in Germany. He was privately offered the crown on the day before the official election. But he did not think himself able to undertake 'the burden of the empire'. He had no personal ambition. He was too old, too cautious, too well acquainted with the troubles that lay before the ruler of Germany to think of accepting office. He felt especially that a stronger hand than his was necessary to knead into a unity of subordination the unruly and restless factions of

Germany. Perhaps, too, he may have cherished the idea that the young Emperor would follow the advice of one to whom he owed the Imperial crown, and that in the near future at least the sagacity and experience of Frederic might guide the stronger hand of Charles. He refused the crown, and urged the election of the King of Spain, and after this there was no more to be said.

So on the 28th of June 1519, when, according to the ancient custom, the Alarm Bell of Frankfort gave the signal, and the Electors, in their scarlet robes of State, came together in the dim, narrow little chapel of the Church of St Bartholomew where the conclave was always held, the Electors had already made up their minds, and Charles was unanimously chosen to be the head of the Holy Roman Empire and the ruler of the Medieval State.

Charles was at Barcelona when the news reached him, and the affairs of his Spanish and then of his Netherlands States prevented his coming to be crowned until 20th October 1520. When the German princes assembled at Aachen (Aix-la-Chapelle), for there since the beginning of the Empire the coronation took place, they saw a young man of twenty, who sat his horse and managed his lance as well as his neighbours, but who looked in weak health, whose face, though good-natured enough, showed signs of weary melancholy, and who seemed to leave all business to his ministers. There was not a trace of that masterful ambition which was soon to show itself. He came to Worms in December, called together his first Diet, and the nobles of Germany with the representatives of the free cities crowded the town to meet their new master.

Before describing the business, and especially the ecclesiastical affairs, which were presented to this famous Assembly, it may be well to glance at the political condition of Germany at the accession of Charles V to the Imperial throne. For it is to be remembered that at the Diet of Worms the past and future confronted each other in two men – the Emperor Charles and the monk Martin Luther. The young Emperor, with his melancholy, listless expression, concealed in his brain the vast, and as he was in the end to learn, the impossible design of setting back the clock of European history two centuries at least, and of reproducing again the Holy Roman Empire of the earlier Middle Ages. Luther represented in great part forces invisible to the Emperor, which were to wreck all his schemes, send himself into a convent, and at least inaugurate a new Europe. The conditions of Germany – political, social and religious – were the conditions on which both forces acted, and by which both were modified and sent into channels not of their own choosing.

Charles was elected to be head of the Holy Roman Empire, as his grandfather Maximilian had been; and some idea of what underlay the expression may be conceived when one reads across Albert Dürer's portrait of the latter, 'Imperator Caesar Divus Maximilianus Pius Felix Augustus', just as if he had been Trajan or Constantine. The phrase and the thought it conveys carries us back to the times when the Teutonic tribes swept down on the old Roman lands of Western Europe and took possession of them. They were rude barbarians, and tried to adopt and assimilate the wider civilisation of the conquered, with its system of jurisprudence and its modes of government. They crept into the shell of the old Empire of the Caesars, and lived more or less uncomfortably within it. One main thing to be noted was the increased political influence of the Church, for Churchmen had been trained in and had not forgotten the traditions of the old imperialism, and taught them to their barbarian conquerors. Hence in the Middle Ages it came to pass, as Mr Freeman says, that

'The two great powers in Western Europe were the Church and the Empire (and that the centre of each, in imagination at least, was Rome). Both of these went on through the settlements of the German nations, and both in a manner drew new powers from the change of things. Men believed more than ever that Rome was the lawful and natural centre of the world. For it was held that there were of divine right two Vicars of God upon earth, the Roman Emperor, His Vicar in temporal things, and the Roman Bishop, His Vicar in spiritual things. This belief did not interfere with the existence either of separate commonwealths and principalities or of national Churches. But it was held that the Roman Emperor, who was Lord of the World, was of right the head of all temporal States, and that the Roman Bishop, the Pope, was the head of all Churches. Now this part of the theory was never carried out, if only because so large a part of Christendom, all the Churches and nations of the East, refused to acknowledge either the Emperor or the Bishop of old Rome. But it was much more nearly carried out in the case of the Roman Bishop than it was in the case of the Roman Emperor. For the Popes did really make themselves spiritual heads of the whole West, while the temporal headship of the Emperors was never acknowledged by a large part even of the West.'

As the modern nations of Europe came gradually into being, the real headship of the Emperor became more and more shadowy. But both headships contrived to prevent the national consolidation of the countries in which the possessors dwelt. Machiavelli says: 'We owe to Rome that we are become divided and factious, which must of necessity be our ruin, for no nation was ever happy or united unless under the rule of one commonwealth or prince, as France and Spain are at this time.' And the shadowy Empire kept the Germans separate, and filled her princes and nobles with ideas which stood in the way of all national union. For the theory was that all princes directly under the Emperor were sovereign, and Germany was full of small sovereign kinglets who clung tenaciously to their kingship, even when it could only be exhibited in that form of war which we should now call highway robbery.

The political condition of Germany was something like this. The Empire was elective, and it had been settled by the 'Golden Bull' of 1356 that the election was to be in the hands of seven prince electors, four of them on the Rhine and three on the Elbe. There were ecclesiastical princes, the Archbishops of Mainz, Trier and Köln; and four were laymen, the Electors of Saxony and Brandenberg, the King of Bohemia and the Count Palatine of the Rhine. During an interregnum the management of affairs was in the hands of the Count Palatine and the Elector of Saxony. The internal affairs of Germany were managed, under the Emperor, by a national Council called the Diet, a feudal and not a representative assembly, which met and voted in three Chambers – the Electors (excepting the King of Bohemia, who had no place in the Diet), the Princes or great territorial magnates lay and ecclesiastical, and the free Imperial cities, i.e. those cities who had got their charters directly from the Emperor. But nothing could be even submitted to the Chamber of the cities until it had first passed through the other two Chambers.

The Diet had very little real power, and was of use chiefly for providing public discussion, for it could not enforce its own decrees. Power in Germany had been for long coming into the hands of the great territorial magnates, and the cities were all armed and independent republics. The power of the Emperor depended on the amount of force he could bring to bear upon Germany from his own hereditary dominions. The disorganised nation had not even the semblance of common government. Ranke says that when Charles met the Diet at Worms in 1521 everything was in confusion:

'No form of central government had been established, no finance system nor army organisation were in existence; there was no Supreme Court of Justice, and private war had not been put down. Besides this, the various classes within the Empire were at variance with each other – the nobles with the princes, the knights with the cities, the clergy with the laity, and the upper and middle classes with the peasants. Added to all this a comprehensive religious movement had sprung up from the depths of the national consciousness which had within the last months openly defied the supreme ecclesiastical authority.'

All these difficulties confronted the young Emperor at Worms.

It may be added that he was the subject of the most extravagant hopes, and that his presence in Germany was looked to with enthusiasm. Nor was the exaltation of feeling to be wondered at. No one man for centuries had been in possession of the power which belonged to Charles. He had inherited the hereditary lands of Austria, and had added to them the over-lordships of Hungary

and Bohemia. He was master of the Netherlands, the richest part
of Europe in trade and manufactures, with cities which more than
rivalled the past glories of the Italian towns. He was King of Spain,
with all the Spanish possessions in Italy and the wealth of the
newly discovered continent at its command.

Men did not pause to think that the world had been growing
much more complicated, and that these large dominions meant a
variety of conflicting interests which it was beyond the power of
man to harmonise in one homogeneous government. They saw the
outside power, they recognised the opportunity, and when Charles
devoted himself to none of their projects the disappointment was
all the more bitter.

The young Emperor had his dream also, and a most natural one
then, though strange enough to us now. He had the highest idea of
his Imperial rank, and his dream was to restore the medieval Empire and establish it in a splendour unknown even to Frederic II,
whom his contemporaries called the 'Wonder of the World'. He
had only to humble France, to make Italy his own, to set the Pope
back into his place as chief pastor of Christendom, to organise
Germany – and the Empire would be restored to its old position.
That was his policy from the very first; every calculated step he
took was towards this end. Everything encouraged him. All Europe except England was under a jurisprudence which spoke of
one Christendom under one Imperial rule. The keenest intellects of
the day drew their aspiration from the literature of old Imperial
Rome, and those Imperialist ideas were their political atmosphere.
It had been for centuries the tradition of Europe that only a strong
Emperor could hold in check a tyrannical and rapacious pontiff.
And the peasants knew that a strong central power saved them
from oppression.

Charles understood all these things; but one thing he did not
understand and could never be made to understand, was the power
of a deep-seated religious conviction when once it had embedded
itself in the hearts of the people. He never could see in the movement which Luther represented anything more than a band of men

who were to be diplomatically caressed if the Pope became too exacting, to be bribed if they became troublesome, or to be crushed underfoot if they refused to move out of the path of his State policy.

It is not easy to say when the Middle Ages begin or when they end; the phrase is only a convenient way of speaking. But that a man in the position of Charles should conceive the ambition of restoring the Empire of the Hohenstaufens, and that his contemporaries should think it a most natural and feasible project, shows the Middle Ages had not yet departed. That a movement like Luther's, preaching the indestructible liberty of the individual human soul, should prove itself stronger than this most powerful of monarchs, and should in the end utterly wreck his scheme, is proof that the Middle Ages had gone. The time is an epoch, and Luther was the epoch-maker.

2. Luther at the Diet

The general business of the Diet need not concern us. It was arranged that there should be a Council of Regency to manage the affairs of the Empire when Charles was absent in Spain. An Imperial Court of Justice was also established, and an impost sanctioned to defray its expenses. The two Courts were excellent things, but were rendered useless by the fact that no real powers were given to them. All felt that the important business was the settlement of the disputes between the ecclesiastical and the civil powers, and that this involved the discussion of the excommunication of Luther.

One day, while a tournament was beginning and the Imperial standard had just been hoisted to authorise the sports, the members of the Diet were hastily summoned to the Emperor's presence to hear him read a letter from the Pope. It asked the Emperor to put into execution the Bull of excommunication against Luther, and reminded him that as head of the Holy Roman Empire the unity of the Church must be as precious to him as it had been to former Emperors. It is probable that Charles had made up his mind about Luther before he came to Worms, and that he was very much less influenced by his confessor and others than has been supposed. He had a bargain to make with the Pope. For one thing, the Pope had been interfering with the Inquisition in Spain, and trying to soften its severity; and Charles, like his maternal grandfather, Ferdinand of Aragon, believed that the Inquisition was a great help in curbing the freedom-loving people of Spain, and had no wish to see his instrument of punishment meddled with. For another, it was evident that Francis I was about to invade Italy, and Charles wished the Pope to take his side. If the Pope gave him his way on both these points then he was ready to treat Luther as a heretic, if not he might follow the advice of his Spanish secretary: 'Your Majesty should show some favour to a certain Martin Luther, who is to be found at the Court of Saxony, and is a cause of some anxiety to the Court of Rome from the things which he preaches.'

The papal legate was Aleander, selected because he was believed to be acceptable to Charles, and his letters are curious reading. According to his own account, he had got Luther's books burnt in the Netherlands without the Emperor or his councillors knowing what writings they had condemned to the flames. He had surrounded Charles with spies, by bribing one of his secretaries with fifty gulden and his doorkeepers and others with smaller sums. He explains that these Imperial councillors and secretaries, however much they hate the papacy, 'can be made to dance to the Pope's piping as soon as they see his gold.' It is probable that all this fuss amounted to very little. Charles was already a cool diplomatist, who knew exactly what he wanted and the price he was willing to give for it. It must have been a grim pleasure to him to explain to the legate that the Pope's letter could not be acted upon until the Electors at least had discussed it. It was read to the Electors, and the princes, and Aleander tried to convince them in a nine hours' speech that Luther ought to be placed under the ban without further hearing. But the German princes, however little they cared for Luther's evangelical doctrines, were very much in earnest to get rid of the exactions of the papal Curia; and resolved that before coming to any decision about the excommunication they should appoint a committee to draft their grievances against Rome. When the list was read to them they remembered what a valuable ally Luther was, and they insisted that it did not consist with the dignity of the Emperor to condemn a man unheard. They suggested that Luther should get a safe-conduct, and be summoned to appear before the Diet to defend himself. The Emperor consented, and the safe-conduct and the summons were sent off to Wittenberg on the 6th of March.

As for Luther, he was eager to go to Worms, and would have gone even had no safe-conduct been sent him. He was burning to testify before the Diet, and was firmly resolved not to recant. While the Diet was deliberating whether he was to be heard or not, Luther, in conjunction with his intimate friend the painter Lucas Cranach the elder, had published a little book called *Passional christi und antichristi*. It is a series of pairs of engravings contrasting the lives of our Lord and the Pope, so arranged that wherever the book was opened two contrasting pictures could be seen at the same time. Below the scenes from our Lord's life were appropriate texts, and below those representing the Pope, texts from the Canon Law. The contrasts were: Christ washing the disciples' feet and the Pope holding out his toe to be kissed; Christ healing the sick and the Pope presiding at a tournament; Christ bending under His cross and the Pope carried in state on men's shoulders; Christ driving the money-changers out of the temple and the Pope and his servants turning a church into an Indulgence mart, and sitting surrounded with piles of money and strong boxes; and so on. 'It was a good book for the laity,' Luther said.

Kaspar Strum, the Imperial herald, reached Wittenberg and delivered the citation and the safe-conduct to Luther on the 26th of March 1521, and Luther found that he was ordered to appear at Worms not later than the 16th of April. He calmly finished some expository writing, and on the 2nd of April he left Wittenberg for the Diet. The town of Wittenberg provided him with a large cart with a canvas covering to protect him from the sun and the rain. Luther took with him a companion-brother of his Order, John

Petzensteiner, his old friend Nicholas Amsdorf, and a young Pomeranian noble, Peter Staven, who was a student at Wittenberg. The four sat in the hay at the bottom of the cart.

Just before starting Luther wrote to his friend Link: 'I know, and am certain, that our Lord Jesus Christ still lives and rules. Upon this knowledge and assurance I rely, and therefore I will not fear ten thousand Popes; for He who is with me is greater than he who is in the world.' And to Melanchthon, who was broken-hearted at the parting, he said: 'My dear brother, if I do not come back, if my enemies put me to death, you will go on teaching and standing fast in the truth; if *you* live, *my* death will matter little.' He stepped into the covered cart, and the little procession started amid the tears and ejaculations of the citizens, the herald with the square yellow banner, blazoned with the black two-headed Imperial eagle, hanging over his bridle arm, blowing his trumpet, riding before.

The road led past Leipzig, then through Thuringia by Naumburg, Weimar, Erfurt, Gotha, Eisenach, Hersfeld, Grünberg, Friedberg, Frankfort, and Oppenheim to Worms. The journey was full of incidents; it seemed, the indignant papists said, like a royal progress; crowds came to see and bless the man who had stood up for Germany against the papacy, and who was going to his death for it. At Erfurt forty members of the university, with their rector at their head, rode out to meet Luther, and escorted him to the old familiar monastery, where he lodged and spent the Sunday. He preached to an immense crowd from the text, 'Peace be unto you; and when He had said so, He shewed unto them His hands and His side.' It was from the gospel for the day (John 20:19-23), and the sermon has come down to us. He preached also in the Augustinian Convent churches at Gotha and at Eisenach. The excitement of the journey, the worship of the crowds, the numberless fatigues began to tell upon him. He was ill at Eisenach; he wrote to Spalatin from Frankfort that he was in great bodily weakness; but his courage and clearness of vision never faltered.

The papal party at Worms began to feel alarmed at the demonstrations on the journey, and thought it might be advisable to prevent him reaching the town. They hinted at a compromise, and Glapio, the Emperor's confessor, went to Sickingen to propose a private interview with Luther at the Ebernberg. But Luther would have none of it. He could see Glapio at Worms; he would obey the Imperial citation, come what might. Even the Elector grew alarmed. Spalatin wrote to Luther reminding him of the fate of John Huss, who had been burnt at the Council of Constance in spite of the Imperial safe-conduct. The message reached Luther at the last stage of the journey at Oppenheim, and he replied 'that he would go to Worms if there were as many devils there as tiles on the roofs; if Huss had been burnt, the truth had not been burnt with him.'

In the early forenoon the watcher on the lookout tower blew his trumpet to announce that the herald with Luther in charge was in sight. The princes sent out six knights with some men-at-arms to escort him into the town; the people were at their forenoon meal, but when the news reached them all rushed out into the streets, to see the monk sitting in his cart clad in the habits of his Order, with a curious travelling cap on his head.[1] The escort made their way with difficulty through the excited, gaping, jostling mobs, and brought Luther to the doors of the house of the Knights of St John, where he was to live in safe proximity to his Elector.

Next day, late in the afternoon, he was summoned before the Diet. The Emperor presided; below him sat the six Electors; the princes, lay and clerical, filled the hall. On a table there was a pile of books – Luther's writings. He had never been in such a presence before; his voice seemed to fail him; men thought that his spirit was broken at last. He was asked whether these books – the titles were read over to him – were his; and if so, whether he stood by what he had written, or whether he would recant. He begged for time to consider his answer. It was granted till the following day, and he went back to his lodging.

The evening and night was a time of terrible depression, conflict, despair and prayer. Before the day broke the victory had been won, and he felt in a great calm.

---

[1] Cf picture by Daniel Hopper in Hirth's Cultsergesch. Bilderbuch, 1 No 37.

He was summoned on the following evening (18th April); the streets were so thronged, even the roofs crowded with people to gaze on him, that the officials had to take him by side streets and lanes to reach the Diet. He had to wait two hours before he was received. The throng of members was so great that the Electors had found it difficult to get to their places; the darkness had fallen, and the hall was lit with flaring torches. There was the same table with the same pile of books. This time Luther was ready with his answer; his voice had recovered its clear musical note, and his demeanour was calm and fearless.

An old tradition tells us that as he was entering the hall, old General Frundsberg, the most famous of German warriors, who was to be the conqueror of Pavia, and to lead an army of Germans to the sack of Rome, clapped him on the shoulder and said: 'My poor monk! my poor monk! thou art on thy way to make such a stand as I and many of my knights have never done in our toughest battles. If thou art sure of the justice of thy cause, then forward in the name of God, and be of good courage; God will not forsake thee.'

John Eck, the 'orator' of the Archbishop of Trier – not be confounded, as he often is, with the other John Eck who was professor at Ingolstadt – conducted the proceedings as on the previous day. He asked Luther whether, having acknowledged the books to be his, he was prepared to defend them, or to disavow some of them.

Luther replied at some length – a two hours' speech, it was said – but the substance of it was that his books were not all of the same kind; in some he had treated of faith and morals in a way approved by all, and he could not retract what friends and foes alike commended; other of his books were against the papacy, whose doctrine and example were ruining Christendom, body and soul, and to retract these would be but to strengthen its odious tyranny; in a third class he had written against those who had upheld the Roman tyranny, and he was quite prepared to admit that he might have been more vehement in his charges than became a Christian, and yet he was not prepared to retract them either; but he was ready to listen to anyone who could show him that he had erred. He spoke in German.

When he had done, the Emperor, who did not understand German, asked him to repeat what he had said in Latin, which Luther did. Then the Emperor, through Eck, told Luther that he was not there to question matters which had been discussed and settled in General Councils long ago, and that he must give a plain answer, 'without horns', whether he would retract all that he had said contradicting the decisions of the Council of Constance; if so, then he would be dealt with leniently with regard to what else he had written.

Luther replied: 'Since your Imperial Majesty requires a plain answer I will give one without horns or hoof! It is this: that I must be convinced either by the testimony of Scripture or by clear arguments. I cannot trust the Pope or Councils by themselves, since it is as clear as daylight that they have not only erred but contradicted themselves. I am bound by the Scriptures which I have quoted; my conscience is thirled to the Word of God. I may not and will not recant, because to act against conscience is neither honest nor safe.' This he said both in German and Latin. Then after a pause he added in German: 'I can do nothing else; here I stand; so help me God! Amen.'

The Emperor asked him, through Eck, whether he really declared that Councils could err! Luther 'hardened himself like a hard rock' and answered that it was manifest that Councils had erred often; that the Council of Constance had given decisions against the clearest passages of Holy Scripture, and Holy Scripture compelled him to say that Councils had erred. 'It cannot be shown that any General Council has erred,' said Eck. Luther answered that it could, and in many a place. Here the Emperor interfered. He had heard quite enough, and the audience was restless and noisy. He dismissed the Diet, and Luther was sent back to his lodgings, escorted by guards. The excitement, the crowd, the speaking, had worn him out; his face was wet.

When the multitudes in the streets saw him on the threshold escorted by guards, they began to cry that he was being taken to prison, and there was danger of a riot. But Luther calmed them by calling out that the guards were taking him to his lodging. With great difficulty a passage was forced, and Luther reached his door, where friends had already gathered. When he got among them he stretched out his hands, crying out, 'I am through! I am through!' While they were talking together excitedly a message came to Spalatin from the Elector. The good old prince only wanted to say to his chaplain how delighted he had been with Luther's appearance before the Emperor: 'How excellently Father Martin spoke both in Latin and in Germany before the Emperor and the Estates; he is too bold for me.' The Germans, friends and foes, were proud of the stand he made, and praised his speeches. The Emperor, however, had not been much impressed. 'He will never make a heretic of me,' he said. The Spaniards and the Italians were only moved to rage.

Next day the Emperor proposed formally that Luther should be condemned, but the Germans pressed for delay, and suggested that a commission should be appointed to confer with him. The negotiations with the Pope were not yet ended, and the Emperor consented. The commission, with the Archbishop of Trier at the head of it, had several meetings with Luther, and the archbishop showed himself most conciliatory; but the conference always broke down at the point that Luther refused to submit himself to any authority except the Holy Scriptures.

Luther had written out his account of the proceedings at the Diet, and had summarised his answers; the printers sent the sheets all over Germany. The excitement of the common people rose to a white heat. He was their champion, who, for the sake of the Fatherland, had faced both Pope and Emperor. They grew impatient, thinking that their hero was still in Worms, and still in the clutches of the Emperor and of his Spaniards.

The confidential agents of the various Powers noticed the tremendous popularity of Luther. The English envoy wrote to Wolsey:

'The Germans everywhere are so addicted to Luther that rather than that he shall be oppressed by the Pope's authority a hundred thousand of the people will sacrifice their lives.' The Spanish envoy, evidently ignorant of his master's negotiations with the Pope, wrote: 'Here you have, as some think, an end of this tragedy, but I am persuaded that it is only the beginning of it. I see that the minds of the Germans are greatly enraged against the Roman See, and they do not seem to care for the Emperor's edicts; for Luther's books are sold openly at every step and corner of the market-place and streets. From this you will easily guess what will happen when the Emperor leaves. This evil might have been cured with the greatest benefit to the Christian commonwealth, had not the Pope refused a General Council, had he preferred the public good to his own private interests. But while he insists that Luther shall be condemned and burnt, I see the whole Christian commonwealth hurried to destruction unless God help us.'

German princes came to Luther's lodgings to congratulate him; among them young Philip of Hesse; he grasped Luther by the hand, saying, 'You were in the right, Doctor; may God keep you.' Franz von Sickingen threatened to attack the town in spite of the Emperor's presence if Luther came to any harm. A placard was found posted up on the walls of the town hall, declaring that four hundred knights, with eight hundred men-at-arms, had bound themselves to take vengeance on the Romanists if Luther was harmed. It was unsigned, but beneath it were written the ominous words, 'Bundschuh! Bundschuh! Bundschuh!' – the old watchword of peasant revolt.

At last Luther got leave of the Emperor to quit the town and return to Wittenburg. Meanwhile the legate was urging the unconditional condemnation of Luther, when a conversation with Charles's confidential minister made him see the state of matters. 'If *your* Pope,' said the minister, 'is going to throw our affairs into confusion, we will make such an entanglement for him that he will not easily get free from it.' '*Your* Pope,' thought the legate, and hastened to complete the bargain Charles wanted to make. The

Pope pledged himself to interfere no more with the Inquisition in Spain, and to support Charles against Francis in Italy. Then at last the Emperor set himself to suppress Luther.

But it was not so easy to do this. Some of the German princes had no desire for it, and one of them, the good Elector, was sure to withstand it. So Charles waited for some days to get rid of them. Then the Emperor, after formally closing the Diet, requested the princes to remain a day or two longer to finish some unimportant matters. They met on the 25th May, not in their hall, but in the Emperor's apartments. He produced the ban against Luther, and, after some objections, it was agreed upon. Next day, a Sunday, the legate brought the official document to Charles, who signed it. The Emperor, however, dated the 8th of May, the day on which he had made his bargain with the Pope, to make people believe that it had been issued formally after discussion, and perhaps also to remind the Pope that there was a bargain.

The ban of the Empire, thus fraudulently obtained, granted Luther twenty days' safe-conduct after his departure from Worms; after this – twenty days after the 26th April – everyone was forbidden, under severe penalties, 'to give the aforesaid Luther house or home, food, drink, or shelter, by words or deeds.' It only remained to secure Luther's person and burn him as a heretic. Luther had suddenly disappeared, however, and no one knew where he was, and the wildest conjectures were started. Aleander came nearest the truth when he said that he believed that 'the old fox', meaning the Elector of Saxony, had hidden him somewhere.

CHAPTER 6

IN THE WARTBURG

Luther left Worms in the covered cart which had brought him there, with the same travelling companions and some friends who accompanied him on horseback, among them Jerome Schurf, the Wittenberg jurist who had acted as his legal adviser at the Diet. The little company wished to shun observation as much as possible, and the herald rode far behind. They returned by the way they had come. When they came to Hersfeld, Abbot Crato, the head of the Benedictine monastery there, received them with all respect, lodged them for the night, and insisted on Luther preaching before he started next day. Luther preached at five o'clock in the morning. They reached Eisenach, Luther's 'dear town' on Wednesday, and stopped there for the night.

Next day the little company separated, the majority taking the straight road to Gotha, while Luther, Amsdorf, and the companion Augustinian monk, leaving Eisenach in the afternoon, turned south to let Luther visit his kinsfolk at Möhra. Heinz Luther, who lived in the old family house, welcomed and lodged his nephew, and Luther preached in the parish church early in the forenoon of Saturday (4th May).

In the afternoon the three companions left Möhra, making for Gotha by Schweina and the Castle of Altenstein, a group of Luther's relations accompanying them on foot as far as the castle. About two miles to the east of Castle Altenstein the road begins to wind through wooded slopes, and a hill stream runs alongside. When the cart reached the ruins of a wayside chapel – the spot is still shown, and is now marked by a monument to the Reformer – two knights and some horsemen dashed at the cart from the ambush of the wood; the driver was ordered to stop; Luther was dragged from the cart, his grey felt travelling cap falling off in the rush and left upon the road. The band rode eastwards for a short distance, then took a woodland path. Luther was set on horseback, and the raiders set off along a winding track in the beech woods to the Wartburg, from which they had started. A ride of eight miles was before them, through the glades of dense beech wood, the horses over the fetlocks in the dead leaves of the last year, and all around the young shoots bursting with sap and blossoming into dainty beech green, the hares leaping noiselessly into the underwood, and the shy deer watching the riders from behind some distant tree-trunk. The troop had to go slowly, for in these deep glades round the Wartburg, even in the first week of May, the winter's snow, crushed into ice, lay in many a hollow that had to be crossed, and it was eleven o'clock at night before Luther drew rein at the courtyard door, heard the kindly welcome of Herr von Berlepsch, the Elector's trusty castellan, and was conducted with all honour to the rooms which had been got ready for him.

This was the hiding-place, the 'Patmos' Luther calls it, which his Elector had provided for him; and there he remained in complete seclusion for ten long months. He doffed his monkish habits, and wore the hose and doublet of a soldier, with a sword-belt and the sword clanking at his heel. He let the hair grow on his tonsured head and shaven face. He was no longer Dr Martin but Knight George, a friend of the Elector's who needed shelter for a time. He was free to go where he pleased within the castle precincts, and a trusty servant man-at-arms accompanied him in his walks and rides in the woods surrounding. He could write to his friends, provided the letters were sent by the Elector's own servants to Spalatin. He had his books and his pen. Sometimes a friend, provided he was a very trustworthy person, was allowed to see him; but that did not happen very often. Lucas Cranach got himself smuggled in to paint the portrait of 'Junker George', and let future ages see what Luther looked like when dressed as a knight.

The grim stronghold whose dark turrets look down on the trees, with its memories of courage and justice, of song and of saintship, represented all that was best in medieval Germany, and was the fitter casket to hold the most precious life that the Fatherland had then produced. But the stout old Landgraves who ruled there centuries ago, and who rode up and down the steep causeway, with their weapons clanking behind them, have all faded out of recollection, and the memories of song and saintship alone survive. It was to the Wartburg that there came in 1207 all the most famous of the Minnesänger to prove their gifts and win the crown of minstrelsy, when the boy Walther von der Vogelweide sang the praises of spring, and the grey-haired Remar der Zwete chanted the charms of autumn, while Heinrich of Osterdingen chose winter as his theme, and Wolfram of Eisenbach carried off the crown by his lay of the summer-time. It was in Wartburg that St Elizabeth lived the happiest part of her life with husband and children, where she fed the hungry, clothed the naked, housed the homeless, and nursed the sick, where she founded almshouses in which Luther saw the brothers doing deeds of mercy three hundred years afterwards.

The guest who was now hidden away in the old fortress combined the memories of both minstrelsy and piety. His songs and hymns are the property of the German people, and he taught them that saintship did not mean, what it did to poor Elizabeth, the sacrifice of all family affections and giving up the honest work of daily life in the world.

The rooms Luther inhabited in the Wartburg remain in the state in which he used them. The visitor can see his bed, his table, his bookcase, his chair, and his footstool.[1] The great window beside which he wrote is still there, and the descendants of the rooks he delighted in still 'hold Diets' in the treetops far below the panes. The view is magnificent away down to Cassel in billow on billow of wooded hills, where the dark pines, the lighter larches, the beeches and the birches, and the oaks, make a sea of many coloured green.

---

[1] The ink-stain on the wall made by Luther flinging his ink-bottle at the devil is comparatively modern, and was unknown for many a decade after his death. A similar stain made in the same way, it was said, was long shown in the Castle of Coburg.

He complained of idleness and soft living. He took walks in the woods, and delighted to find wild strawberries. He once or twice took part in the hunt, and saw hares and partridges taken with nets and dogs – 'an occupation for idle men,' he says. Restless at being caged up while others were bearing the brunt of attack, he was also disturbed by noises which he attributed to the devil. But he loyally obeyed his Elector's wishes, until the troubles in Wittenberg compelled him to leave his 'Patmos'.

What he called idleness most men would count hard work: a multifarious correspondence, answers to the theological faculty of Paris, attacks on the Bull, a series of sermons on the Epistles and Gospels for the day, tracts on celibacy and monastic vows, and, above all, the translation of the New Testament into German from the original Greek. This is what he calls, writing to Spalatin, sitting the whole day at leisure reading the Greek and Hebrew Bibles.

Luther's stay in the Wartburg will, however, always be noted for three things especially – his tussle with the Archbishop of Mainz, his tract on *Monastic Vows*, and his translation of the New Testament.

Albert, archbishop of Mainz, the old patron of Tetzel, and now a cardinal, being as sadly in need of money as ever, had bethought himself of a new expedient to raise funds. He published that he had added several wonderful relics to his collection in his church at Halle. There was part of the body of the patriarch Isaac, some pieces of the manna which had fallen in the desert, a few twigs of the burning bush which Moses had seen, some thorns from the crown of our Lord, and some of the water that He had changed into wine at the wedding at Cana! All these, with others to the number of nine thousand, were to be exhibited in the collegiate church of Halle, and all pilgrims who came to see and adore would receive an Indulgence when they contributed alms to that foundation. This proclamation roused all Luther's righteous wrath. He composed a pamphlet on *The New Idol (Abgott) at Halle*, and told Spalatin that he meant to attack the cardinal. The Elector, who was anxious that no more should be done to disturb the peace of the realm, sent word to Spalatin that Luther's pamphlet must not appear, and the court chamberlain quietly suppressed it. Luther, however, without consulting anyone, wrote a letter to the archbishop telling him that Luther was not dead; that the God who had protected him against the Emperor lived still, and could gainsay an Elector of Mainz with four Emperors to back him, and that if the new sale of Indulgences was not stopped, he, Luther, would testify. The man's power was so great that Albert replied in a letter so abject that Luther could not believe it to be written seriously, and the new attempt to introduce Indulgences was abandoned. Scarcely stronger evidence could be given of the influence and power which the prisoner of the Wartburg had suddenly attained by his appearance and behaviour at Worms.

The bold declaration of Luther about the marriage of priests in his *Address to the Nobility of the German Nation* had produced its natural effects, and some parish priests had married wives. This led to reflections about the lawfulness of monastic vows, and to the violent disruption of the convent life in some places, and Luther was anxious to publish his thoughts on the subject. It was all the more needful because one of his former allies, Archdeacon Carlstadt, had begun to teach that the married state was the only lawful one, and that none but married men should be set apart for office in the Church. Luther's views, put shortly, were that the married state is honourable and natural, that the marriage of priests was clearly sanctioned in the Word of God, and that the chastity required of monks and nuns by their vow of celibacy was only possible when the man and woman possessed the special gift of continence spoken of by St Paul (1 Corinthians 7:7). Besides, monastic vows and others of the same kind were the fruit of a work-righteousness, and were therefore denials of faith rather than marks of a real Christian life. Nevertheless there should be no compulsion in the matter, for God was not served by force but by voluntary service. His letters and treatises really solved the question for Saxony. At a chapter of the Augustinian Order held at Wittenberg under the presidency of Vicar-General Link, it was resolved that all monks had free permission to leave their convents if they desired to do so; and that those who voluntarily remained must keep the rule strictly, and exert themselves either in preaching or in manual labour for the support of the community. This became in time the general usage all over Electoral Saxony, and might have continued long had not the horrors of the Peasants' War destroyed what remained of the convent life in Saxony.

Luther's greatest gift to Germany from the Wartburg was his translation of the New Testament. It was priceless religiously, but its benefit to Germany did not stop there. Other translations of the Bible into the German language had been made long before Luther began his work. Janssen, the learned Roman Catholic, author of the *History of the German People from the close of the Middle Ages*, tells us that no fewer than fourteen complete versions of the whole Bible in High German and five in Low German had appeared before 1518. For it is a mistake to believe that the medieval Church attempted to keep the Bible from the people. That was reserved for the Roman Catholic Church, which was founded at the Council of Trent. But these translations, made from the Latin Version, were mostly uncouth, and not very easily understood by the common people. Luther may almost be said to have created the German language as a vehicle of literary expression. Ulrich von Hutten, for example, was made to see what the German language could express from his study of Luther's German writings. Besides, Luther, a Thuringian born, was brought up on the boundary between the two German languages, and used neither High German nor Low German, but a third, which united the two. His Bible in this way gave Germany a common language. This new intellectual possession preserved the unity of the German people through times of political and ecclesiastical division in a way that no Emperor ever did or could have done. He resolved that his translation should be a book for the 'common man'. 'One has to ask,' he says, 'the mother in her home, the children in the street, the common man in the market-place, and to look at their mouths to see how they speak, and thence interpret it to oneself, and so to make them understand. I have often laboured to do this, but have not always succeeded or hit off the meaning.'

He took incredible pains with his work. Some MS of his translations survive, and we find that he has struck out passages as often as fifteen times in the endeavour to find exactly the right expression. Many versions are much more literally accurate, but none takes the reader so directly into the heart of the original as his does. It took the exclusive interpretation of the Bible out of the hands of the ecclesiastics, and made man feel God speaking to him face to face. Every German with reference enough for it could now stand beside Moses on the Mount. The translation finished by Luther in the Wartburg was revised by Melanchthon and others at Wittenberg. Three printing-presses were then set to work, and on 21st September 1522 the first edition of the New Testament in German was published. It was speedily exhausted, and a second was ready in December. The book was illustrated by Lucas Cranach; it was published without date or name of printer or translator; the price was 1½ gulden.

The translation of the Old Testament was not begun in the Wartburg. Luther felt that he required help for such a great task. After he was back in Wittenberg, a band of scholars set themselves to the work, and it was slowly accomplished and published in installments. In 1534 the first complete edition appeared entitled, *Biblia, das ist die ganze heilige Schrifft, Deudsch. Martin Luth. Wittenberg* MDXXXIV. By this time no less than sixteen revised editions of the New Testament had been issued, and more than fifty reimpressions.

Amid his multitudinous studies, correspondence, and writing of every kind, Luther's great heart was being fretted and worn by the news which came to him from time to time of his own town of Wittenberg. His comforting sermons published in pamphlet form, his cautions and exhortations by letter, seemed to produce no effect. He had dreamed of a renovated Germany, with a school in every parish, high schools in convenient centres, and libraries, all provided out of the worse than useless wealthy convent endowments; of children taught at home and in school the 'fundamentals' which to his mind, true to the memories of his own home training, were the Lord's Prayer, the Apostles' Creed, and the Ten Commandments; of an evangelical pastorate of married parish priests, free from the vices and hypocrisy of the old clergy, proclaiming the full grace of God, and warning against the soul-destroying error of work-righteousness; of the limitation of the power of the clergy, and the transference of the direction of the social duties to the magistracy and the community – all being brought about gradually by the quiet working of the Word of God on heart and conscience, and nothing done in undue haste or by compulsion. Events were advancing at a rate neither he nor anyone had thought of only a few months before. His Theses, his Leipzig Disputation, and above all his appearance before the Diet, had kindled a train which had long been laid. What this was, must be told when we come to the double flare up of the combustible elements in Germany, in the brief revolt of the knights and the prolonged conflagration of the Peasants' War. The ecclesiastical events alone need concern us now.

One question was solving itself quietly; more than one parish priest, after obtaining the consent of his congregation, had married; this conduct obtained Luther's approval. But many were demanding the abolition of all monastic vows by ordinance to be enforced by violence. Although this question had been solved by the timely decision of the Augustinian Order assembled in full chapter, the populace were subjecting the monks, who refused to quit the cloister and who appeared in the streets in their monastic dress, to all manner of petty insults.

Changes in worship were also hotly demanded, the celebration of the Eucharist in both kinds, new modes of receiving the elements to bring out the primitive idea of a supper, the abolition of the sacrifice of the Mass, and the abolition of the use of vestments. The populace riotously disturbed the service of the Mass, stormed into the churches to tear down images and pictures, and made many unseemly tumults.

Then there appeared a strange movement, headed by Archdeacon Carlstadt, which repudiated all human learning, disorganised the university, and persuaded the schoolmaster to send the boys home to their parents. Carlstadt himself, in order to carry out his idea of 'simplifying himself', assumed the peasant's dress, and worked on his father-in-law's farm. All these things were aggravated by the presence in the town of certain men who came from Zwickan, famed for its weaving industry, Nicholas Storch and Mark Stübner, men who were called the 'heavenly prophets', and who preached a thorough and radical reconstruction of all the public religious life.

Luther had been so anxious about all these things that he had gone to Wittenberg secretly, remaining hid in Amsdorf's house, to satisfy himself about the actual state of matters, and he had returned to the Wartburg in great depression of spirit. When he heard that the Council of the Regency, on complaint of Duke George of Saxony, the head of the Albertine line and a strong opponent of the Reformation, had called upon the Elector to put down by force all the innovations introduced into the town, he could restrain himself no longer. He wrote to the Elector that he must leave his place of refuge, and asked him to do nothing to protect him should the Imperial officials seize him according to the decree of the Diet.

We get a glimpse of him on the road from the Wartburg to Wittenberg from the pen of John Kessler, a young Swiss student, who was travelling with a companion to enrol himself in the university.

Kessler relates that at the town of Jena they entered the 'Black Bear' Hotel to lodge for the night. 'There we found a man sitting alone at the table, and before him lay a little book. He greeted us kindly, asked us to draw near and place ourselves by him at the table, for our shoes were so covered with mud and dirt that we were ashamed to enter boldly into the chamber, and had seated ourselves on a little bench in a corner near the door... We thought nothing else but that he was a trooper, as he sat there according to the custom of the country, in hose and tunic, without armour, a sword by his side, his right hand on the pommel, and his left grasping its hilt. His eyes were black and deep, flashing and beaming like a star, so that they could not well be looked upon.' Then they talked about Switzerland, their studies, their earnest desire to see Luther, and so on. 'With such conversation we grew quite confidential, so that my companion took up the little book that lay before him, and looked at it. It was a Hebrew Psalter. Then he laid it quickly down again, and the trooper drew it to himself. And my companion said, "I would give a finger from my hand to understand that language." He answered, "You will soon comprehend it if you are diligent; I also desire to understand it better, and practise myself daily in it." Meanwhile the day declined, and it became quite dark, when the host came to the table. When he understood our fervent desire and longing to see Martin Luther, he said, "Good friends, if you had been here two days ago you would have had your wish, for he sat here at table, and in that place."'

After some more conversation the host called Kessler apart, and informed him that he believed the stranger to be Martin Luther, and Kessler managed to whisper the news to his companion, but neither could believe that Luther could be dressed in such a way, and concluded that the host must have meant Ulrich von Hutten. When the meal came in they wished to be excused from partaking, but the stranger invited them to seat themselves as he meant to pay their score. Then two merchants came in, and having removed their cloaks and spurs, sat down at the table, and one of them produced an unbound book, which proved to be a copy of Luther's *Commentary on the Epistle to the Galatians*. The merchant asked Luther whether he had seen it, and he replied that it would be sent to him.

'During the meal Martin said many pious and friendly words, so that the merchants and we were dumb before him, and heeded his discourse far more than our food. Among other things, he complained with a sigh how the princes and nobles were gathered at the Diet of Nürnberg on account of God's Word, many difficult matters, and the oppression of the German nation, and yet seemed to have no purpose but to bring about better times by means of tourneys, sleigh-rides, and all kinds of vain courtly pleasures; whereas the fear of God and Christian prayer would accomplish so much more... After this the merchants gave their opinion, and the elder of them said, "I am a simple, unlearned layman, and have no special understanding of these things; but as I look at the matter I say, Luther must either be an angel from heaven or a devil from hell. I would gladly give ten florins to be confessed by him, for I believe that he could and would enlighten my conscience."

'...On Saturday (they had got to Wittenberg by this time) we went to Dr. Jerome Schurf to deliver our letters of introduction. When we were called into the room, lo and behold! There we found the trooper Martin, as before at Jena; and with him were Philip Melanchthon, Justus Jonas, Nicolas Amsdorf, and Dr. Augustin Schurf, who were relating to him what had happened at Wittenberg during his absence. He greeted us, and laughing, pointed with his finger and said, "This is Philip Melanchthon of whom I spoke to you."'

CHAPTER 7

THE PROGRESS OF THE REFORMATION

1522–1525

Luther got back to Wittenberg on a Thursday, and spent the next two days in learning all about the condition of affairs in the town. On the Sunday his familiar face appeared in the pulpit, and for eight successive days he preached to his people. He enforced the need of charity and forbearance even in essentials, he counselled his audience against all violence, he made no personal references, and in the end he was master of the situation. In his exhortations against all violent action, especially in matters of religion, he says: 'The Word created heaven and earth and all things; the same Word will also create now, and not we poor sinners. *Summa summarum*, I will preach it, I will talk of it, I will write about it, but I will not use force or compulsion with anyone; for faith must be of free will and unconstrained, and must be accepted without compulsion. To marry, to do away with images, to become monks or nuns, for monks or nuns to leave their convents, to eat meat on Friday or not to eat it, and other like things – all these things are open questions, and should not be forbidden by any man.'

'It is His Word that must act, and not we. And wherefore do you say? Because I do not hold the hearts of men in my hand as the potter holds the clay in his. Our work is to speak. God will act. Let us preach. The rest belongs to Him. If I employ force, what do I gain? Changes in demeanour, outward shows, grimaces, shams, hypocrisies. But what becomes of the sincerity of the heart, of faith, of Christian love? All is wanting where these are lacking; and for the rest I would not give the stalk of a pear. What we want is the heart, and to win that we must preach the gospel. Then the word will drop today into one heart, tomorrow into another, and so will work that each will forsake the Mass. God effects more than you and I and the whole world combined could attempt. He secures the heart; and when that is won all is won.'

By Luther's advice the old methods of performing service were restored, the clergy wore vestments again, the Eucharist was given in the old way, but for those who wished it a separate altar was placed where the communicants could partake of the cup as well as the bread, and gradually all went to that altar, and the change came about peaceably. Luther himself went back to the Augustinian convent and resumed his monk's dress. The university classes were again crowded, and the boys were again sent to school, the master having recovered from his momentary aberration.

As soon as Wittenberg was pacified, Luther was asked to make preaching tours through towns, mostly in Electoral Saxony[1] – Zwickau, the town of weavers, where it is said twenty-five thousand persons assembled to hear him, to Altenberg, the old princely residence of Saxony ere the grand division of lands was made, to Dorna, to Weimar (at the invitation of Duke John, the Elector's brother) and to Erfurt. When at home he was chiefly busied with his Bible translation, but composed one notable short treatise, foreseeing, no doubt, that something on the subject would soon be required. This was entitled, *On the Secular Power, and how far Obedience is due to it*. The intention of the tract was to show that the secular power was as much an ordinance of God, and as much

---

[1]Saxony in the time of the Reformation was divided most irregularly as territories were concerned, for they wound out and in through each other, into the two divisions of Electoral Saxony, with Wittenberg as capital and university town, and Ducal Saxony with Leipzig as capital and university town. Electoral Saxony was held by the Ernestine line and Ducal Saxony by the Albertine line. Luther's Elector was the son of Ernest, and Duke George the son of Albert, the boy-heroes of the Prince-Stealing Raid, the theme of many a *Fastnachtspiel*, and still commemorated by local celebrations in the Altenberg region. The younger or Albertine line ousted the elder or Ernestine line from the Electorship in the person of Maurice of Saxony, Duke George's nephew and successor. It is now represented by the King of Saxony. The elder line split into many small dukedoms, and is represented by the Duke of Saxe-Coburg-Gotha, our Queen's second son.

meant by Him for the good of man, as the ecclesiastical power, which proclaimed itself to be divine. His position is that the commands of our Lord forbid Christians taking vengeance for personal wrongs, that it is necessary for the general good that wrong-doing should be punished, and to this end our Lord has assigned the sword to the secular power. Princes and magistrates are as much set apart by God for this good end as Churchmen for the service of the Church, and they as truly command our veneration and obedience. There is a limit to this obedience. The secular power has no divine rule over the human conscience, and it has nothing to do with testing doctrines. That belongs to bishops and not to princes.

During the months which had elapsed since the Diet of Worms, and while the fever of the reform movement was spreading itself over the land, Germany had been watching with much patience the gradual establishment of what was called a Reichsregiment or permanent Imperial Council, meant to govern Germany during the absence of the Emperor, and perhaps to act as some restraint on Imperial despotism. This had long been an aspiration, and now seemed in the way of becoming an established fact.

Once started on their work, one can discern that if the times had not been so difficult, if the warring interests had not been so utterly conflicting, or even with all these if they had got a fair backing from the Emperor, whose work they were doing, the Council might have made something of the terribly distracted Germany. They were almost at the beginning called upon to face the economic problems which were perplexing the land, and the sketch plan which they produced shows that this Council had in their minds a united Germany, whose various territories and classes of men were to support each other against all outsiders. They drafted a great customs union, which was to include all German lands, and some lands that were not German (for they included the Netherlands) which had laid hold on the sea approaches of the Rhine.

They were soon forced to give some attention to the religious question. Duke George of Saxony was deeply concerned that so many religious tumults should have taken place in his cousin's university town of Wittenberg, much afraid that they might extend further perhaps into his own ducal Saxony. Early in 1522, therefore, he brought forward a proposal that the Council should commission the three bishops of Naumberg, Meissen and Merseberg to visit Wittenberg and other places where disorders had occurred, and restore, by pains and penalties if need be, the public worship to the old use and wont. Luther had returned to his post, and had mastered the situation not a day too soon. As it was, the representative of the Elector could remind the Council and Duke George that the work of the Commission had already been done; the disorders had been put down, and most of the old uses had been restored in public worship. As for the other things, they were trifles. What if the Eucharist *was* celebrated in both kinds, what if one or two parish priests *had* married, or a pair of monks *had* left their convent? Those things were not heresies against the faith, but mere evasions of some recent commands of Popes, which were not of much consequence. It was in vain that Duke George declared that Luther's presence in Wittenberg was an insult to the Empire. He was informed that the Council were able to judge when the Empire was insulted, and when they saw any insult would punish it.

When the summer of 1522 came round, it was the turn of the Elector of Saxony to take his place in the Council, and the thorny question of the religious commotions began to be treated in his wise, tolerant fashion. What benefit might have come to unfortunate Germany if he had not refused the Imperial throne on that evening in the end of July 1519! Readers are familiar with his portrait by Albert Dürer, which shows us a corpulent, benevolent, elderly gentleman 'looking out from under his electoral cap, with a fine, placid, honest, and yet vigilant and sagacious aspect'. He belonged to the band of old princes who had suggested the Council. He had taken a personal part in its institution. He had been frequently consulted on points of official procedure. His placid nature, his wide experience, the veneration in which he was held from his sagacity and talent for business, all gave him a position of unusual authority. 'It might be said,' says Ranke, 'that at this period he ruled the Empire, so far as it was possible to speak of ruling it.'

It was to this Council that Pope Adrian VI sent a letter and a legate about the religious matters in Germany. The new Pope was a very different man from Leo. He had been a Dominican monk and the tutor of Charles V. He was a pious man according to his lights, and was deeply sensible of the evils which were corrupting the Church. He was not afraid to confess them, and to promise honestly to do what in him lay to end them. But he was a firm believer in the scholastic theology of the Middle Ages, and he had all the Dominican feeling that obedience to ecclesiastical and papal authority must be enforced. He accordingly demanded the enforcement of the Bull of his predecessor and of the Edict of Worms against Luther.

The legate brought his requests before the Diet which met at Nürnberg at the close of 1522. The Diet was in no mood to grant his demands. Germany had abundant grievances against Rome, and Luther had voiced these more effectually than any other person. They could not burn him and then proceed to demand the very thing for which he had been condemned. Besides, the princes felt sure that the land would be plunged into civil war if the Edict of Worms was carried out. Even Albert of Mainz had forbidden the Franciscans to preach against Luther, from dread of popular disturbances. All the members of the Diet knew something of the state of popular unrest arising from many causes, among which the exactions of the Church were not the least. These only required occasion to flame out into popular revolt against all constituted authorities.

The Diet determined to come to no decision about the Pope's demand until they had received some definite answer from Rome to a statement of their ecclesiastical grievances. They drafted the famous 'Hundred Grievances' of Germany against Rome, and gave that to the legate for their answer. This done, they debated how to deal with the religious question at home. They held long discussions over it, and at last came to a conclusion which was the outcome of many a compromise. It was to the effect that nothing should be preached in Germany but the true, pure, sincere, and holy gospel, in accordance with the teaching and interpretation of well-known works approved by the Church. Almost every word in the decision represents a compromise; and what made it valuable was that it represented the way in which Germany, if left to itself and apart from the foreign policy of the young Emperor, would have treated the Reformation movement. The one permanent result of it was that it gave a legal standing to the reformed religion in those parts of the country where that was making progress.

Luther had published his opinion that it was lawful and scriptural for communities, who were of the evangelical faith, to choose for themselves pastors, and gather round them in worship. He had seen that the decision of the Nürnberg Diet gave a quasi-legal authorisation for changes in worship, and had accordingly published a *Wittenberg Order of Public Worship*, an *Order of Baptism*, and an evangelical Hymn-book, containing eight hymns. All these publications of his went far and wide, and no doubt helped to encourage the minds of those who looked to him for guidance in many parts of Germany. The Hymn-book especially, which was enlarged during the course of the year, aided the work more than anything else.

We find, after this Diet of 1523, a silent, widespreading movement going on all over Germany. There was no concerted action, no plan of operation, no active incitement, but everywhere evangelical preachers appeared and congregations were formed. These preachers were for the most part monks who had left the cloister – Augustinians in largest number, but also Benedictines, Franciscans, and even Dominicans. Sometimes parish priests called their parishioners together, and explained that they had accepted the teaching of Luther, and for the most part their congregations were glad to follow them. Sometimes the priest explained that he could no longer conscientiously conduct the service in the old fashion, and that, as his superiors would not allow him to use the church, he would preach to them in the fields. The people followed him, and after they saw that no use was being made of the church, they insisted on going back there and worshipping in the reformed fashion. One pastor preached to his people under the trees in the churchyard, and the congregation came armed to protect him, and found that they had no need to bring their weapons. Sometimes evangelical communities formed themselves, and had no pastors; then they wrote to Luther to send them one. Thus Wittenberg became a sort of evangelical metropolis, and Luther an unconscious metropolitan. The movement was so universal in all German-speaking lands, so silent, so natural, that Ranke can compare it to nothing else save the warm rays of the spring sun quickening and making sprout the seed which has laid 'happed' in a tilled and sown field.

Some princes came forward as open supporters of the movement, foremost among whom, to Luther's great delight, were the Counts of Mansfeld in his native Thuringia. The free cities also ranked themselves on the evangelical side – Nürnberg, Ulm, Strasburg, Frankfurt-on-the-Main, Breslau, and others. The more important towns in Electoral Saxony – Zwickau, the town of weavers, Altenberg, Eisenach, and others – had their reformed pastors.

German notables, perplexed by the strenuous wishes of their people, came to consult Luther. The townspeople in the Culmbach region, for example, urged thereto by Nürnberg, the great city near them, began to feel impatient that they had still to endure the Romish services, and wished to make a clean sweep of them all. Their superior, George, Margrave of Anspach, and cousin to the Archbishop Elector of Mainz himself, rode off to Wittenberg 'with six attendants only', alighted at Luther's door, had long, earnest conversation with him, and rode back again, all his doubts removed, to be a loyal supporter of the evangelical cause to the day of his death. His brother too, Albert of Brandenberg, Grand Master of the Teutonic Knights of East Prussia, in desperate trouble between the King of Poland on the one hand and his German commanderies and the Diet on the other, took the same road more than once (June 1523, again in 1524), and got the emphatic advice that the Order had become a thing serviceable neither to God nor to man; that the best thing he could do was to throw off his Grand Master's cloak, dress as a plain German noble, marry, and make East Prussia an evangelical principality. All of which Albert did, and East Prussia became the first principality to adopt the evangelical faith officially and completely.

So the Reformation spread through Germany far and near in simple, natural fashion, without any attempt at preconcerted action, or any design to impose a new form of Church government, or a new and uniform order of public worship. Luther was not without hope that the great ecclesiastical principalities would become secular lordships, that the bishops would assume the lead in ecclesiastical reform, and that there would be a national Church in Germany, altered in externals as little as possible, enough only to permit free scope to evangelical preaching and teaching. It is true that before the year 1524 had ended, the Pope's legate managed to bring together the princes of Austria and Bavaria, and the ecclesiastical States in South Germany, in a Convention at Ratisbon, and there to induce them to agree that, provided the sales of Indulgences and various ecclesiastical extortions were put an end to, no further concessions should be made in doctrine, and that any pretence of favouring new theological ideas should be firmly checked. It is true that the Emperor had set himself firmly against the whole Reformation movement, and that in his hereditary dominions of the Netherlands he had sent the first martyrs for the faith to the flames. It is true that there were not lacking symptoms of restlessness and discontent over wide areas of Germany. Still, all these things did not prevent such a skilled and wary statesman as the old Elector from confidently expecting a peaceful, and, so far as Germany was concerned, a unanimous and hearty solution of the religious difficulty. The storm burst suddenly which was to shatter all these optimistic expectations, and to change fundamentally Luther's conception of what was to be expected from the 'common man' in Germany.

This was the Peasants' War.

CHAPTER 8

POLITICAL AND SOCIAL REVOLTS

1. The Revolt of the Nobles

Two sudden risings, significant of the social and economic troubles of the time, materially affected the course of the religious movement which centred round Luther. These were the 'Revolt of the Nobles' under Franz von Sickingen, and that terrible conflagration which has been called 'The Peasants' War'.

We have alluded to the economic changes which were affecting society everywhere, but especially in Germany, during our epoch (pp. 11-13), and seen that they bore most heavily on two classes in the society of the Middle Ages – the lesser nobility and the peasants with the lower classes in the towns; and it was from these two oppressed classes that the risings came.

The lesser nobility, the *Freiherrn* or free nobles of the Empire, had once held a commanding position in the social life of the Middle Ages. They had been the warrior caste, and had possessed the position in life which naturally falls to the men who do the fighting. The feudal structure of society gave them a real independence, and when land was the one great source of wealth their position as an aristocracy was unchallenged. The Swiss peasant revolts had proved the superiority of trained infantry over the clumsy chivalry of knights and squires. The great landowners, who could afford to maintain small armies of paid soldiers, made the free nobles feel themselves reduced to a position of galling inferiority. The commerce of the towns had furnished a new source of wealth, to which the free nobles had no legitimate access, and in which they could only share, either by taxing heavily the merchant trains as they passed under the cliffs on which their castles were perched or laboriously forded some rushing and unbridged streams within their territorial domains, or else by rushing down from their eyrie-like towers and capturing both traders and merchandise. The very names of the two Imperial houses now ruling in Germany (Hohenzollern or Upper Tolls and Hapsburg or Gled's Tower) show the aristocratic methods of money-getting in the Middle Ages. But the sturdy German burghers did their best to put this highway robbery down by Hanse Leagues among themselves and Swabian Leagues with the princes. The German free nobles were discontentedly feeling themselves reduced to a very inferior position in a society in which they claimed a first rank. Some of them accommodated themselves to the new style of things by becoming the followers of the greater landowners, and gained a comparative security while losing their independence. Others levied blackmail in districts where quiet people gladly paid for some rude protection. A third class gathered round them bands of trained mercenaries, and rivalled the Italian Condottieri in their exploits as mercenary leaders, selling their swords to the highest bidder.

Foremost among the last class was Franz von Sickingen, commonly, but rather inappropriately, called 'the last flower of German chivalry.' He was much like a premature Wallenstein or one of those Italian soldiers of fortune of the latter Renaissance period, such as Giovanni dei Medici of the Black Bands, save that being a German he possessed a fund of natural morality and piety lacking to the great Italian soldier, and had Ulrich von Hutten and not a Pietro Aretino for his confidential friend. He began life by serving under various princes, and having gradually made his way, amassed wealth by attacking and ransoming cities instead of wayfarers. He had three castles strongly fortified and placed in strategic positions, and he kept up a greater state than most princes. He was the patron of Humanists and men of learning. He had been attracted by Luther's teaching, and we have already seen (p. 77) Ulrich von Hutten expounding the evangelical faith to his patron in the afternoons at Ebernburg. His wife, Hedwig von Flesshaim, was a pious lady much given to good works, and his castle was a well-ordered household. He had espoused Charles's side in the election, had even lent him money for his canvas; and he was powerful enough for Charles to ask him to make war in a district in France when the Emperor wished to embarrass his rival. His portrait by Hopper shows a high square forehead, a close-packed brain, firm nose, mouth and chin, a face full of courage and craft, humour and decision of character, and, in addition, curiously 'modern' looking.

This was the man to whom the knights turned in their extremity, and he was willing enough to be their champion. The free nobles of the Upper Rhine met at Landau on the 13th of August, 1522 and signed a 'Brotherly Agreement' in which they declared their wrongs. They protested against the Swabian League, which acted as accuser, judge and executioner all in one; against the Imperial Privy Council, which sought out and punished the weaker offenders and let the powerful ones go unscathed; and against the grasping greed of the princes, who were ruining the free nobles with their new-fangled Courts of Justice, the administration of their feudalities, and their increasingly severe feudal dues. They claimed their old independence, and refused to be tried by other than their peers. Franz was named Hauptmann, and was expected to redress their wrongs.

The aim of the nobles was, like the dream of Charles, to return to a state of society that had for ever fled. It is difficult to believe that the brain behind that 'modern' looking face, could have thought the thing possible; still more difficult to understand the medley of forces he tried to weld together in his attack on the power of the princes. He may have seriously believed that he was actually clearing the way for a religious reform, for a man's inner religious convictions can make strange alliances in most ages. There is no reason to doubt the reality of his ecclesiastical aspirations, or to think that he was posing for effect when he insisted on public worship at Ebernburg being modelled on the reformed service at Wittenberg, assisted at the marriage of his chaplain, wished the cup given to the laity at Holy Communion, banished pictures from his churches, and objected to prayers to the saints; but along with all these things there was the perception that the ecclesiastical principality of Trier would make an excellent secular lordship if it could only be won, and that the man who secured it would 'become an Elector and more'. He knew that Luther did not believe in attaching a reformation of religion to an armed rising, and that he had told Hutten so frequently. But he also knew the wild words that Luther had flung out against the ecclesiastical princes, and how loudly they were re-echoing in the hearts of the lower clergy and the people. We need not be surprised then at the alliance he tried to make between his raid on the Archbishop of Trier and the evangelical Reform movement.

But what is difficult to see is how he could ever have hoped for an alliance between the nobles and the cities. It is true that the burghers were indignant for the time being at the Imperial Council; that they were feeling the position of inferiority in which their delegates were placed at its meetings; and at the disproportionate weight of Imperial taxation which was laid on their shoulders. But no two classes in the Empire had less in common than the free nobles and the burghers. It was the interest of the burghers to see that the roads were kept safe; it was the free nobles who made the roads dangerous for all the law-abiding trading classes. What had Frankfort in common with the nobles at a time when its own delegate to the Imperial Council, worthy Philip Fürstenburg of the Tailors' Guild, had to leave his carriage on the way to be pillaged by lawless knights, and make his way on foot by bypaths with a trusty journeyman craft-brother to Nürnberg where the Council met? Yet Franz summoned Frankfort to aid him.

Hutten, that stormy petrel of the epoch, even appealed to the peasants, and compared his patron to Zisca, who had cleared Bohemia of useless priests and monks, confiscated their possessions to the common good, and ended the robberies of Rome. But the peasants knew full well that their most pitiless oppressors were those free nobles whose cause he was championing, and were soon to feel that his soldiers pillaged peasants' farmyards as well as convents and bishops' abodes.

The very army which Sickingen led showed that a restoration of the medieval knighthood was a thing of the past. It was a body of drilled and paid soldiers, and had the usual equipment of artillery. There was no appearance of the old medieval militia of knights and squires.

Yet his rising was regarded by many as the most dangerous thing that had happened or could happen to the Empire – so difficult is it to see the proportions of contemporary events! He sent the usual feud letter to the Archbishop of Trier, and set out on his march in the beginning of September 1522, all Germany wondering what was to come of this thing.

The expedition was a complete failure. The archbishop defended his capital like another Pope Julius II. The siege had only lasted a week when the besiegers' powder ran out. Sickingen had to withdraw his forces and retire to Ebernburg, where he hoped to pass the winter.

The princes, however, were on the alert. The Imperial Council had sternly forbidden Sickingen's raid, and now they were resolved to punish him and his abettors. The Cardinal-Elector of Mainz, who had not gone at once to his neighbour's assistance, was heavily fined; his chamberlain, Frowen von Hutten, a cousin of Ulrich, was driven from his castle and deprived of his estates. In the spring the three princes, the Archbishop of Trier, the Count Palatine of the Rhine, and the young Landgrave of Hesse, blockaded Sickingen in his castle of Landstuhl, captured the messengers he sent out to secure help, and battered down his walls with cannon. Franz himself was desperately wounded, and the strong place was surrendered.

When the princes entered they found Sickingen dying. 'What hadst thou against me, Franz,' said the Archbishop of Trier, 'that thou hast laid waste me and my poor folk?' – 'Or against me that thou didst overrun my land in the days of my minority?' said the Landgrave. 'I have to answer to a greater Lord,' said the dying man. His chaplain asked him if he wished to confess, and Franz answered that he had already confessed to God in his heart. Then the chaplain gave him absolution. He was about to elevate the Host, the princes had uncovered their heads and knelt, when Franz expired. The princes said the Lord's Prayer over the body and departed.

They none the less determined to stamp out the rising. The castles of Sickingen and his allied nobles were seized and kept by the princes who had made the campaign against him. The wonderful treasures of Ebernburg fell to the share of Philip of Hesse. The Swabian League thought that the time had come to put an end to the Franconian robber knights. They held a memorable meeting at Nördlingen, and resolved to proceed against all who did not make submission. An army was gathered, with George Truchsess as general; the towns of Augsburg, Ulm and Nürnberg furnishing artillery. The League began by attacking the strongest castle in the whole district of Franconia – Bocksberg, near the quiet little town of Mergentheim, where invalids in these calmer days congregate to drink mineral waters. This was taken and destroyed. The defenders of the other castles were too frightened to make much resistance. The grim tower of the Absberg, the castle of the ruffian Hans Thomas, who, not content with robbing, used to cut off the hands of his victims and occasionally send them to the authorities in Nürnberg, was seized, and its walls of enormous thickness were blown asunder with gunpowder. The work was done very thoroughly; the von Giechs, the von Aufsesses, the von Absbergs, the von Brandensteins, and the von Rosenbergs were reduced to submission, and highway robbery and mutilation by knightly persons was largely suppressed.

The fall of Landstuhl and the end of Sickingen are therefore more than the capture of a castle and the death of a warrior. They mark the crowning victory of the great magnates over the free nobles and the beginning of the new era of political development which was the feature of the age. Only the internal circumstances of Germany prevented a national centralisation round a national king, as in England, France and Spain. The centralising principle found expression rather in the concentration of authority in the hands of local territorial magnates and in the division of Germany into a number of separate and independent principalities; and this formed a field which invited the intrigues of the Roman Curia, and led to the disastrous Thirty Years' War, where the bitterness of contending creeds, the fierce rivalries of mutually jealous petty sovereigns, and the fiendish desire of France and the Curia to bleed Germany to death, prolonged the most ferocious internecine struggle that Europe has ever seen. All these things came from the economic ferment which sent Franz von Sickingen to attack the princes, in the hope of restoring their ancient position and privileges to the free nobles of the German medieval Empire.

Few impartial writers will venture to trace anything but a remote and indirect connection between this revolt of the nobles and the preaching of Luther. Sickingen himself may have calculated upon the effects of Luther's denunciation of the ecclesiastical princes, and Hutten certainly hoped that the rising led by his patron would introduce a new era of light and intellectual and religious liberty. Both, however, knew very well that Luther did not desire their help, and that he disapproved of the appeal to arms. Sickingen himself was too cool-headed a man to be carried away by the violent language of a religious preacher. His enterprise rested on political calculations which were outside the sphere of Luther's thinking.

2. The Peasants' War

When we consider the causes which produced the Peasants' War, however, it must be acknowledged that there was an intimate connection between that disastrous outburst and Luther's message to the German people. When the voice of a bold and earnest preacher sounds over a land, the conviction of the speaker awakening an answering conviction in the hearers, when it proclaims the old gospel in such a new form as to pierce the sham religion of the age, when it comes at a time when all men are restless and most men are intolerably oppressed, when it appeals especially to all who feel the yoke galling and the burden heavy, it is sure to be followed by far-resounding reverberations. It awakens responses, some of them very unexpected, in the depths of the life of the common people, and is able to call into being a movement which may last for centuries. The voice of Luther in the age of the Reformation awoke echoes whereof he never dreamt, and its effects cannot be measured by some changes in doctrines or by a reformation of ecclesiastical organisation. It is easy to show that the Reformation of Luther had nothing in common with the revolt of the peasants in the country districts and with the insurrections of the working classes in the towns – as easy as to show that there was little in common between the 'spiritual poverty' of St Francis of Assisi and the vulgar communism of the Brethren and Sisters of the Free Life, between the doctrines of Wyclif and the gigantic labour strike headed by Wat Tyler and priest Ball, between the preaching of John Huss and the extreme Taborist fanatics. The fact, however, remains that the 'common man' in each case did appropriate and remodel, after his own fashion, the exhortations of the religious leaders, and apply them in wholly unexpected ways.

The times of the Reformation were ripe for revolution. The fields had been ploughed, sown and harrowed; the voice of the Reformer came like the sun in the early summer to quicken all the seed into life.

We have referred to the social and economic conditions of the time already, but it is necessary to point out again how they were affecting the lot of the labouring classes in town and country. The growth of commerce, the shifting of the centre of trade from Venice to Antwerp, caused by the capture of Constantinople and the closing of its port, together with the discovery of a sea route to the East, had disorganised the old city Guild life, which was still further overthrown by the growth of great merchant companies whose world-trade require large capital. The rise of this capitalist order severed the poor from the rich, dug a great gulf between them, and created, in a sense unknown before, a proletariat class within the cities, liable to be swollen by the influx of discontented or ruined peasants from the country districts. The sudden accession of wealth led to diffuse display in dress and adornment of houses, in eating and in drinking, which in turn led to a corruption of morals that reached its height in the city life of the first quarter of the sixteenth century, and which must have intensified the growing hatred between rich burgher and poor workman.

The territorial magnates, unwilling to be left behind in the race for luxurious living, increased their feudal dues, and oppressed the lesser nobles, who in the race for wealth had no recourse but to squeeze still further their unfortunate peasants. The ferment which this restless competition between classes, this unwearied hunting after luxurious living, this embittered separation between poor and rich, and the envenomed class hatreds resulting therefrom, were producing, created great rifts in the social structure of medieval feudalism. Into it all came the sudden rise of prices, which intensified every economic evil, and swelled all the roads and streets with crowds of sturdy beggars, the refuse of all classes of society, from the broken knight and the disbanded mercenary soldier to the ruined peasant, the workman out of employment, the begging friar, and the 'wandering student'.

This was the society to which Luther spoke, and its discontent was the sounding-board which made his words reverberate. His message was democratic.[1] It destroyed the aristocracy of the saints, it levelled the barriers between the priest and the layman, it preached the equality of all men before God, and the right of every trusting man to stand in God's presence whatever might be his rank or condition of life. It did not content itself with simply preaching sin and repentance and pardon. The Reformation voiced the grievances of the people; it attacked the merciless exactions of the Churchmen, and it had also hard words on occasion for the oppressors among the secular princes and the free nobles, and for the luxurious and money-getting life of the burghers. Luther's *Appeal to the Nobility of the German Nation* touched upon almost all the open sores of the time, and seemed to warn against disasters not very far off.

It must be remembered, too, that no other man of the great

---

[1]See Stern, Die Socialisten der Reformationszeit.

men of the earth, and we place Luther in the very front rank, ever flung about wild words in such reckless profusion. He had, as all men have, the defects of his qualities. He had the gift of strong smiting phrases which seemed to cleave to the very heart of the subject, of words which lit up the matter with the vividness of a lightning flash, and he had them at command in the utmost profusion. Whatever he said or wrote remained stuck fast in the memory and the imagination, and he launched letters or pamphlets from the press about almost everything – written for the most part on the spur of the moment and when the fire burned. His words fell into souls full of the fermenting passions of the time, readier to remember the incitements than the cautions, and longing to translate speech into action. They drank in with eagerness the thought that all men were equal before God, and that men have divine rights which are more important than all human prescriptions. They refused to believe that such golden ideas belonged to the realm of spiritual life only, and that the commands and exactions of Popes, Curia and bishops, were the only human prescriptions to be resisted. The successful revolt of the Swiss peasantry and the victories of Zisca, the people's leader in the neighbouring Bohemian lands, were illustrations, they thought, of how Luther's sledge-hammer words could be changed into corresponding deeds.

Other teachers besides Luther were listened to. Many of the Humanists, professed disciples of Plato, were accustomed to expound to admiring friends and scholars the communistic dreams of the *Republic*, in which the State was all and the individual nothing or very little, and to indulge in theories 'of the study' of which Sir Thomas More's *Utopia* is the most brilliant example. These, listened to in the classrooms by the 'wandering students', were expounded and illustrated in a manner undreamt of by the scholarly Platonist, to peasant audiences and gatherings of workmen, and received unexpected applications.

The missionaries of the movement were innumerable, and belonged to all sorts and conditions of men. Poor priests exhorted their parishioners. Wandering monks who had deserted their convents, students who were on their way from one university town to another, working men journeying according to the German fashion from one centre of their trade to another – everywhere found eager audiences. They sat at the tables of the public-houses in the lower parts of the towns, they mingled with the villagers on the village green under the lime trees, they talked in the rude language of the people, and their speech was garnished with many a biblical quotation and many a trenchant illustration gathered in their wanderings in Switzerland or Bohemia.

The propaganda carried on by means of the printing-press must not be forgotten. Luther had discovered the power of the printed word in the German language, and the exponents of the rights of the 'common man' made a very effective use of it. Small fly-sheets and pamphlets, sometimes with rude woodcuts, printed in thick letters on coarse paper, passed from hand to hand. They were read to small excited audiences, who discussed them eagerly. They are full of biblical ideas, if not exact quotations, and are stored with the broad, coarse humour of the period, which Luther himself did not disdain to use. The weapon was a new one – so new that the authorities never seemed to notice it – and was never more effectively employed. The most popular was 'Karsthans' or 'Mattock John', the Reformation equivalent of the 'Jack Upland' or 'Piers Ploughman' of the times of the English Lollards, and their most prominent characteristic is their embittered hatred of the clergy and of clerical exactions, loose living, and hypocrisy. 'Jack Upland' describes the fat friar of the earlier English days with his dew-lap wagging under his chin 'like a great goose egg' and contrasts him with the poor peasant and his wife going shoeless to work along the ice-bound roads, their steps marked with the blood which came from their cut feet. 'Mattock John' is much more theological, and discusses Luther and Eck, and the doctrine of papal authority, etc. These pamphlets commonly took the form of dialogues between peasants and monks, noblemen and peasants, clerics and artisans. They were sold at the markets and church festivals, and hawked about the towns and villages. All the burning questions of the day were discussed in these popular pamphlets, which found their way everywhere, added to the ferment of the times, and prepared the way for common action and a statement of common principles when the time for revolt came.

It would seem that there was no preparation for any organised insurrection throughout all Germany; no confederation of leaders or formulation of demands, until after the rising had actually begun. The Zwickau prophets had preached something very like a general revolution. Thomas Münzer, his mind aflame with the wrongs of the commonalty, had made wide tours throughout many parts of Germany, and had striven to create something like combined action. It is very doubtful, however, whether his personal influence extended much beyond Thuringia. Common distress, the same surface causes producing the evils which were felt, the common class hatreds were sufficient of themselves to give the outbreak an appearance of combined action which it did not really possess.

The first rising, according to the common story, came almost accidentally. The Countess of Lupfen ordered her husband's peasantry on a *holiday* to gather wild strawberries for the castle table, and to collect snail-shells on which she might wind her silk thread. It seems a small matter, but it filled up the measure of exasperation, and produced the first serious rising. Whether this traditional story is correct or not, it is certain that this region, the eastern side of the slopes of the Black Forest, furrowed by small tributaries of the Rhine, where the peasants, looking across the river, could almost see and envy their fellow-peasants in free Switzerland, gave the signal for the general uprising.

On 24th August, 1524 a body of peasants met at the little town of Waldshut, about half-way between Basel and Schaffhausen, under the leadership of Hans Müller, an old mercenary soldier, and pledged themselves to rebel against the conditions of their life. The peasants, carrying a flag with the Imperial colours of red, black and yellow, fraternised with the townspeople, and the formidable 'Evangelical Brotherhood' was either then formed or the roots of it were planted. The news spread among the peasants and towns of

Baden. It crossed the Rhine into Elsass, it went up the valley of the Mosel. From the south of the Black Forest it spread northwards through Franconia and Swabia. In its beginnings it took the route marked out by Joss Fritz's *Bundschuh* organisation twelve years earlier, and its whispered programme was at first almost the same – the differences being due to the altered conditions of the times, especially in the religious environment. The commonalty wished to make a clean sweep of all controlling castes between the peasants, the townspeople, and the Emperor. 'Their name was legion; not only were there endless numbers of princes, bishops, dukes, landgraves, margraves, counts, lords, abbots, who exercised sovereignty of one sort or another, but the old Imperial cities were ruled by little oligarchies of old families, who, by close combination, possessed as much real sovereignty as any prince. The land was thus broken up into numerous States, great and small, each entrenched against the other; and custom-houses, different coinages, bad roads, brigand knights, and bands of robbers divided them still more.'[1] These ruling classes, it was believed, defied and hindered the just rule of an Emperor, and prevented all peaceable living.

The Swabian League, the only Imperial organisation which possessed any controlling power in South Germany, was thus confronted with the most formidable popular uprising that Germany had yet seen. It was compelled to negotiate with the leaders of the revolt. Had the demands of the peasants and townsmen been met in a fair spirit of compromise, the country would have been spared much. All the evidence goes to show that the demands of the people, once formulated, were not unreasonable, and that the leaders would have accepted some compromise. But the negotiations were begun, on the part of the ruling powers, only to gain time, and as soon as forces could be collected were shamelessly broken off and the insurgents massacred. When the atrocities of the peasants are mentioned, it should be remembered that the bloodshed was begun by the ruling classes, after having appeared at least to accept the terms proposed to bring about peace. It is scarcely to be wondered

[1] R Heath, *Anabaptism*, p 10.

if the insurgent peasants attempted to avenge their slaughtered brethren. But even a casual reading of the contemporary documents shows that, if we except the few outstanding cases which histories always enumerate, the Peasants' War stands forth as an example of how little bloodthirsty the oppressed German peasantry showed themselves during the short period of their success. Their moderation in revenging wrongs by bloodshed forms a striking contrast to the horrible bloodbath into which the conquering princes plunged almost every district of Germany when the revolt was overcome. The peasants sacked and burned castles and monasteries, they filled themselves drunk at nights with the wines they found in the noble and ecclesiastical wine-cellars, but as a rule they did not shed blood wantonly.

The rising, so sudden, so widespreading, so simultaneous, spread terror among all the ruling classes. The flames of insurrection were kindled all over Germany. From Swabia and Franconia they spread to Thuringia, then through the Vorl-Arlberg, the Tyrol, Salzburg, and up into the Duchy of Austria.

Manifestos were issued, summarising the grievances of the peasants, and of the working-classes in the towns, and also giving the political aspirations of more educated leaders, who had wider outlooks.[1] In almost all of them ecclesiastical demands are mingled with the political and social requirements. The right to choose and dismiss the pastor is one of the commonest, and there is frequently a clause added to ensure evangelical preaching. The peasant demands appeared in several forms, with a varying number of articles. They were, however, summed up in the famous 'Twelve Articles', which became the Peasant Charter of the rising, although the classic form was continually modified in various districts. The

---

[1] The full text of the famous 'Twelve Articles' has been given by Dr Belfort Bax in his *Peasants' War*, London, 1899, pp 64-75. This book gives by far the best account of the movement accessible to the English reader. The curious ideas the author has of the characters of Luther and Melanchthon do not seriously interfere with his description of the great rising. Dr Belfort Bax has pilloried a slip of mine, made long ago, which was discovered just when it was too late to correct it. It has been pointed out and apologised for several times, but *litera impressa manet.*

peasants asked the abolition of villeinage, the withdrawal of all or most of the ecclesiastical and feudal exactions, freedom to hunt, to fish, and to take wood for fuel and building under proper restrictions, the restoration of the common lands, and a return to their old rights and Communal Courts of Justice, for fair rents settled by honest valuators, and in some cases for the cancelling of loans which had been granted to peasants on the security of their holdings. The townspeople asked that the ecclesiastical and conciliar immunities should cease; they demanded improvements in the administration of justice, a readjustment of local taxation, the popular election of the Council, and a better treatment of the poor.

The more comprehensive manifestos contained demands for a thorough reconstruction of the Imperial administration on a scheme which involved the destruction of all feudal and local Courts of Justice, and contemplated an organised administration, based on the Communal Courts to be revived, and ascending to the Imperial Court of Justice. They also called for a unification of coinage, weights and measures throughout the German Empire, a confiscation of ecclesiastical endowments for the purpose of lessening taxation and for the redemption of feudal rights, a uniform rate of taxes and customs dues, restraint to be placed on great capitalists, the regulation of business and trade by law, and the admission of delegates from every class of the community into the public administration.

In every case the Emperor was regarded as the lord-paramount. There was also a declaration of the sovereignty of the people, made in such a way as to suggest that the teachings of Marsilius of Padua had insinuated themselves into the minds of some of the leaders of the commons. The main thought with the peasant was to secure his fair share of the land; and when that was denied he printed in burning letters in the blaze of castles and monasteries, which reddened the midnight sky all over Germany. The main thought of the workman was to secure an adequate representation on the city council, and he made it emphatic in tumults which drove the patrician Council from the town hall and installed people's delegates.

During the earlier months of 1525 the rising carried everything before it. The smaller towns made common cause with the peasants; prominent nobles were forced to join the 'Evangelical' or 'Christian Brotherhood'; princes like the Cardinal-Elector of Mainz and the Bishop of Würzburg had to come to terms with the insurgents; a wave of destruction spread over the whole land. But the movement had no solidity in it. It produced no creative leader, save in the Tyrol, where the wisdom of Gaismayr, aided by the mountainous nature of the country, enabled the people to make a permanent stand, and wring some real concessions out of the governing classes. Everywhere else there were divided counsels. Leaders like the bankrupt Duke of Würtemberg and the freebooting noble Götz von Berlichingen could only harm any movement they joined or were compelled to join. The insurgents became demoralised by their drunken revels. They refused to obey orders, on the ground that they were all brethren, and the whole movement began to show signs of dissolution before the princes had recovered from their terror and begun to stamp it out in bloody massacre.

On the side of the ruling classes there was at least some unity of purpose. They had their mercenaries, who were trained soldiers, armed and drilled according to the best ideas of the time. They had military experience and skill in the art of war. Had it not been that the Italian campaigns of Charles V had drained Germany of the greater part of its soldiery, the poorly armed, undisciplined, and badly led bands of peasants and artisans would have succumbed much earlier. As it was, long before the end of 1525 the rising was stamped out, and that with atrocious severities. One chronicler asserts that more than a hundred thousand fell on the field of battle or elsewhere, and Bishop Georg of Speyer has, after careful examination, asserted that the number was a hundred and fifty thousand. No attempt was made to cure the ills which were at the roots of the rising. All counsels to redress the clamant grievances were thrown to the winds. The oppression of the peasantry was intensified. The last vestiges of local self-government were stamped out, and the unfortunate people were doomed for generations to exist in the lowest degradation. The few months of terror and paralysis gave birth to a fiendish cruelty of suppression. The year 1525 was one of the saddest and most terrible in the annals of the German Fatherland.

3. Luther's Relation to the Revolt

The question meets us: What had Luther to do personally with this tragedy which overtook his land of Germany?

It would not be difficult to show that the Peasants' War had no place in the thoughts of Luther for the regeneration of Germany. His ideal was always a religious Reformation brought about by preaching and teaching, and owing nothing to violence – in *action* at least. He has expounded this thought over and over again. He never had any sympathy with an armed rising to effect the legitimate reforms. But he seemed singularly unable to measure the inevitable effects of his own sledge-hammer words on minds excited by oppression or by passion. He had a singular lack of self-control in the use of violent and incendiary speech. He saw and pitied the growing oppression of the peasantry, and denounced it in his own trenchant fashion. He reproved the greed of the lords by saying that if a peasant's land produced as many coins as ears of corn the profit would go to the landlord only. No man had been so outspoken against the tyranny of the princes and over-lords as Luther; no one had denounced more strongly the mad race after luxury which was at the root of most of the evils.

But Luther, rightly or wrongly, was convinced that no good could come of armed insurrection, and that any lasting good must be patiently worked and waited for. He had detected the signs of the coming evils in the crowd of beggars which was a moral pest in the beginning of the sixteenth century all over central Europe, and he advised that every town and country district should assess themselves to support their poor. He dreaded the revolutionary spirit that betrayed itself in the Zwickau prophets and in Münzer and Carlstadt. He felt sure that those guides were leading the poor people who followed them to their destruction. Before the storm

burst he did his best to show that no good would come from insurrection. After it burst, he risked his life over and over again in the
visits he paid to the disaffected districts to warn the people of the
dangers they were running. He did not believe in the more ambi-
tious schemes of the leaders of the rising. He saw clearly enough
that, in the condition in which Germany was, the one element of
permanent political strength which the country possessed was the
princes. He had sympathy with the demands of the 'Twelve Articles', and long before they were formulated he advocated a return
to the old common law of Germany. He expressed his approval of
the substance of the 'Twelve Articles' after they were recognised
to be the 'charter' of the German peasant. But, true to the principles that had always been his, he declared that to press them by
armed insurrection was not the way to bring them into force.

He has been accused of sycophancy to the constituted authorities. He has been censured for 'sitting on the fence' when he blamed
both nobles and peasants in the *Exhortation to Peace, on the Twelve
Articles of the Peasants in Swabia.* But that 'Exhortation' ex-
presses the opinions he had entertained years before these Swabian
Articles had been formulated. In this tract he sharply rebukes those
princes, nobles and bishops who 'tax and fleece their subjects, for
the advancement of their own pomp and pride, until the common
people can endure it no longer'. He praises some of the Articles,
but warns against attempting to extort agreement to them by force
of arms. He proposes that 'a few counts and nobles should be
chosen from the nobility and a few councillors from the towns,
and that matters should be adjusted and composed in an amicable
manner, that so the affair... may be arranged according to human
laws and agreements.' The tract must have been written about the
end of the third week in April 1525, while Luther was at Eisleben,
called there to establish a school in his native town. Münzer was
then at Mühlhausen, where his intense earnestness and sincerity
carried all before him. The citizens regarded him very much as the
Florentines looked on Savonarola. For a while the rich fed the
poor, and he almost established a community of goods. The news

from South Germany excited him, and he appealed madly to arms. He sent out fiery proclamations to citizens and peasantry:

> 'Arise! fight the battle of the Lord! On! On! On! the wicked tremble when they hear of you. On! On! On! Be pitiless! although Esau gives you fair words (Genesis 33). Heed not the groans of the godless; they will beg, weep, and entreat you for pity like children. Show them no mercy, as God commanded Moses (Deuteronomy 7), and as He has revealed the same to us. Rouse up the towns and the villages; above all rouse the miners... On! On! while the fire is burning; let not the blood cool your swords! Smite pinkepank on the anvil of Nimrod! Overturn their towers to the foundations; while one of them lives you will not be freed from the fear of man! While they reign over you it is of no use to speak of the fear of God! On! while it is day! God is with you.'

These words were meant to rouse the miners of Mansfeld, and were intended to bring fire and sword into the district where Luther's parents were living. If they failed in their original intent, they sent bands of insurgents through Thuringia and the Harz, and within fourteen days about forty monasteries and convents were destroyed and the inmates (many of them poor women with no homes to return to) were sent adrift.

It was then that Luther determined to make one last personal effort to bring the misguided people to more reasonable courses. He made a tour through the disordered districts. He went west from Eisleben to Stolberg (21st April); thence to Nordhausen, where Münzer's sympathisers rang the bells to drown his voice, and where he was in great personal danger; south to Erfurt, which he must have reached before the 28th April, then north again to the fertile valley of the Golden Aue and Wallhausen (1st May), and south again to Weimar (3rd May). Here news reached him that his Elector was on his deathbed, which made him hurry home to Wittenberg, which he reached on the 6th of May.

It was on this journey, or shortly after his return, that Luther wrote his vehement tract *Against the Murderous Thieving Hordes of Peasants*. He wrote it while his mind was full of Münzer's calls to slaughter, when the danger was at its height, with all the sights and sounds of the turmoil and destruction in eye and ear, while it still hung in the balance whether the insurgent bands might not, after all, carry all before them.[1] In this terrible pamphlet Luther hounded on the princes to crush the rising. When all is said that can reasonably be said in explanation of his action, we cannot help feeling that the language of this pamphlet is an ineffaceable stain on Luther, which no extenuating circumstances can wipe out. It remains the greatest blot on his noble life and career. After speaking of the duties of the authorities, he proceeds: 'In the case of an insurgent, every man is both judge and executioner. Therefore, whoever can knock down, strangle, and stab such, publicly or privately, and think nothing so venomous, pernicious, and devilish as an insurgent ... Such wonderful times are these that a prince can merit heaven better with bloodshed than another with prayer.' To which we may add, 'such wonderful times' that a preacher of the gospel of Christ thought that he could do his Master's work best by hounding on men to slay in cold blood these poor benighted peasants! When did the majority of German princes need to be told to misuse their commonalty?

The thoughts and sayings of the wise old Elector were in striking contrast. It adds an additional element of pain to the thought of Luther's action, that he must have written his furious pamphlet either immediately before or immediately after the death of the Elector. Frederic the Wise had been much distressed at the news of the peasant rising in the south. He wrote to his brother, Duke John, on the 14th of April: 'The poor are in many ways burdened by us of the secular and ecclesiastical upper classes; it may therefore be God's will that the common man should reign; but if that is not His divine will, and if that will not be to His glory, it will not happen; let

---

[1] It is somewhat difficult to say where Luther went, and on what days, during this attempt to calm the people. He had made a journey through the same districts in the previous year, and the two are sometimes confused. But the dates and the places above given may be taken as correct. The Thuringian peasants were defeated at Frankenhausen (near which Luther must have passed at least once in this journey) on the 15th of May.

us pray God to forgive us our sins, and let us leave it all to Him.'
He thought that he and his brother should let things alone as much
as possible. The news of the rising among his own subjects troubled him greatly. In his last illness, on to his death on the 5th May,
he kept hoping that all grounds of complaint might be removed by
reasonable compromise, and that all the negotiations would go on
peaceably and have a good ending. He wrote anxiously to Luther
to come and see him before he died. But he passed away ere
Luther could reach the castle. He was the best loved prince in
Germany, and was taken away just when his counsels would have
helped most. It is recorded that the children used to watch for him
as he rode through the streets, to catch his kindly smile, and to
greet 'Our Elector' as they called him. Perhaps the thought of the
pain that the rising had caused the good prince added to the feroc-
ity of Luther's pen; but it is not pleasant to think of the pamphlet
coming from Luther at the moment of the Elector's death.

Luther's enemies were quick to make capital out of his worse
than blunder. Doggerel verses by Emser, one of his most persistent
opponents, compared Luther to Pilate, who washed his hands after having done the deed. Luther tried to make some amends. He
declared that he had meant his words to apply only to those who
were actually engaged in bloodshed and rapine; and he publicly
asserted that the authorities, when they were victorious, ought to
extend full pardon to the guilty who had been beaten in the fight;
but he was to learn that it is much easier to justify wrathful passions than to calm them. It is not likely that Luther's ferocious
words made the sufferings inflicted on the peasants any more severe than they would have been; and it does not seem that his
recommendations to mercy had very much effect.

The Peasants' War had a lasting and disastrous effect, not only
on the Reformation, but on Luther himself.

Up to the tragical year 1525, the Lutheran movement absorbed
all the various elements of discontent in Germany, and Luther
seemed to have the whole land behind him. This year was the
parting of the ways. The conservative ecclesiastical Reformation,

of which Luther was the exponent, was rudely separated from a large amount of the popular aspirations which had given it such an appearance of strength. The political destiny of Germany appeared definitely shaping for territorial centralisation round the greater princes and nobles, and the dream of a united and democratic Germany was rudely dispelled. The conservative religious Reformation followed the political lines of growth, and resulted in the formation, not of a National Church of Germany, but of territorial churches under the rule and protection of such of the territorial magnates as embraced the Reformed faith. The more radical religious Reformation broke into fragments, and appeared in the guise of the maligned and persecuted Anabaptists, who also, to some extent at least, appropriated the social aspirations which had been crushed in the Peasants' War. The terrors of that time were eagerly used by the servants of the Roman Curia to separate Germany into two hostile camps – the one accepting and the other rejecting the ecclesiastical Reformation, which in this way ceased to be a national movement in any real sense of the word.

As for Luther himself, the Peasants' War imprinted in him a deep distrust of the 'common man' which prevented him from believing in a democratic Church, and led him to bind his reformation in the fetters of a secular control, to the extent of regarding the secular government as having a quasi-episcopal function. He did his best within Germany to prevent attempts to construct anything like a democratic Church government. His dislike and distrust of the 'common man' was largely at the basis of his inability to understand or appreciate the heroic Ulrich Zwingli and his fellow-Switzers – a misunderstanding which worked many an evil to the German Reformation, and produced much of the disasters of the horrible Thirty Years' War. For years after the publication of his pamphlet against the peasants his life was scarcely safe in many of the rural districts of Germany. If he sinned, it may be said that few men have suffered so severely for it.

CHAPTER 9

MARRIAGE, FAMILY AND PUBLIC LIFE

1. Marriage

The religious movement which Luther led in the sixteenth century contained no thought more startling nor impregnated with more far-reaching ethical consequences than the position which was assigned to marriage. It is vain to look for anything like this in any of the medieval religious revolts. The Reformation may be distinguished from all other partial anticipations by the way in which it dealt with this one question. It destroyed at one blow the amazing blasphemy, which in the Middle Ages was received as an unquestioned divine conception, that the order which God Himself has established in the world is comparatively unholy, and that the union between husband and wife, which is hallowed in the Holy Scriptures by comparing it with the union between Christ and His Church, is one which must sully the lives of Christians who share it. It is difficult for us who live so far removed from the shadow of medieval religious life to appreciate the change of view, nor is it possible to describe it by contrasting propositions laid down by medieval and by evangelical theologians. With regard to this one question at least, Luther's teaching changed the whole atmosphere of the spirit's life; and just as all organic beings cannot live in one climate, so certain circles of thought lose all their convincing power when the moral atmosphere is changed. The difference of mode of thought went far beyond the Lutheran ecclesiastical Reformation. It can be seen working in the arguments which Romanists now use to defend the retention of the celibate life – arguments which appeal to the new circle of thoughts created at the Reformation, and which the medieval Church had never occasion to use.

The Reformation worked a revolution in the conception of piety and the pious life when it asserted that every kind of honourable and honest secular calling could be as much a vocation as the call to a monastic and celibate life. It made the family hearth as sacred as the monastic cell, and saw that the mother who spent a sleepless night at the bedside of a sick child was holding a vigil as sacred as that of a nun prostrate on the flags of the convent chapel. It made the thought possible that the heaven that is about us in our infancy is the haven of a pious home. Such thoughts might have been in the minds of thousands in the Middle Ages. We know that Luther's sturdy old father held them. But they formed no part of the recognised teaching of the Church, and they did not create a moral atmosphere in which the family life could be lived and hallowed. The Reformation did this, and created religion in common life in consequence. In doing so its influence went far beyond the boundaries of its ecclesiastical reconstruction.

Within the circle of ecclesiastical reformation the thought worked great changes. The marriage of the clergy put an end to the disgraceful concubinage of the medieval parish priests, which was almost universal in the later Middle Ages. The home-life of the Lutheran parish priest was generally a model to his rough parishioners, and the great numbers of the men foremost in every department of public life in Germany who have come from these homes show how the clerical and the citizen life have been combined by the Lutheran ideal.

It would have seemed as if the story of the Reformation was incomplete if the voice of the daring preacher, who had awakened the conscience of mankind to all these new thoughts, had spoken from a hermitage and not from a home. Yet Luther himself for long had an instinctive disinclination for a marriage life. He had early in his career become convinced that there was no reason why parish priests should practice celibacy if they preferred a married life. He believed that men and women who had been forced to take monastic vows in early years, and without a distinct sense of vocation to that life, were at liberty to leave their cloisters. He was not at all persuaded, however, that men like himself, who had deliberately, and without any external constraint, embraced the monastic life, and taken its vows of celibacy, ought not to keep their oaths. Even when he reached the conclusion that those vows were plainly based on such an erroneous idea of righteousness, and were so misleading that they ought not to be kept, he did not feel inclined to break them in his own case, and that although he had often been urged to marry. He abandoned his monastic garb some months after his return to Wittenberg from the Wartburg, and wore instead the usual dress of the German professor. But he lived on in the old convent, deserted by all the monks except himself and prior Brisger, without even a lay brother to look after them and perform the usual menial services. While Münzer was sneering at 'the soft-living flesh at Wittenberg', Luther was often reduced to dine on bread and water from lack of any other kind of provender. Melanchthon tells us that when he remonstrated with Luther that his bed was damp and not been made for days, Luther told him that he had been so hard at work all day that when the night came he was unable to do more than to tumble down on the bed and fall asleep.

Yet since the spring of 1523 the overworked man had been busied with the matrimonial affairs of others. From the time that he had made visitation tours in the region of Grimma, his writings had found their way into cloisters of the district, and among others into a convent of Cistercian nuns at Nimtzeh, which lay a little to the south of Grimma, and not far from Leipzig. Many of the nuns in this convent, which was reserved for ladies of noble birth, became convinced of the unlawfulness of the vows they had taken, and wished to return to their homes. They wrote to their relations and asked leave to return home, but none of those noble families could brook the disgrace, as it was then reckoned, of receiving into their houses a recusant nun. Then the ladies wrote to Luther. After some correspondence, the matter was entrusted to a worthy burgher of Torgau, Leonhard Koppe by name. Tradition says that nine of the nuns, all who dared the venture, met in the cell of Catherine von Bora, who had planned the rescue, on the 4th of April 1523, got out of the window into the court, and were assisted over the wall by Master Koppe, who was waiting for them with a large country cart and some empty beer-barrels. The nuns were put into the beer-barrels, and after three days' journey, part of it through the hostile territories of Duke George of Saxony, they reached Wittenberg safely, where Luther was able to find shelter for them in the houses of some of the most respectable citizens of the town.

This convent-breaking made a great sensation, and was vehemently condemned. Luther justified it in a telling pamphlet in which he told the history of a poor girl, Florentina, of Upper Weimar. She had been immured in a convent when she was six years old, and at the age of eleven had been made to take the veil. When she was fourteen years old she felt that she had no vocation for a nun's life, and was then told by the abbess that she was a nun for life, and had to make the best of it. She seems to have heard of Luther, and the young girl wrote to him. Her letter was intercepted, and she was punished by severe penances. She tried to communicate with her relations, and when this was discovered she was beaten, chained by the foot, and finally condemned to lifelong imprisonment in a cell. She escaped, and her story became known. Luther published it to let people know what 'cloistery' was like, and said that he could tell many a similar story.

His letters are full of his successes and failures to get the nine nuns married, Catherine among the rest. The others seemed for the most part contented with the partners proposed to them. Not so Catherine. She was a dignified maiden of four-and-twenty, with a high fair forehead and bright black eyes. Her history was a type of hundreds. She belonged to a noble but impoverished family in the Meissen district, who were glad enough to get a daughter provided for by sending her to a convent; had entered Nimtzch when she was ten years old, and had taken the veil when she was sixteen. It was a 'family arrangement', practised generation after generation in noble German households. Magdalena von Bora had been the victim in the previous generation, and Catherine found her aunt an inmate of the convent when she went there in 1509.[1]

The young nun found a home at Wittenberg in the family of Dr Reichenbach, the town-clerk. Her maidenly dignity of demeanour was universally observed, and attracted the attention of King Christian of Denmark when he was the guest of Lucas Cranach in October 1523. Luther himself was a little afraid of her, and thought her very proud.

How Luther and she came together and agreed to become man and wife is unknown. Luther said more than once that such matters ought to be left in the hands of God and the two persons most concerned, and he kept his own counsel. The marriage took place during the storms of the Peasants' War. On the evening of the 13th of June 1525, he invited his friends, Bugenhagen the parish priest of Wittenberg, Justus Jonas the provost of All Saints, Lucas Cranach the painter and his wife, Dr Apel, professor of laws, who had himself married a nun, to witness the ceremony. Bugenhagen officiated, using the common German form of matrimony. The pair were asked whether they would take one another for man and wife; they were then directed to take each other by the right hand, and they were declared 'to be joined together in holy matrimony, in the name of the Triune God'.

This concluded the ceremony, and Luther and Catherine von Bora were man and wife. A few days later the wedded pair gave a modest breakfast to their more intimate friends and the magistracy of Wittenberg sent formal congratulations through Cranach, and along with them a present of wine. A fortnight later, on 27th June, the wedding was celebrated at a feast to which relations and distant friends were invited. At this, to Luther's great joy, his father and mother were present, and old Hans Luther at last thoroughly forgave his son his lapse into monasticism. Good Leonhard Koppe from Torgau, whose cart and beer-barrels had brought this about, was not forgotten in the ceremony. The breakfast and the feast

---

[1]Magdalena von Bora left the convent some time after her niece, and was a member of Luther's household; she is the 'Aunt Lene' of the Letters and Table Talk. Magdalena, Luther's favourite daughter, was named after her.

which followed were all in accordance with the usual medieval wedding usages among the Germans – only to be distinguished from most by the modest frugality displayed. The university presented the married pair with a beautifully chased silver goblet, with the inscription: 'The Honourable University of Wittenberg presents this wedding gift to Doctor Martin Luther and his wife Kethe von Bora.' Luther was forty-two and Catherine twenty-six years of age when they married.

The Elector (formerly Duke John, the brother of Frederic, whom he succeeded) gave Luther the old Augustinian convent for a house; and as prior Brisger was called to be pastor at Altenburg a few months after the wedding, the newly married couple had the empty buildings all to themselves. The first year of their wedded life was a time of pure happiness to Luther; the second one of great trials. His 'Kaethe' was no ordinary woman. She was a good housewife, which she had need to be with such a husband, but she was much more besides. She took a great share, and an increasing share as the years went on, in all her husband's work. He liked her to sit with him in his study. He consulted her about most of his correspondence. Her name comes into his letters continually, and she becomes one of the circle of inmates who are together working out the great Reformation in Germany.

Catherine's biography has yet to be written, and the wonderful influence she exerted has to be gathered from innumerable minute references to her work scattered throughout Luther's huge correspondence. For one thing, her loving care prolonged Luther's life. He had overworked himself recklessly. He was subject at times to fits of the gloomiest depression, which reacted upon his bodily condition. Catherine persuaded him to take an interest in his garden – the old convent garden with the pear-tree under which he sat with Staupitz, and was persuaded, sorely against his will, to undertake the teaching of theology; to dig a well; to write to friend Link to send him choice seeds from Nürnberg – seeds of melons, cucumbers, and other plants; to instruct friend Lange to send him seeds of the great radishes for which Erfurt was famous. These requests come at the end of letters in which he is denouncing the iniquities of Duke George, of Henry VIII, or of some other emissary of Satan sent to buffet him. Why need he mind them after all, he says, when the garden and gardening are so delightful? Then comes the birth of his firstborn, Hans, named after the old father at Mansfeld; and Luther bubbles over with bliss. 'His young fawn with his doe' thanks Spalatin for his blessing; 'the little one' is the lustiest eater and drinker that man can see; he begins to walk and gets into every corner of the study; 'Hanschen' thanks friend Haussman for a rattle, 'in which he glories and rejoices wondrously'; and so the tiny thread of life embroiders quaintly the grave web of correspondence about the most serious business.

The year 1527 was a harassing one. Luther fell dangerously ill. As he lay near death the baby's smile brought comfort the one moment and the next sadness, to think that he must leave behind him a widow and a fatherless child without means of support, nothing but a few silver tankards that had been presented to him. 'Dear Doctor,' said Catherine, 'if it be God's will then I also choose that you be with Him rather than with me. It is not so much I and my child that need you as the multitude of pious Christian people. Take no thought for me.' Her courage kept him up; her careful nursing drew him back from death.

But the troubles were not over. There followed one of the severest periods of gloom and spiritual distress, almost as severe as in the old days in the Erfurt convent. This had scarcely passed when the dreaded plague visited Wittenberg. The university and the Court left the town to settle for a season at Jena, and the Elector entreated, all but commanded, Luther to follow. But he would not. He would be no hireling, he said, to flee when the sheep needed him most. He remained in the smitten city, and Catherine – soon to become a mother again – and baby Hans stayed with him. The plague began in the fishers' quarter, and Luther soon counted eighteen corpses buried at the Elster Gate, not far from his house. It crept up to the centre of the town, where the first victim, the burgomaster's wife, died while Luther was with her. It attacked his friends. The wife of Dr Schurf was seized, and did not recover until the beginning of November; the wife of the chaplain died of it, and Luther insisted on Bugenhagen and his family leaving the pestilence-stricken house and coming to live with him. It entered his house; Frau von Mocha, sister-in-law to Carlstadt, who was living with the Luthers, was seized. Catherine's second child, Elizabeth was born, and only her superb coolness and courage saved the mother. Little Hans fell ill, but not of the plague as it was at first feared. So the weary months passed. Then Luther could write: 'My little boy is well and happy again. Schurf's wife has recovered; Margaret has escaped death in a marvellous manner.' During this anxious time he was further distressed by the news that persecution for the faith had begun in South Germany, and that the Bavarian pastor Leonard Kaiser had been burnt at the stake. His pent-up feelings found expression in the famous hymn:

'A safe stronghold our God is still,
  A trusty shield and weapon;
He'll help us clear from all the ill
  That hath us now o'ertaken.'

The plague ceased; the students and professors returned to Wittenberg; and Luther had his old friends about him again. He recovered his health and his spirits.

2. Home Life and Family Cares

The empty Augustinian convent which became Luther's house was an unfinished building when the Reformation began, and required many a repair and addition ere it was fit for the household which gradually gathered round Luther. It stood with its back to the wall of the town, the front windows and door opening into the large garden, and the back windows looking out over the Elbe. It was a three-storeyed building, with the usual high roof covered with red tiles. The family latterly consisted of Luther and his wife, their three sons and two daughters, Aunt Lene or Magdalena von Bora, Catherine's aunt, two orphan nieces, Lene and Else Kaufmann, daughters of Luther's sister, and another young girl, Anna Strauss, who seems to have been a grandniece.

Like the other Wittenberg professors, Luther had students who boarded with him, and in his case they were often men of some age and distinction, who were glad to have this opportunity of intimate intercourse with him. It is from the recollections of these boarders that we know something of the inner life of Luther's home. They tell us that the Reformer was sometimes moody and silent at table, brooding over the troubles and difficulties of the time, but that he generally led the conversation on all manner of interesting subjects. He liked to spend an hour or so after dinner in singing or listening to music. The children always sang to him; and at this hour friends came to talk with him as he sat in the garden, his children and boarders around him.

When Luther and his wife began to keep house they must have been in very straitened circumstances. He had married a portion-less nun; and on till 1532 his professorial salary was only two hundred gulden, or about £160, according to the present value of money. He had besides, his house, and occasional presents of eatables and wine from the town council of Wittenberg when he had to entertain distinguished strangers.

Then Luther was a man of overflowing charity. Wandering students, monks who had broken their convents, beggars of all kinds got what money he had. If he had no money, he gave away silver cups he had received as presents, and must have been the despair of his long-suffering wife. It is said that on one occasion in these early years he told a poor student who came begging that he had no money, but that he might take and sell 'this'; and in spite of his wife's frowns, he handed over the little silver christening cup that had been given to baby Hans.

Catherine was, however, a notable housewife; she made the long-neglected garden profitable; she kept pigs and poultry; she planted all manner of fruit trees; she made Luther rent and then buy three other gardens, stocked a fish-pond, kept cows, and farmed in a small way. She showed Luther that he was getting into debt, and proved to him that his indiscriminate charity did no good.

Luther regarded this last as a notable discovery, too good to be kept to himself, and he published it in a very daring manner. He got hold of a curious old book, the *Liber Vagatorum*, which we may translate 'The Book of Scoundreldom' – book collectors know the quaint medieval cant-German in which it is written, and the strange woodcuts with which it is illustrated – and he actually published it, with a most characteristic preface, in which he says:

> 'This little book about the knavery of beggars was first printed by one who calls himself "Expertus in Truffis", i.e. a fellow right well knowing in roguery, which the book very well proves... Princes, lords, counsellors of State, and everybody should be prudent and cautious in dealing with beggars, and should learn that, whereas people will not give and help honest paupers and needy neighbours as ordained by God, they give by the persuasion of the devil, and contrary to God's judgment, ten times as much to vagabonds and desperate rogues... For this reason every village and town should know their own poor, as written down in the register, and assist them. But as to outlandish and strange beggars, they ought not to be borne with, unless they have proper letters and certificates; for all the great rogueries mentioned in this book are done by them. If each town would only keep an eye on its own paupers, such knaveries would soon cease. *I have myself of later years been cheated and befooled by such tramps and liars more than I like to confess.*'

From which it may be seen that after two years Catherine had done something with her husband, and that he presented to his native land the outline of a 'Charity Organisation Society'.

After 1532 the Luther household was in much more comfortable circumstances. The professorial salary was increased to £240, and there were also added payments in kind – corn, wood, malt, etc. – which meant a great deal more. Great princes made presents, and Luther was able to buy a small property near Leipzig, called Zulsdorf, and to build a house on it. Catherine was greatly attached to it, and went there so often that the thing would excite our wonder, were it not that it seems that the property was bought from

Catherine's brother in order to help him in some money difficulties. We can understand the very peculiar pleasure with which the noble lady, who had been cast off by her family, became the proprietress of part of the old family estate; and how Luther would secretly enjoy her absorption in her small property, though he never ceased 'chaffing' her about it.

This household of wife, family, dependants, and guests was a very haven of rest for the storm-tossed man. His devotion to his wife was unbounded, and it may well have been; for few wives have done or could do so much for such a husband. 'I am apt to expect more from my Käthe, and from Melanchthon, than I do from Christ my Lord. And yet I know that neither they nor anyone on earth has suffered or can suffer what He has suffered for me.' These words belong to his earlier married life. 'I would not part from my Käthe, no not to gain all France and Venice'; he declared that if his Käthe died and he were a young man nothing would induce him to marry again; and late in life, speaking from his own experience, he says, that 'next to God's Word, the world has no more precious treasure than holy matrimony. God's best gift is a pious, cheerful, God-fearing, home-keeping wife, with whom you may live peacefully, to whom you may entrust your goods, your body, and life.'

Perhaps his profound respect for her and trust in her comes out nowhere more strongly than in his 'will'. He bequeathed her everything that he had – lands, houses, the goblets and jewels he had received in presents, to be at her sole disposal; and he did so for three reasons – (1) because she had been to him 'a pious, faithful, and dutiful wife, always loving, devoted, and beautiful'; (2) because she alone knew his affairs and would have to pay his debts; and (3) because it was more fitting that his children would be dependent on their mother than the mother on her children.

He carried out the principle he had laid down in his *Table Talk*: 'Between husband and wife there should be no question of *meum* and *tuum*. All things should be in common between them, without any distinction or means of distinguishing.' Of course he talked roundly of marital supremacy and the impossibility of getting a thoroughly obedient wife unless he carved one out of stone for himself; he laughed at his Käthe's command of language, and assured an English guest that he ought to take her as his teacher in the German tongue, for she knew more about it than he did; but he had a deep desire to spare her any pain. When the country was in a disturbed state after the Peasants' War he refused to go to a friend's wedding 'for the tears and fears of my Käthe prevent me'.

There is one letter of his to his wife, which is seldom or never quoted, and which shows the high opinion which Luther had of her judgment even on deep theological matters. He wrote it from Marburg, where he was at the conference with the Swiss theologians, and where he did not certainly show himself at his best. In that letter he gives the only fair statement he ever made about the views of his Swiss opponents, and seems anxious to persuade her that it was not his obstinacy but the prevalence of the plague which broke up the negotiations. He tells her, what he confessed to no other creature, 'that we (the Swiss and the Lutherans) are united on all points except that our opponents maintain that it is mere bread in the Lord's Supper, *but acknowledge therein the presence of Christ spiritually*'; and he goes on to say that everyone is become mad with fear of the 'sweating sickness'; 'yesterday fifty were taken ill of it, and one or two have died.'

His affectionate playfulness ripples over all his correspondence with her, and was no doubt appreciated with due wifely fondness, although it must have been trying to have one's letters addressed *on the outside*: 'To my dear Master, Frau Katherine Luther'; 'To my kind and dear Master, Frau Katherine v Bora, Doctoress Lutheress, at Wittenberg.' In this letter he wrote: 'It is an annoyance to me to have bad wine to drink, when I remember what good wine and beer I have at home, besides a pretty wife – or shall I say it – Master?' but that was inside. Other outside designations are: 'To my gracious girl, Katharine Luther v Bora and Zulsdorf, at Wittenberg, my darling.' This one begins inside: 'Grace and peace, my dear girl and wife Käthe. Your Grace must be informed that we

are all here fresh and sound – God be praised; we eat like behe-
moths (yet not much), and drink like Germans (yet not much), and
are joyous.' 'To the rich lady of Zulsdorf, Frau Doctor Katherine
Luther, dwelling in the body at Wittenberg and wandering in the
spirit to Zulsdorf; to be delivered into the hands of my darling; if
absent, to be opened and read by D Pömeran, Pastor'; 'To my
heartily beloved wife, Katharine Luther, Lady of Zulsdorf,
Doctoress, Lady of the pig Market, and whatever else she may
be'; inside this we find: 'Grace and peace in Christ, and my poor
old love as before. Dear Käthe, I have been very weak on the
road... M L, your old darling.' 'To my dear wife, Katharine Luther,
Doctoress and self-tormentor, at Wittenberg; to the hands and feet
of my gracious lady'; inside this one we have 'Dear Käthe, read St
John and the Small Catechism, of which you sometimes say, "All
in this book is said of me." For you must needs take God's cares
upon you, just as if He were not the Almighty... All the letters you
have written have come here, and today the one which you wrote
last Friday... I mention this that you may not be angry.' On the
outsides of other letters we have such epithets as 'The deeply
learned lady', 'the saintly, anxious-minded lady', 'my dear and
kind wife'.

The letters show how much she did for him; she corresponded
with ladies who could assist her husband (the Electress Sibyl, wife
of John Frederic, had almost as great a regard for Catherine as her
husband had for Luther), she looked after the printing of Luther's
sermons and pamphlets, and saw that the printers did not run short
of paper; she even bought special presents which Luther might
give to the children when he came home from a journey; and she
had wonderful tact in soothing people whom Luther's roughness
had offended. She managed the large household with its boarders,
and presided at the table in her husband's absence.

One thing she could not do, and it rather worried her anxious
mind when she thought of the young family and the precarious
health of her husband; she could not get Luther to charge any fees
for lecturing, to take any salary from the town for his services as

pastor in the town church, nor take one farthing for all the books he wrote. On this last head he was stolidly immovable, though his wife showed him that he might surely have a share in the profits as well as the publishers. She had calculated that if Luther only took as much for writing his books as was given to scholars by the publishers for translating some of them into foreign languages, they might lay past nearly four hundred gulden a year. But Luther was inexorable. He would take no money for his writings – a resolution which, as Catherine saw, benefited no one but the publishers of his books.

Luther had the greatest delight in his children. 'I am sufficiently contented,' he writes, 'for I have three noble children, which no papist theologian has; and the three children are three kingdoms which belong to me by inheritance more surely than Ferdinand's Hungary, Bohemia, and the Romish Kingdom.' When baby Elizabeth died (she lived scarcely eight months), Luther was broken-hearted. 'She has left me,' he writes, 'a strangely sick almost womanly heart, such pity moves me for her; I could never have believed before what is the tenderness of a father's heart for his children.'

A second daughter, Magdalena, the 'Lenchen' of the *Letters*, was born just a year after her sister's death. She was Luther's favourite child, perhaps because she came before his grief was spent, perhaps because she was the very image of her mother. She grew to be a beautiful and charmingly affectionate girl, and died when she was a little more than thirteen years old. Her death was very peaceful. Her father often asked her, 'Lenchen, my little daughter, thou wouldst like to stay with thy father; art thou also content to go to thy Father yonder?' 'Yes, dearest father; as God wills,' she said. When the end came, Luther fell on his knees at her bedside, weeping and holding her in his arms, prayed that God would receive her. He tried to console his wife by saying that they had sent a saint to heaven – 'Yes, a living saint! May we have such a death! Such a death I would gladly die this very hour.' When they came back from the grave, he said: 'My daughter is now provided for in body and soul. We Christians have nothing to complain of;

we know that it must be so. We are more certain of eternal life than of anything else; for God, who has promised it to us for His dear Son's sake, cannot lie. Two saints of my flesh has our Lord taken.' That evening he said: 'We must take great care of our children, and especially of the poor little maidens; we must not leave it to others to care for them. I have no compassion on the boys. A lad can maintain himself wherever he is, if he will only work; and if he will not work he is a scamp. But the poor maidenkind must have a staff to lean on.' All the infinite tenderness in his great heart was called forth in his thoughts about his little 'Lenchen'. His youngest child, Margarethe, was also a great favourite. He writes that she could sing hymns when she was four years old. He wrote hymns, words and music, for his children to sing. The best known is:

'From heaven above to earth I come,
To bear good news to every home;
Glad tidings of great joy I bring,
Whereof I now will say and sing.'[1]

The Luther house which contained this happy family has been renovated out of all recognition, and the room now shown as Luther's study was probably the family room – it could not have been the study. One thing, however, remains very much what it was – the great arched stone doorway which Catherine planned with Master Lucas Cranach as a surprise gift for her husband when he was away on one of his many journeys.

---

[1]Luther's children were: Hans, born 7th June 1526. He studied at Wittenberg, became a lawyer, was in the service of Duke Albert of Prussia, and died a councillor of the Court at Weimar.

Elizabeth, born 10th December 1527, and died 3rd August 1528.

Magdalena, born 4th May 1529, and died 20th September 1542.

Martin, born 9th November 1531. He studied theology, but was always delicate. He married the daughter of the burgomeister of Wittenberg, and died in his thirty-third year.

Paul, born 28th January 1533. He studied at Wittenberg, became a physician, and was court physician to the Elector of Saxony at Dresden.

Margarethe, born 17th December 1534; she married a Prussian noble, Adeligen von Kunheim.

'On the one tip of the arch was her Doctor's face, aet suae 57. On the other (where a lesser soul might have been forgiven for putting her own fair face) his own device of arms – a dark cross on a red heart in a white rose on a blue ground in a golden ring. Luther, I think, has an interpretation of it for himself – mine is "Christ and Him crucified contained in a sinner's love, making it flower out into a clear conscience and a pure life, with an open heaven above and a golden heaven before." Was it not a beautiful thought of hers? – something she had laid awake thinking for nights not a few – something she called Master Lucas Cranach in to talk over more than once, before the plans quite pleased her – something she carried out finally and hastily, with many fears lest the work should be caught unfinished, with many questions from the children as to what, and how, and why, and when, while her Doctor was away on one of those worrying visitations – something "brought forth with singing" and clapping of hands one fine day, when the familiar horse-hoofs came clattering up the street, and the dear Greatheart, her husband, flung heavily out of the saddle, and landed right down on the very stones which cried out to him of his wife's love. How glorious and noble and perfect such a "love in life" seems!'[1]

We can recall the picture of Luther at the Leipzig Disputation, holding a bunch of violets in his hand, looking at it, and tasting its perfume, while he thundered against Eck, the Pope, and the Councils. This home of his, with wife and children and family friends, was his bunch of violets in his later life. While at Wittenberg the evening talks in his garden, where he sat with wife and friends under the pear tree, and the children brought him flowers and were taught to distinguish the voices of the birds that were singing, were a great refreshment. Of a rose he would say: 'A man who could

---

[1]Robert Barbour, *Letters from the Land of Luther*, pp 102-105. Luther's own explanation of the meaning of his device was: "A black cross on a red heart; for, in order to be saved, it is necessary to believe with our whole heart in our crucified Lord, and the cross, though bringing pain and self-mortification, does not corrupt the nature, but rather keeps the heart alive. The heart should be placed in a white rose to show that faith gives joy, comfort and peace, and because white is the colour of the spirits and angels, and the joy is not an earthly joy. The rose itself should be set in an azure field, just as this joy is already the beginning of heavenly joy and set in heavenly hope, and outside, round the field, there should be a golden ring, because heavenly happiness is eternal and precious above all possessions.'

make one rose like this would be accounted most wonderful; yet God scatters countless such flowers around us! His gifts are so infinite that we do not see them.' Or seeing a little bird gone to roost for the night: 'That little bird has chosen his shelter; above it are the stars and the deep heaven of worlds; yet he is rocking himself to sleep without caring for tomorrow's lodging, calmly clinging to his little twig, and *leaving God to think for him.*' Or when the slow creaking of the mill was carried far on the still afternoons: 'The heart of man is like a millstone in a mill; when you put wheat under it, it turns, and grinds and crushes the wheat into flour; if you put no wheat it still grinds on, but it grinds itself and wears itself away. So is the human heart; unless it be busied with some employment, it leaves space for the devil, who wriggles himself in, and brings with him a whole host of evil thoughts, temptations, tribulations, which grind away the heart.' Or when Catherine sat beside him with her distaff and flax, spinning her linen thread: 'What a martyr the flax is! When it is ripe it is plucked, steeped in water, beaten, dried, carded, spun, and woven into linen, which is cut and torn and pierced... So must good and godly Christians suffer much from the ungodly and wicked.' Or when he was very ill and they brought him proof-sheets: 'God has touched me sorely. I have been impatient; but God knows better than I do whereto it serves. Our Lord God is like a printer who sets the letters backwards, so that here we cannot read them. When we are printed off in the life to come we shall read all clearly and straightforward. Meanwhile we must have patience.'

'I know few things more touching than those soft breathings of affection,' says Carlyle, 'soft as a child's or a mother's, in this great wild heart of Luther. So honest, unadulterated with any cant; homely rude in their utterance; pure as water welling from the rock. What, in fact, was all that downpressed mood of despair and reprobation which we saw in his youth, but the outcome of pre-eminent thoughtful gentleness, affections too keen and fine... Luther to a slight observer might have seemed a timid, weak man; modesty, affectionate shrinking tenderness the chief distinction of him. It is a noble valour which is roused in a heart like this, once stirred up into defiance, all kindled into a heavenly blaze... The common speech of him has a rugged nobleness, idiomatic, expressive, genuine; gleams here and there with beautiful poetic tints. One feels him to be a great brother man. His love of music, indeed, is not this, as it were, the summary of all these affections in him? Many a wild unutterability he spoke forth from him in the tones of his flute. The devils fled from his flute, he said. Death-defiance on the one hand, and such a love of music on the other; I could call these the two opposite poles of a great soul; between these two all great things had room.'

3. The Emperor and Luther

Things had been going badly with the Evangelical party since the Peasants' War. That mad outlook had been industriously used by the Romanists as a proof of what the Evangelical doctrines would lead to if tolerated. The Emperor had resolved that the Evangelical cause should be crushed, and that his Edict of the Diet of Worms should be carried out. He sent down orders to Germany that this should be done when the Diet met at Speyer in 1526.

Political events beyond Germany stayed off the collision for a while. Charles had totally defeated Francis at the battle of Pavia. The Pope, afraid of the power of Charles and of its effect in Italy, had made a secret alliance with Francis. Charles, determined to resist the Pope, no longer cared to crush the Lutherans; therefore, at the Diet of Speyer, it had been resolved that, 'Each State should, as regards the Edict of Worms, so live, rule, and bear itself as it thought it could answer it to God and the Emperor.' This left each principality and Imperial city free to do what it pleased in the matter of religion; but it was felt by both sides that the truce was but temporary. The Romanist States had made a league, and it was felt by many of the Protestants that they, too, ought to be united. Doctrinal differences between the Swiss and some of the Imperial cities on the one side, and the followers of Luther on the other, stood in the way of a close alliance, and young Philip of Hesse had proposed a conference at Marburg. The conference had produced a great deal of good, but it had been wrecked by the obstinacy of

Luther, in spite of proved and acknowledged unanimity on all points of doctrine but the one of the meaning of Christ's presence in the Sacrament of the Supper. Meanwhile, the Emperor had settled his quarrel with the Pope, and was again demanding that the Edict of Worms should be carried out in Germany. A second Diet at Speyer was held in 1529, the decision of 1526 was reversed, and the Evangelical States protested. Civil war might have ensued had not the Turks threatened Vienna, and had not Luther patriotically insisted that all should unite to drive away the danger menacing Christendom.

Charles had now reached the summit of his power. He had crushed France, had humbled the Pope and compelled him to enter into an alliance, and had conquered the Turks. He had only to crush the Reformation to attain his scheme of restoring the Medieval Empire in all its old glory. He came down to Germany to hold a Diet at Augsburg, with the express design of compelling the Evangelical princes to abandon the cause of Luther and of the Reformation. With all Charles's keenness of diplomatic vision and power of measuring men, he could never understand spiritual forces. He thought that he had only to appear in Germany, and exercise his persuasive powers on the German princes, to overthrow the Evangelical movement. He had sent messages to the Evangelical princes, and had expressed hopes which might soon become commands.

He entered Augsburg in extraordinary state, the flower of all Germany, princes evangelical and papal, riding out to meet him as far as the bridge of the Lech. In the evening he summoned the foremost Evangelical princes to meet him – John of Saxony, Philip of Hesse, old George of Brandenburg among them. He had told them firmly that all the licence hitherto permitted must cease, and that tomorrow they must walk with him in the *Corpus Christi* procession. The princes refused, and young Philip was about to argue the matter theologically, but the Emperor sternly refused to hear him. Then George of Brandenburg stood forth and told the Emperor that he and his fellows could not and would not obey. It was a short, rugged speech, though eminently respectful, and ended with these words, which flew over Germany, kindling hearts as fire lights flax: 'Before I would deny my God and His Evangel, I would rather kneel down here before your Majesty, and have my head struck off' – and the old man hit the side of his neck with the edge of his hand. 'Not head off, dear Prince, not head off,' said Charles in his Flemish-German ('Nit Kop ab, löver Först, nit Kop ab!'). Charles walked in the procession through the streets of Augsburg on a blazing hot day, stooping under a heavy purple mantle, and with a superfluous candle sputtering in his hand; but the Evangelical princes remained in their lodgings.

It had long been felt that this Diet would be a critical time for the Evangelical faith, and the Elector John had been anxious to have a summary of Evangelical doctrine prepared for him, to be used when he met the Emperor. He had accordingly summoned Luther, Melanchthon and some other theologians to meet him at Torgau to prepare Evangelical 'Articles of Faith'; and Luther, with his companions, had presented the Marburg Articles with some additions. It was felt, however, that something fuller was needed; and Luther and Melanchthon had been busied at Coburg, whither they had gone with the Elector, in drafting a 'Confession'. The work was interrupted by a summons from the Emperor asking the Elector to meet him at Augsburg at the end of April, and the Elector left for the city where the Diet was to be held, taking the other theologians with him but leaving Luther at Coburg.

Luther was worried and anxious, feeling like a caged eagle. He knew Melanchthon's strong desire for some conciliatory confession with which everyone could agree; he knew that his Elector had neither the influence nor the strength of mind of his brother; he feared the impetuosity of young Philip of Hesse; he was left for weeks at a time without any news; he was fretting himself ill and longing to be back at Wittenberg, where he could at least 'teach his students'.

His secretary wrote woeful accounts of him to the Wittenberg home circle. Catherine knew how a little bit of home would cheer him. She got their good friend Lucas Cranach to paint their baby Magdalena, then a year old, and the picture was sent on to Coburg.

Luther hung it up where he could always see it from his chair, and the sweet little face looking down at him gave him the courage to endure during these long months of waiting. The old father died at Mansfeld during this enforced stay at Coburg (29th May), and Luther could not go to see his widowed mother. Posts brought him word that the 'Confession', completed by Melanchthon, had been read in German in the Diet on the 25th of June; that the Romanists were preparing a refutation, and that meanwhile all manner of conferences were going on; that the Romanist reply was ready on 3rd August; that Philip of Hesse had left the Diet abruptly on the 6th, to raise troops to fight the Emperor, it was reported; that Melanchthon was being entangled in conferences, and was said to be giving up everything. How he must have fretted! A man, required to exercise a woman's courage – the courage to wait on in suspense! The child's face smiling down on him as he sat and fretted seemed to give him calm.

He wrote to his Elector's legal adviser at the Diet, exhorting him to remember that God was more powerful than the Emperor, and then went on:

'I have lately seen two wonders; the first as I was looking out of my window and saw the stars in heaven and all that beautiful vault of God, and yet I saw no pillars on which the Architect had fixed this vault; yet the heaven fell not, and all that grand arch stood fast. Now there are some who search for the pillars, and want to touch and grasp them, and since they cannot, they wonder and tremble as if the heaven must certainly fall, for no other reason but because they cannot touch and grasp its pillars. If they could lay hold on them then they think the heavens would stand firm! The second wonder was: I saw great clouds rolling over us with such a ponderous weight that they seemed like to a great ocean, and yet I saw no foundation on which they rested nor were based, nor any shore which restrained them; yet they fell not on us, but frowned on us and flowed on. But when they had passed by, then there shone forth both their floor and our roof which had kept them back – the rainbow! A frail, thin floor and roof, which soon melted into the clouds, and was more like a shadowy prism such as we see through coloured glass, than a strong and firm foundation, so that we might well distrust that feeble rampart which kept back that fearful weight of waters. Yet we found that this unsubstantial prism was able to bear up the weight of waters, and that it guarded us safely! But there are some who look more at the thickness and massy weight of the waters and the clouds than at this thin, light, narrow bow of promise. They would like to feel the strength of that shadowy, vanishing arch, and because they cannot do this, they are always fearing that the clouds will bring back the Flood.'

The flood was threatening. The Evangelical theologians did make the needful stand; 'the Romanists,' said Luther to his wife, 'positively desire to have the nuns and monks again in the cloister'; there was no hope of a compromise; the Emperor announced that he gave the Evangelical princes until the 15th of April 1531 to make their submission; everything seemed making for internecine strife.

Yet the frowning clouds passed away. Troubles in other parts of his widespreading dominions prevented Charles from carrying out his threats. The Evangelical Church had time to root itself and organise itself. The religious war did not break out until Luther had passed away from earth.

CHAPTER 10

LAYING THE FOUNDATIONS
OF THE EVANGELICAL CHURCH

1. Luther's Idea of the Church

The years 1530 to 1555 are usually described by Church historians
as the time of laying the foundations and building the structure of
the Evangelical Church of Germany. From the year 1526, which
saw the decision of the Diet of Speyer that in matters of religion
and with reference to the Edict of Worms every State was to live,
enact, and maintain itself as it trusted to answer to God and to his
Imperial Majesty, if not from the earlier decision of the Diet of
Nürnberg in 1523, Luther, amid his multifarious labours, had always regarded this one thing as his supreme task.

But the very important question at once arises – What had
Luther in view when he set himself to this work, and what did he
mean to do? There were many disturbing elements, all of which
tended to obscure the main purpose in Luther's mind from contemporaries and from students of history. The political condition
of the times, so constantly changing; the policy of the Emperor,
sometimes plainer, sometimes obscure, always an object of suspi-
cion; the attitude of the German bishops, sometimes conciliatory,
sometimes resolutely opposed to the Evangelical movement; unexpected divisions among those who favoured religious reform, which
in turn frequently took the shape they did from social and political
environment; above all, the catastrophe of the Peasants' War and
what that led to and revealed – all these things give an almost
kaleidoscopic appearance to Luther's work in the establishment of
the Evangelical Church of Germany. The stream of his purpose
was turned now the one way now the other as the successive

obstacles met it, and it took now one now another course, following, though with very distinct limitations, the path of least resistance. For Luther was the reverse of doctrinaire. He was, with some interesting reservations, an opportunist, in the good sense of this modern word, and had the defects of the opportunist character, which works rather for the more immediate than for the remoter results.

In the earlier years of Luther's struggle against Rome, his preaching and teaching had forced their way throughout all classes of the population of Germany. His popularity was increased by the incessant use he had made of the printing-press and by his heroic action in presence of the Emperor and the Diet. His friends were astonished at his success, his enemies never counted on such a speedy and widespread popularity. The good Elector always cherished the hope that if the gospel was allowed to spread quietly throughout the land its truth would gradually permeate all Christendom, or at least all Germany, and that a peaceful victory would be gained without much tumult or even much external change.

Luther himself had the same idea. All he wanted was room for the preaching of the gospel, which declared the true way of pardon. This of itself would, he thought, in due time effect a peaceful transformation of ecclesiastical life and worship. The earlier Diets of Nürnberg and Speyer had provided a field, always enlarging, for exhibiting this quiet transformation; and Luther, with the concurrence of his Elector, took advantage of it. He had hoped that the greater ecclesiastical princes would, with the consent of the diet, secularise their territories, and that the ordinary bishops would continue their oversight of the Church. He was as indifferent to forms of Church government as John Wesley, and, like Wesley, every step he took in providing for a separate organisation was forced upon him as a practical necessity. He cherished the hope that the new wine might be stored in the old bottles as late as the Diet of Augsburg in 1530 and the Diet of Speyer in 1545. The Augsburg Confession itself (1530) concludes with: 'Our meaning is not to have rule taken from the bishops; but this one thing only is required at their hands, that they should suffer the gospel to be purely taught, and that they would relax a few observances, which cannot be held without sin.' Meanwhile the common people in Germany were remaining uninstructed in the gospel of the grace of God, and it was impossible to wait for the tardy appreciation by the bishops of the Evangelical movement, or for the almost vanishing hope that a General Council held on German soil would reconcile the religious differences. Something had to be done, and that at once.

It must be remembered that Luther and all the Reformers of the sixteenth century held very strongly and clearly that there was a *Visible* Catholic Church of Christ, that the Evangelical movement which they headed was the legitimate development of the centuries of saintly life within that Visible Catholic Church, and within its Western branch especially. They did not for a moment suppose that in sharing in this movement they were separating themselves from the Catholic Church of Christ in its visible sense. It is true that they all taught that there was an Invisible Catholic Church, and that this Invisible Church was based on the predestination of God. But if their ideas on this subject be carefully examined, it will be seen that they did not take the thought of predestination in the sense of the abstract metaphysical category which it assumed in the hands of doctrinaire theologians of the seventeenth century. It was their way of showing that the whole of the believer's religious life and what it leads to depended in the last resort on God and not on man. They opposed the decree of God (predestination) to the decrees of man (of Popes and Councils). Hence neither Luther nor any of the Reformers thought that in making provision for the preaching of the Word, the administration of the Sacraments, the exercise of discipline, and whatever was required for the existence and good government of Christian congregations, they were founding a new Church, and were going forth from the Visible Catholic Church of Christ. They refused to concede the name Catholic to their opponents, and in the various conferences between the two parties, both before the Diet of Augsburg and after it, the Roman Catholics were always officially designated 'the adherents of the old religion'; and in the official document which states the terms of the Religious Peace of Nürnberg (1532), the two parties are respectively called the 'adherents of the old religion' and the 'associates of the Augsburg Confession'.

On the other hand, neither Luther nor any of his fellow Reformers thought that the existence of a Catholic Visible Church of Christ depended on what has ambiguously been called an apostolic succession of bishops, who through conferred gifts of ordination create priests, who in turn make Christians out of heathen by the Sacraments. His thought of the 'Freedom of the Christian Man', or the idea of the spiritual priesthood of all believers, as he interpreted it, prevented him from imperilling the existence of the Church Catholic on an external succession of office-bearers. If he had thought that an episcopal ordination in the Roman or Anglican sense was essential, there was a sufficient number of evangelical bishops to secure it; but no use was made of them in this way.

The true succession from the apostles lay within the Church, in the succession of generations of saintly souls, who, with confession of sin and faith on the promises of God, had found pardon and impulse to lives of new obedience by going directly to God for them. Neither communion with Rome nor an historical succession of bishops were marks of the Visible Catholic Church in his eyes. He had no objections to episcopal rule, nor even to a primacy in the See of Rome. He respected everything which had belonged to the past, and especially to that medieval Church into which he had been born. But these things were not required to make the Church. They were only modes of exercising the needful disciplinary control, and if they failed to conform to the precepts of the Word of God and had become full of human corruptions, thus degenerating into hindrances rather than remaining helps to the furtherance of the true religious life of the soul, they ought to be done away with, and something else should be put in their place. The fact that the human soul needs absolutely nothing in the last resort but the Word of God dwelling in it, ought to give men courage and calmness in demanding the change. The principle of the spiritual priesthood of all believers was able to deliver men from all fear in demanding such a reformation as the Church required to allow it to do the work God has given it in charge.

He had a very clear idea about what the Church needed to enable it to do the work for which God had called it into being. This is what he says:

> 'The Church of Christ requires an honest ministry diligently and loyally instructed in the Holy Word of God after a pure Christian intelligence, and without the addition of any false traditions. In and through such a ministry it will be made plain what are – Christ and His Evangel, honest repentance and the fear of God, how to attain to the forgiveness of sins, and the properties and power of the Keys in the Church.'

In this way the people will learn what Christian freedom is, and how the conscience becomes free in Christ. There is need of schools that boys and maidens may be taught these things and all good morals in their youth. There is need also of the gift of knowing such languages as Latin, Greek and Hebrew. For all this there must be some real supervision, to see that all these things are done. Bishops, in the medieval sense of the word, might be superfluous, but their true function, that of oversight, was a thing indispensable.

These were the thoughts in Luther's mind when he busied himself about the reconstruction of the Church in Germany. His first idea was that much of this might be left in the hands of the people, with some oversight from the bishops; but this first idea was soon abandoned. The Peasants' War slew all his trust in the 'common man' in Germany at least. It was vain also to expect anything from the bishops. One or two had declared themselves on the side of the Reformation; but the higher ecclesiastics, as a class, had become more and more estranged from the movement. Even if the bishops had shown themselves sympathetic, Luther soon saw that their dioceses were in many respects ill-fitted by territorial arrangement for the inspection and control of the parishes. The only constituted authorities that could do what he conceived ought to be done were the secular princes; and to them Luther turned.

The first thing to do was to ascertain exactly the state of matters in the country districts of Electoral Saxony. This was done by means of 'Visitations', and the example of the Elector was speedily followed by other evangelical princes. Luther persuaded the Elector to appoint a regular commission to visit every part of his dominions; to report what needed to be done; and to give advice about the best means of accomplishing it. The commission was a mixed one of lawyers and pastors; the lawyers to examine into and report upon the legal provisions available for the support of churches and schools, and for the care of the poor; while the pastors were to inquire into the fitness of the country clergy, the spiritual needs of the people, and matters of that kind. The visitors required some common standard to test the condition of matters; and Melanchthon prepared 'Articles of Visitation', which, after careful revision, were published in March 1528, with a preface written by Luther. Luther's preface was the 'pastoral epistle' of the visitation.

The necessity was great, and the visitation was held simultaneously in several parts of Electoral Saxony. The correspondence of Luther during the years 1525-27 shows how urgent the need of such a visitation appeared to be to him. He had been up and down the country several times. He was a 'man of the people', and no one was afraid of speaking to him. The parish priests were always ready to lay their difficulties before him. In his letters he pictures the abounding poverty of those parish priests, a poverty increased by the fact that the only application of the new views made by many of the people was to refuse to pay all clerical dues. This was their idea of Reformation. He saw that the 'common man' respected neither priest nor preacher, that in country districts where there was no supervision, the houses of the priest and of the parish clerk were fast decaying, and he feared that if things were allowed to go on as they were doing there would soon be neither priest's house, nor schools, nor scholars.

The visitations made it clear that Luther had scarcely exaggerated matters. What was discovered was gross ignorance on the part of people and priests alike. The district round about Wittenberg was by far the best; but in the outlying districts a very bad state of things was disclosed. In a village near Torgau the visitors found an old priest who was hardly able to repeat the Creed or the Lord's Prayer, but who was held in the highest reverence for his power as an exorcist, and who derived a good income from the exercise of his craft. Priests had to be evicted for gross immoralities. Some kept beer-houses and practised other worldly callings. Village schools were rarely to be found, and the people were grossly ignorant. Some of the peasants complained that the Lord's Prayer was so long that they could not learn it; and in one place the visitors found that not a single peasant knew any prayer whatsoever.

2. The Visitation of Wittenberg 'Circle'

Perhaps the best way of seeing what this visitation was like is to take one single district – that of the 'circle' of Wittenberg. The commissioners were Martin Luther and Justus Jonas, theologians, with Hans Metzsch, Benedict Pauli, and Johann of Taubenheim, jurists. They began in October 1528, and spent two months at their task. They went about it with great energy, holding conferences with the priests and with the representatives of the community. They questioned the priests about the condition of the people, and the people about the priests. In towns their conference was with the Council or Rath, and in the village with the male heads of families. Their common work was to find out what was being done for the 'cure of souls', the instruction of the youth, and the care of the poor. By 'cure of souls' (*Seelsorge*) they meant preaching, dispensation of the sacraments, catechetical instruction, and the pastoral visitation of the sick. It belonged to the theologians to estimate the capacities of the pastors, and to the jurists to estimate the available income, to look into all legal difficulties that might arise, and especially to clear the entanglements caused by the supposed jurisdiction of convents over many of the parishes.

They found a good deal of confusion. This small district was made up of the outlying portions of three dioceses. It had not been inspected within the memory of man. At Klebitz the peasants had driven away the parish clerk, and put the village herd in his house. At Bülzig there was neither parsonage nor house for parish clerk, and the priest was non-resident. So at Danna; where the priest held a benefice at Coswig and was besides a chaplain at Wittenberg, and where the clerk lived at Zahna. The parsonages were all in a bad state of repair, and the local authorities could not be got to do anything. Roofs were leaking, walls were crumbling, it was believed that the next winter's frost would bring some down bodily. At Pratau the priest had built all himself – parsonage, outhouses, stable and byre. All these things were duly noted to be reported upon.

As for the priests, the complaints made against them were very few indeed. In one case the people said that their priest drank, and was continually seen in the public-house. Generally, however, the complaints, when there were any, were that the priest was too old for his work or was utterly uneducated, and could do little more than mumble a Latin mass. The priests had dealt very wisely in all matters of change. In some parishes they administered the Sacrament of the Supper according to the old and also according to the new rites, and the people seemed to prefer the new. In one parish, where there were two churches, the priest used the one for the old service and the other for the new. At Bleddin the peasants told the visitors that their pastor, Christopher Richter, was a learned and pious man who preached regularly on all Sundays and festival days, and generally four times a week in various parts of the parish. It appeared, however, that their admiration for him did not compel them to attend his ministrations with very great regularity. The energetic pastors were almost all young men who had been trained at Wittenberg. The older men, peasants' sons all of them, were scarcely better educated than their parishioners, and were unable to preach to them.

The visitors made strict inquiry about the habits of the parishioners with respect to attendance at church and at the Lord's Table. They found very few parishes indeed where three, four, five,

or more persons were not named to them who never attended
church or came to the Lord's Table; in some parishes men came
regularly to the preaching who never came to the Sacrament. What
impressed the visitors most was the ignorance, the besotted ignorance, of the people. They questioned them directly; found out
whether they knew the Apostles' Creed, the Ten Commandments,
and the Lord's Prayer; and then questioned them about the meanings of the words. 'What do you mean by saying that God is Almighty?' said Luther to a peasant. 'I do not know,' was the answer. 'I can well believe that,' said Luther; 'the most learned theologian must give the same answer.' But 'do you know that God is
your Father?' 'No.' 'When you say, "Our Father which art in
heaven," who is the Father?' 'I do not know,' was the answer.
Luther came back from the visitation in greatly depressed spirits,
and expressed his feelings in his usual energetic language. He says
in his introduction to his *Small Catechism*, a work he began as
soon as he returned from the visitation:

'In setting forth this Catechism or Christian doctrine in such a simple, concise, and easy form, I have been compelled and driven by
the wretched and lamentable state of affairs which I discovered lately
when I acted as a visitor. Merciful God, what misery have I seen, the
common people knowing nothing at all of Christian doctrine, especially in the villages! And unfortunately many pastors are well-nigh
unskilled and incapable of teaching; and although all are called Christians and partake of the Holy Sacrament, they know neither the Lord's
Prayer, nor the Creed, nor the Ten Commandments, but live like
poor cattle and senseless swine, though, now that the gospel is come,
they have learnt well enough how they may abuse their liberty.'

The visitors found that the pastors never studied theology because they had no books, or very few. They named the pastor of
Schmiedeberg as a notable exception; he had a library of twelve
volumes, which was a wonderful thing! It could not be expected
that such men could preach to much edification; and the visitors
recommended that copies of Luther's *Postils* or short sermons on

the Gospels and Epistles be sent to all the parishes, with orders that they should be read by the pastors to the congregations. The aged and incapacitated pastors were very gently dealt with. At Liesnitz, old Pastor Conrad was quite unable to perform his duties. It was arranged that he should have the stipend and parsonage for life, but that he should give fourteen gulden to a coadjutor, who was also to act as parish clerk, and the proprietor of the place promised to feed the coadjutor at his table. The visitors also found that schools did not exist in the villages at all, and they were disappointed with most of the schools they found in the smaller towns. They saw nothing for it but that the pastors must become the village school-masters. The pastors were instructed not to forget to warn their people to send their children to school, and they were requested to make the catechising of the children part of their church services on the Sunday. Various proposals were also made for the purpose of making the schools in the towns more efficient, and the church 'cantor' or precentor was to train the children to sing the evangelical hymns.

In their inquiries about the care taken of the poor they found that there was not much need for anything to be done in the villages; but the case was different in the towns. In most of the towns there were old foundations meant for the poor, but all manner of misuses and misappropriations of the funds were discovered. Suggestions were made for replacing these on a better foundation.

This very condensed account of what took place in the Wittenberg 'circle' shows the work of the visitations; a second and third visitation was needed in Electoral Saxony ere things were put right; but in the end good work was done. The Elector refused to take any of the confiscated convent lands and possessions for civil purposes, and stipends for the pastors and salaries for the school-masters, with provision for the poor, were gradually secured throughout Electoral Saxony.

Visitations somewhat on the Saxon model went on all over Germany, and out of them came the various ecclesiastical ordinances for the Evangelical States, out of which grew by slow stages the present Consistorial system of the Lutheran Church. If the whole movement towards an ecclesiastical organisation be carefully studied, it will be seen that it advances by slow stages as necessity calls for some new development, and that there is no thought of giving the people, because they are members of the Church, any share in its organisation and rule. The shape which it finally took was a return to the medieval form of Church local control. The Consistorial Courts of the Lutheran Church in Germany are very like the Consistorial Courts of the medieval bishops, only instead of the bishop appointing the members of the Courts, and holding them responsible to him, the members are appointed by and are responsible to the supreme local civil authority, whatever form that assumed. This remains a striking distinction between the Evangelical (Lutheran) and the Reformed (Calvinist) types of ecclesiastical organisation.

One interesting outcome of the Saxon visitations was Luther's Catechisms, Short and Large, and a new and greatly enlarged hymnbook. It is more than likely that in preparing all three Luther had in view his own training as a child in the old Mansfeld home; and that he desired to give all German children the means of receiving the same evangelical education which he had received from his father and mother. The Short Catechism is Luther at his best. It is difficult to think that anyone but himself could have written it; and the preface is as characteristic. He tells the pastors who make use of it that they must above all things avoid the use of different texts or forms of the Ten Commandments and the Lord's Prayer. 'If you preach to scholars or wise men you may show your skill, and vary these articles and twist them as subtly as you can. But with the young, always keep to one form and teach them... word for word, so that they may repeat them and learn them by heart.' When the children know the words perfectly, then the teacher may proceed to explanation, and this is to be done question by question. The second commandment is not to be explained till the first is clearly understood. When the Short Catechism is thoroughly understood, then the Large one is to be gone through in the same way. He closes thus: 'Our office has now become a different thing from what it was under the Pope; it has now become a real and saving office. Therefore it is more troublesome and full of labour, and is more encompassed with danger and temptation, and, moreover, brings little reward and thanks in this world. But Christ Himself will be our reward if we work faithfully. And so may the Father of all mercies help us, to whom be praise and thanks everlasting, through Christ our Lord.'

The Short Catechism is divided into six sections – The Ten Commandments, The Creed, The Lord's Prayer, The Sacrament of Holy Baptism, How the simple folks should be taught to confess, and The Sacrament of the Altar – and it has two Appendices, the first of which gives Prayers for private use morning and evening, and Grace before and after meals; while the second is a selection of pious thoughts, mostly in Scripture language.

One example may suffice to show how Luther wrote his Catechism:

> '*The Sacrament of the Altar...*
>
> 'Who, then, are they who receive this Sacrament worthily?
>
> 'Answer. Fasting and bodily preparation are in truth a good external discipline, but he is truly worthy and prepared who believes the words: "*Given for you and shed for the remission of sins.*" But he who does not believe them is unworthy and not prepared. For the words "*for you*" demand truly believing hearts.'

Luther was accustomed to repeat this Catechism to himself every morning. He thought that men whose business was theology needed more than others to be constantly reminded how simple after all the foundations and essentials of the faith were.

The Large Catechism repeats the thoughts of the Short one at a sevenfold length. These two Catechisms and the tract on the *Liberty of the Christian Man* contain all that is essential and all that is best in Luther's teaching. The Short Catechism and the Augsburg Confession are the two creeds which every Lutheran Church cherishes.

3. Luther as an Educational Reformer

Another result from these visitations was the foundation of something like a universal common-school system for all Germany, and especially for the rural districts. The education of boys and maidens, not merely of the upper and burgher classes, but of the whole people, was an end for which Luther strove unweariedly. In his *Address to the Nobility of the German Nation*, he proposed that a number of the useless convents should be restored to their primary use, that of educating boys and girls. His correspondence is full of desire to see good and sound education spreading throughout Germany. In 1524 he wrote his celebrated call *To the Burgomasters and Councillors of Cities in the German Land*, urging them to provide a large and generous system of education in their towns. His first and most earnest desire was that every child, no matter how poor the parents were, should be trained to read, write, and cipher. If it were objected that the parents need their services in order to gain a living, he replies that his idea is that boys should spend a few hours a day at school, and the rest of the day they can be at home learning their trade, and thus study and work will go hand in hand and mutually help each other. The real difficulty, he says, is the absence of any earnest desire to educate the young, and thus provide accomplished citizens to aid and benefit mankind. Remember, he says, that 'the devil much prefers blockheads and drones.' But while Luther pled for a minimum of education for every child, he insisted that all children of bright understandings should have very much more. He shows how good high schools for girls as well as for boys can be established by using many needless ecclesiastical foundations for the purpose. Then he urges the Town Councils to establish good libraries, for they give the best education.

This extensive reorganisation of education which took in as one whole the training of the youth of the Fatherland from the poorest village schools up to the universities was more to Luther than a 'devout imagination'. He produced it in actual life wherever he could. He encouraged the Town Council of Wittenberg to establish a school for girls, and himself invited Else von Kanitz to be the schoolmistress. 'You shall be in my house,' he wrote (2nd May 1527), 'and at my table, so that you may be free from danger and cares; so I beg you not to refuse me.' One result of the first Saxon Visitation was a Girls' School at Grimma, and Magdalena von Staupitz, sister or niece (I cannot make out which) of Luther's old convent superior, went there as schoolmistress. Luther received funds for the institution of bursaries for poor students from well-to-do ladies and gentlemen – Frau Dorothea Jörger, with her five hundred gulden, being the first. The Counts Mansfeld could think of no more pleasing present to Luther than the foundation of a high school in the town where his parents lived. He went to open it just before the Peasants' War broke out. Not to multiply proofs, it will be found that in almost every one of the numerous ordinances for the organisation of the Evangelical Church in Germany which Richter has collected, there is distinct and earnest provision made for the godly upbringing of the youth in common schools, which are regarded as essential to the well-being of the Church and of the State.

For all these reasons Luther has been usually regarded as the founder of the modern school and university of Germany. Yet many have called in question the correctness of the common opinion. The growl of Erasmus is well known: 'Ubi Lutheranismus, ibi literarum interitus'; Döllinger, Janssen, and Paulsen all declare that the Reformation movement, and with it the influence of Luther, was hostile to learning; they bring forward facts witnessing to the existence of high schools in Germany long before Luther's time, and to the decay of the high schools and universities in the years following 1520. It is undoubted that there were schools and provisions for learning during the Middle Ages in Germany. There were even a few schools for girls supported by some of the larger towns. Frankfort-on-the-Maine and other German cities had schools for girls, taught by mistresses who were not nuns, early in the fifteenth century. In some convents the education of girls was carried on as far as the state of learning permitted. In 1260 the little Saxon convent of Rodoardesdorf, afterwards Helfte, was almost a medieval 'Girton' under its bright young abbess, Gertrude of Hackeborn. Pages could be filled with the evidence of school and student life during the Middle Ages.

It is also true that in the earlier years of the Reformation movement attendance at schools and at many universities was sadly diminished. The excitement of the times and anxiety for the future easily accounts for this. Noblemen who sent their sons to high school and university in the expectation of placing them afterwards in some wealthy religious foundation – and the richest positions were almost all reserved for men of noble birth – burghers who looked to place their sons in the same way, poor people, peasants, and artisans who had once hoped to get their children off their hands in monastery or village parsonage, saw the possibility of all these benefices being abolished. These fears kept crowds back who some years earlier would have all been students. Besides, the Lutheran movement had kindled undoubtedly a distaste for the old learning of the schoolmen, with its pedantic, long-winded arguments about trifles, and Humanism was beginning to descend to much trifling also. Motives which appealed to the enthusiastic and to the sordid kept men back from devoting themselves to a student life. Luther was as keenly alive to all this as his future critics. 'People are saying,' he writes, 'Why should we educate our children if they are not to earn a living by becoming priests and monks and nuns?' He says that he perceives that schools are deteriorating throughout Germany, and that the universities are becoming weak. The thing was inevitable. It took place everywhere. The old incentives were disappearing, and the new had not time to root themselves in the minds of the people.

Yet the popular opinion is right after all, and it is to Luther that Germany owes its splendid educational system in its roots and in its conception. For he was the first to plead for a universal education – for an education of the whole people, without regard to class or special life-work. His firmest thought was that no village should be without its school. He inspired the German people with the desire to give their children as good an education as possible, and, after all, the creation of a living desire that can grow and make itself felt is the root of the matter. Once called into being, the desire, strengthened by the feeling that it was a holy thing, something owed to God, was more important to the German land than a scholastic organisation apart from the desire. The learned authors of the exhaustive *History of German Education from its Beginnings to our Time*, edited by Dr Schmid, claim that Germany owes almost all that is best in its modern education to the efforts of Luther. He freed it from the crushing weight of scholastic authority. He insisted on making the lessons interesting, and prepared an edition of *Æsop's Fables*, to be used as a reading book; he invented the art of pictorial illustration, and teaching by the eye as well as by the ear; and he bound the whole educational system together, from the lowest village schools up to the universities.

So the foundations of the Evangelical Church were laid, and the work of the Reformation was consolidated. It was done in face of enormous difficulties, and before a definite legal status had been gained. Oversight and discipline, two things absolutely required, were revived, and that in a much more thoroughgoing fashion than the medieval Church in the fifteenth and sixteenth centuries had been able to accomplish. The progress was slow. It could not but be slow. Sanctification is always a *work*, whether in a man or in a community. By degrees the rawness of the new congregations, the evil habits of the old pastors, the carelessness and hostility of the people, the greed of the nobles and of the commons, were surmounted, and a moral regeneration set in. It is scarcely possible to dwell on this, for that would involve a discussion and proof of the degrading immoralities which disgraced German life, of noble and burgher alike, in the fifteenth and sixteenth centuries. The subject is not a pleasant one; but a careful examination of the chronicles of the German towns during the latter half of the fifteenth and the first quarter of the sixteenth century reveal a state of things which is usually passed over by history. All this the Lutheran Church set itself to overcome, and it largely succeeded.

4. Luther and Zwingli

Before passing from this subject it may be well to remember that the Lutheran movement did not include a large number of those who separated from the Roman Church. Indeed, in the second generation, a very large portion of the German Reformation abandoned the strictly Lutheran type of doctrine and organisation, and ranged itself under the Reformed Church. This did not take place until after Luther's death. But his positive refusal to admit brotherly relations with Zwingli and the Swiss was largely responsible for it, and it is necessary to say something about the dispute.

What divided Luther from Zwingli was the question of the presence of Christ in the Sacrament of the Lord's Supper. Looking at the whole controversy now, with all the treatises of the controversialists before us, we can see that there was nothing contradictory between the opinions of Zwingli and those of Luther. The opposed views were, in fact, complementary, and the pronounced ideas of each were implicitly, though not expressly, held by the other. Luther and Zwingli approached the subject from two different points of view, and in debate they neither understood nor were exactly facing each other.

The whole Christian Church has found three great ideas embodied in the Sacrament of the Lord's Supper – the thoughts of Proclamation, Commemoration, and Communion or Participation, and the rite has always been held to have a close relation to the death of Christ on the Cross for His people. We proclaim the death and what it means, we commemorate the sacrifice, we participate in or have communion with the Crucified Christ. This last thought of 'participation' has always carried the mind of the Christian Church, not away from the death of Christ, but through it to the Living Risen Saviour, with whom there is fellowship through the Holy Spirit.

The medieval Church insisted that this sacramental Commemoration and Participation, with all the spiritual blessings it involved, was in the hands of the priesthood to give or to withhold. They alone could bring the Crucified and Risen Christ into such a relation to the worshippers as made the sacramental Commemoration and Participation possible things. Out of this claim there grew the medieval theory of Transubstantiation. It may also be said that the medieval Church represented the thoughts of Commemoration and Participation under two distinct uses of the sacrament – as a Mass, where the priest alone communicates, and as the Eucharist, where the faithful laity join. Or if the expression be too strong it may at least be said that the distinction referred to in the *cultus* gave rise to two separate ways of looking at and objecting to the medieval doctrine – each of which connected itself instinctively with the two thoughts of Commemoration and Participation.

Zwingli approached the medieval doctrine by the first and Luther by the second of those two separate paths.

What repelled Zwingli was the fact that the medieval Church had thrust aside the thought of *Commemoration* and put the thought of *Repetition* in its place. For the medieval priest claimed that he, in virtue of miraculous powers given in ordination, could change the bread and wine before him into the actual and physical body and blood of Jesus, and when this was done, that he could reproduce the agony of the Cross by crushing with his teeth. Whenever Zwingli thought of the medieval doctrine of the Sacrament of the Lord's Supper, he saw with horror a priest who claimed that he was repeating the agony of the Cross by *manducating* the Host. The thing was, to his mind, horribly profane. Besides, it dishonoured the one great Sacrifice; and it departed from the words of Jesus, which imply Commemoration but not Repetition. The commemoration was of the death of Jesus, and the participation a sharing in the Atonement which that death effected. But Atonement is appropriated by faith. Thus we get Zwingli's second thought, that we receive Christ by faith. Commemoration instead of repetition, faith instead of eating with the mouth; these are Zwingli's two great thoughts. But it must also be remembered that Zwingli held that faith always meant spiritual union or contact with Christ. Thus there is a Real Presence of Christ in the sacrament brought about by faith. Then when his theory was complete, and not till then, he gave the explanation of the words of the Institution, that 'is' means 'signifies'.

What repelled Luther in the medieval doctrine was the way in which it trampled upon the scriptural thought of the spiritual priesthood of all believers. He protested against Transubstantiation and private Masses because they were the most flagrant instances of that contempt. When he first began to write on the subject (1519), it was to insist that the 'cup' should be given to the laity. In the sermon there is an interesting statement, which sheds a light on Luther's whole position, to the effect that in the sacrament 'the communicant is so united to Christ and *His saints*, that Christ's life and sufferings and *the lives and sufferings of the saints* become his.' No-one held more strongly than Luther that the Atonement was made by our Lord, and by Him alone. Therefore Luther cannot be thinking of the Atonement when he speaks of union with our Lord and *His saints*. He thinks that the main thing in the sacrament is that it gives real companionship with Jesus, such fellowship as His disciples and saints had. There must be a reference to the death of Christ, for apart from the death there is no companionship possible, but the reference is indirect and through the thought of the fellowship. In the sacrament we touch Christ as His disciples might have touched Him when He walked on the earth, and as His glorified saints touch Him now. This reference to the saints also shows us that Luther saw in the sacrament the presence, not of the crucified, but of the glorified body of Christ. Luther, then, believed that the primary use of the sacrament was to give believing communicants a direct and immediate communion with the Living Risen Christ, such as His saints have in the life of glory. This required a presence (and Luther thought a *local* presence) of the glorified body of Christ in the sacrament; the communicant must be in contact with it. But communion with the Living Risen Christ implies the appropriation of the death of Christ, and of the Atonement won by His death. Finally, the local presence of Jesus in the elements need not involve any special miracle; for in virtue of the ubiquity of the glorified body of Christ it is present everywhere, and is therefore naturally in the elements. This natural Presence becomes a sacramental Presence because of the promise of God which is attached to the reverent and believing participation of the sacrament.

Each theologian held implicitly what the other stated explicitly; Zwingli put the relation to the death of Christ in the foreground, but implicitly admitted the relation to the Risen Christ; Luther put the fellowship with the Risen Christ in the foreground, but admitted the reference to the Crucified Christ.

The one had a very shallow exegesis to help him, and the other a scholastic theory of space; and naturally, but unfortunately, when controversy arose, the disputants attacked the weakest part of his opponent's theory – Luther, Zwingli's exegesis, and Zwingli, Luther's scholastic theory of space.

The most notable attempt to bring about an understanding was made by Philip of Hesse at the Marburg Conference in 1529, where Zwingli and Œcolampadius (real name Heusgen, transformed into Hausschein or House Lamp, and then turned into Greek) represented the Swiss and Luther and Melanchthon the Saxons. The Conference did not bring about agreement on the doctrine of the sacrament, but it proved that on all other points of the Christian faith the Reformed theologians were completely at one. Yet Luther refused to give Zwingli his hand. Long afterwards Zwingli's followers accepted Calvin's theory which combined the doctrines; Luther declared himself satisfied with it, and Calvin signed the Augsburg Confession. After Luther's death, his followers, more Lutheran than himself, refused the compromise, and thus the Reformation was split into two.

CHAPTER 11

THE LAST YEARS OF LUTHER'S LIFE

1. Luther's Political Influence

The last years of Luther's life were spent amid incessant labours, and amid continual ill-health. He had always spent himself when work for the 'evangel' was to be done, and had it not been for the iron constitution he had inherited from his parents he could never have gone through the labours he thought himself forced to undertake. He was twice at death's door.

At Schmalkald, where he went in February 1537 to attend a meeting of theologians to discuss the propriety of accepting the proposal to convene a General Council, he had a terrible attack of 'stone'. He preached nevertheless, and the malady increased. He had a week of intense pain, his body swelled, he was constantly sick, everyone feared and he hoped for death. He was far from wife and children, and was anxious about them. The Elector promised to care for them 'as his own'. To make matters worse the necessary medical appliances were not to be had at Schmalkald, and it was resolved, ill as he was, to remove him. The journey was a prolonged torture, but the jolting of the carriage seems to have effected what the doctors had been unable to do. As soon as the pain left him he wrote to his wife, to remove her anxieties. The journey was accomplished by slow stages. At Weimar, his niece Lena Kaufmann met him from Wittenberg; he got safely back to his Kaethe and his home, where good nursing brought him round again.

In 1541 the terrible malady returned, and his life was again despaired of; but careful nursing restored him. These attacks occurred at times of very trying anxieties. His life was spared, but he was constantly an invalid, and the misused body revenged itself in continual pain. He told his friends during this last illness that his brain was like a knife worn to the heft and incapable of cutting.

His father had died in 1530, when Luther was detained at Coburg; his mother lived a year longer, and died on 30th June 1531. Luther wrote a touching letter to her, which she received on her deathbed. It ends: 'All your children and my Kate pray for you. Some weep; the younger eat and say, "Grandmother is very ill." ' One can see little Hans and baby Lena, wagging their small heads, and repeating the words between the mouthfuls.

It was characteristic of Luther to describe what he saw, and to think in pictures. This breaks forth even in the most abstract questions. When he discusses the doctrine of Christian perfection in the Augsburg Confession, he has a God-fearing German burgher and a barefooted friar in his eye. 'Christian perfection,' he says, 'is this, to fear God sincerely, and to have great faith, and to trust assuredly that God is pacified towards us for Christ's sake, to ask and certainly to expect help from God in all our affairs according to our calling, and outwardly to do good works in our vocation. In these things doth true perfection and the true worship of God consist. It doth not consist in celibacy, in begging, and in wearing dirty clothes.' When he expounds the meaning of 'Give us this day our daily bread,' he calls up the picture of a well-fed, warmly clothed German child trudging to school in a stout pair of shoes to keep its small feet dry. His thoughts naturally shaped themselves in pictures; and he was careful to cultivate this gift.

German art had been changing since the beginning of the sixteenth century. It had begun the change by tracing sketches from common life round the margins of its copperplates or woodcuts of Holy Families, or of scenes from the Bible and from the lives of the saints. Then, emboldened, it had plunged into the delineation of all kinds of ordinary, commonplace life. The revolution in religion said that all human life, even the most commonplace, could be sacred; and the contemporary revolution in art discovered the picturesque in the life of the people. We have from Albert Dürer,

Hans Burgmaier, the brothers Beham, Lucas Cranach, and from many another artist, pictures of the life of the times, in the castles of the nobles, in the streets of the cities, and in the villages of the peasants. Nürnberg was the great centre of this effort to bring art into common life. In 1535 we find Luther writing to his friend Wenceslas Link to collect for him all the *pictures* of the common German life, the rhymes, the ballads, and the stories that had been published there, because he wished to familiarise himself thoroughly with the genuine language and life of the people.

The last years of Luther's life brought him no new tasks; they were ceaselessly occupied in the same kind of work which had come upon him after the Diet of Augsburg. He was the confidential adviser of a large number of the German princes. He was occupied with attempts to unite more firmly together the whole Evangelical movement. He was also on the watch against the attempt of the Roman Curia to recover its old power over Germany.

Luther's intimacy with his own Elector helped to give him the place accorded to him by other German princes. Luther lived under three Electors of Saxony – Frederic the Wise, who had been offered the Empire, and had declined; John, his brother; and John Frederic. Frederic, although he had been Luther's protector in all the early stormy times, although he lived continually in the same town, frequently heard Luther preach, and had corresponded with him, never had any personal intercourse with the Reformer. He sent for Luther, when he was on his deathbed during the storm of the Peasants' War, but Luther did not reach the castle in time to see the old lord alive.

His brother John, long before Frederic's death, had been much more intimate with Luther, had sent for him to preach at Weimar, when he was only Duke John, and was fond of consulting him personally. After he became Elector, the intimacy between the Augustinian convent and the castle was continuous, and Luther was constantly summoned to attend the prince at distant castles when things of importance were being debated. He died in 1532, just after the conclusion of the Treaty of the Peace of Nürnberg, which he had done so much to bring about. He was a man of straightforward piety and of great benevolence. John the Stedfast was his name in that age of sobriquets. Poor man! he grew to be so fat in his latter days that his people had to hoist him on the back of his horse by a sort of windlass!

John Frederic, his son and successor (born in 1503), was twenty years younger than Luther, and we can see that from his boyhood the Reformer had been his hero. He was fourteen years old when Luther published the Theses, eighteen when Luther stood forth at Worms. The *Passional Christi et Antichristi* had taken great hold on his young mind, and he was intensely pleased that he was one of the few who knew who the author was. When he became Elector, he wished Luther to come and live constantly with him in the castle and dine daily at his table. He wrote to him continually in terms of the greatest familiarity, and could never make enough of him. His wife, Sibylla of Cleves, was full of loving admiration of the household in the Augustinian convent. Her portrait by Cranach gives one the idea of a tall lady with a clever, demure face, and eyes and mouth that are longing to laugh, only that must not be while one's portrait is being painted. She was the sister of that Anne of Cleves, the rather stout and large German lady who was too coarse-looking for such a delicate creature as Henry VIII, and whom he called the 'Flanders Mare'. It is curious to think how the sisters were separated. The one coming over to England to share a throne, and finding instead a quiet life in a pleasant English house at Burley-on-the Hill; the other in the heart of the busiest part of Germany, a true and noble wife, sharing her husband's good fortunes, counselling wisely him and his, and in the evening of his days, when he lost the Electorate and almost lost life, sharing in faithfullest fashion every hardship he had to undergo. Her letters to Luther are full of bright feminine humour and sincere womanly piety.

Next to his own Elector, Luther's most intimate friends among the princes were Wolfgang of Anhalt and his three nephews, the lords of Anhalt-Dessau. The history of the three lads is interesting, if there was time to tell it. They had three bitter supporters of the papacy for their guardians, and George, the eldest, intended for the Church, had been made a canon of Merseberg when he was eleven years old. One after another they sought the friendship of Luther, and became strong Protestants. They had a visitation of their small territories made after the Saxon fashion, and George, as a clergyman, insisted on conducting it.

In 1539 Duke George of Saxony's brother, Henry, succeeded to the Albertine Saxony, and with the joyful consent of his subjects, pronounced for the Evangelical faith. Nothing would content him but that Luther should come to Leipzig to preside clerically at such an auspicious event. He had even to preach in the great hall of the castle, where just twenty years before he had stood confronting Eck in the famous Disputation, and had heard Duke George declare that his opinions were pestilential. In the afternoon he preached in one of the town churches, where, on the same occasion, the priests had swept the *elements* off the altar into the sacristy, lest the presence of such a heretic would profane them.

Perhaps the most romantic story belongs to Electoral Brandenberg. The Elector, Joachim I, brother of Albert of Mainz, who farmed the Indulgence, was a strict supporter of the Emperor and the Edict of Worms. He died praying his son, with tears it was said, to remain in the old religion – the son being then committed to the Protestant side. His wife, Elizabeth, was secretly inclined to the Evangelical faith. She longed to partake of the Lord's Supper according to the Evangelical rites, and succeeded, but was not able to keep the matter from her husband's knowledge. Whereupon he threatened to 'wall her up'. The poor lady managed to escape, and made a desperate flight to Saxony, to Torgau first, and then to the Castle of Lichtenstein. There she corresponded regularly with Luther, and had him to stay with her when he travelled that way. But she felt that she must know Catherine, for Luther was always speaking about his wife, especially to lady friends and correspondents. The royal lady, therefore, came to Wittenberg, and spent three months with Catherine in the Luther household. Her children all sympathised with her – the sons at least – and thus Brandenberg, which is today Prussia, became Protestant. Elizabeth, a king's daughter and an Electress, must have enjoyed the Luther family household, with all its bustle, or the visit would have been somewhat shorter. The young Elector, Joachim II, and his brother John had always afterwards an immense esteem for Luther. Their people, too, had been secretly longing for the Evangelical worship, and rejoiced at the change. Electress Elizabeth went back to Brandenberg after her son's accession, and ended her days peacefully at Berlin.

Princely correspondence was not always pleasant, however, even when it came from men who were strong and hearty for the Evangelical faith. Philip of Hesse, the brightest, boldest, and by far the most capable of all the Evangelical princes, had an unhappy home-life. He had married, when barely nineteen, a daughter of Duke George of Saxony, and had been, in that age of sexual licence, a faithful husband to her, in all outward respects at least. We have not the lady's story, it must be remembered; but the husband's is that she was of morose temper, that she had a disagreeable disease, and that she was given to drink. Latterly he declared that married life with her was impossible, and that the terms on which he was with her prevented him going to the Lord's Table and fretted his whole inner life.

It has been suggested that the statements of some of the wilder Anabaptists, justifying polygamy from Old Testament example, first made him think of the possibility of taking a second wife. He had thought of divorce; but he knew that the strong opinions which Luther had on the subject of Henry VIII's divorce made it impossible for him to get the Evangelical theologians to consent to such a thing. Brooding over the whole matter, he convinced himself that there were cases in which a man might take two wives, and that his was a case in point. He got no encouragement, rather dissuasion, at first. He thought himself very hardly treated, and declared, truly enough, that had he been a Romanist he could easily have got a dispensation to keep a concubine. We have on record the yearly sums some bishops made in the beginning of the sixteenth century by the granting of such dispensations. He entrenched himself in the idea that polygamy was permitted under the Old Testament, and was not positively forbidden under the New, and that matrimony was not part of the ceremonial law of the Old Testament, which was manifestly done away with by the coming of Christ.

Matters at last came to a crisis. Philip had fallen in love with a young lady, Margarethe von der Saal, whom he met when on a visit to his sister, the Duchess Elizabeth, at Rochlitz. The young lady, who was some distant relative of Luther's wife, very properly refused to have anything to do with him unless she could be legally married to him; and her mother's idea of a legal marriage was one at which Bucer, the renowned Strassburg theologian, Luther, Melanchthon, or at least two of them, would be present as witnesses, with envoys from John Frederic the Elector, and Maurice, now Duke of Saxony. These two princes were respectively the second cousin and the nephew of Philip's wife.

Philip prepared his own case, recapitulating the arguments given above, adding some precedents he had discovered of princes being allowed to take a second wife, and ending with the compliment that the lady was a relation of Catherine von Bora, and that part of his anticipated joy in the marriage was that it would make him a connection of Luther's by marriage. He won over Martin Bucer to his side, and indeed the blame attaching to the Evangelical theologians must be laid most heavily on Bucer's shoulders.

There is no doubt that this action of Philip was a profound grief to Luther. The Landgrave had been bringing the matter before him for thirteen years with increasing insistence. It can scarcely be said that Luther's answer to the question placed before him by the Landgrave was due to the fear of displeasing a leading Evangelical prince. For it is clear that the proposed second marriage must have been, and was, looked upon as a personal affront by young Maurice of Saxony, whose ability and power everyone recognised. The slight put upon his aunt was an insult to himself and to the family of which he was the head. Luther also knew that his own Elector not only felt that his friend's proposal was against the fundamental laws of Christian morals, but regarded it as an affront upon the House of Saxony. Then Luther, at the very time when the question was finally placed before him by the Margrave, was deeply anxious about the exaggerated reports he had heard of the Anabaptists encouraging polygamy, and was very much afraid lest such views might spread among the peasantry, who, he said, had already very lax ideas about the sanctity of the marriage tie. These things ought to be stated, not to palliate Luther's conduct, for they rather increase the error, but for the purpose of having the whole situation before us.

The official document sent by Luther, Melanchthon, and Bucer is very sad reading. It may be summarised thus: According to the original commandment of God, marriage is between one man and one woman, and the twain shall become one flesh, and this original precept has been confirmed by our Lord; but sin brought it about that first Lamech, then the heathen, and then Abraham took more than one wife, and this was permitted by the law. We are now living under the gospel, which does not give prescribed rules for the regulation of the external life, and it has not expressly prohibited bigamy. The existing law of the land has gone back to the original requirement of God, and the plain duty of the pastorate is to insist on that original commandment of God, and to denounce bigamy in every way. Nevertheless the pastorate, in individual cases of the direst need and to prevent worse, may sanction bigamy in a purely exceptional way; such a bigamous marriage is a true marriage (the necessity being proved) in the sight of God and of conscience, but it is not a true marriage with reference to public law or custom. Therefore such a marriage ought to be kept secret, and the dispensation which is given for it ought to be kept under the seal of confession. If it be made known, the dispensation become *eo ipso* invalid, and the marriage becomes mere concubinage. This is a short summary of the document which caused the scandal.

It may be well to ask whether Luther had any principle before him when he drafted and signed this extraordinary paper? He had, and this paper is the worst instance or outcome of a mode of thinking from which he never completely divested himself. With all his reverence for the Word of God he could never avoid giving the traditions of the Church a certain place beside the Scripture. We find this thought coming continually forward, sometimes quite unconsciously, in much of his reasonings about institutions and in doctrines. He applied that principle here. The medieval Church had been accustomed to insist that it possessed a power of dispensation; and Luther never altogether denied this. In this instance, notwithstanding his denunciations of the dispensations granted in matrimonial cases by the Roman Curia, he declared that the Church did possess this power of dispensation even to the length of tampering with a fundamental law of Christian society, provided that it did not attack a *positive* scriptural ordinance to the contrary. If it had been pointed out to him that he was acting as the Roman Curia had done, he would probably have replied that the Curia took money for its dispensations and that the Evangelical Church did not, and that this fact made the two cases entirely dissimilar.

However he reasoned with himself, he thoroughly repented of his action when it was too late. He was not present at the marriage, though Philip by a stratagem did secure poor doubting Melanchthon as a witness.

Repentance, however, as Luther had often said, does not secure against the consequences of sin, and Luther was to feel this. Nor did Philip escape. Bigamy was a grave offence against the laws of the land. Serious talk arose about bringing Philip up before the Imperial Law Courts and punishing him. The Emperor ended this by declaring that poor Margarethe had never been married at all, and was simply Philip's concubine. The effect of the formal answer of Luther, Melanchthon, and Bucer was simply to deceive a poor maiden. The full consequences of the sin did not manifest themselves in Luther's lifetime, but the beginnings were not lacking. The confederacy of Protestant princes received a shock from which it never recovered; and Maurice of Saxony took his revenge on Philip when he suddenly deserted to the Emperor's side when the religious war broke out, as it did shortly after Luther's death. It must not be supposed that Evangelical theologians approved of Luther's conduct. Most of them disapproved strongly, and the remonstrances of some had the effect of inducing Melanchthon formally to withdraw his acquiescence in the paper he had signed along with Luther and Bucer. Yet the Evangelical cause had to sustain the burden brought on it by this strange document.

2. The Last Scenes

During the last years of Luther's life attempts were unceasingly made to bring about a union, or at least a common understanding, between the North Germans, represented by Luther, and the South Germans, at the head of whom stood Bucer of Strasburg. All throughout the conferences Luther endeavoured to be as friendly as his conscience permitted him; but he would on no account have any personal relations with the Swiss. He could not divest his mind of the error that Zwingli's views on the Sacrament of the Supper were those of his old friend Carlstadt, whom he had never forgiven for his share in bringing on the deplorable Peasants' War. But the heroic death of Zwingli at Cappel in October 1531, seems to have softened all men's minds towards the Swiss, and plans for united action became more possible. The beginnings of those conferences go back to the year 1529, when Evangelical princes and theologians met at Schmalkald to discuss the situation. The first League was formed at the same place in view of the threat of the Emperor to suppress the Reformation by force, a threat which appeared very real at the Diet of Augsburg. In this first League only the stricter Lutheran territories were included, notwithstanding the entreaties of Bucer that the South Germans might be allowed to join. In 1531 happier feelings prevailed, and a mutual defensive alliance was made between the members of the Schmalkald League and the South German cities, Luther making no objection. All the political side of the matter Luther contentedly left to the princes, saying that such matters did not belong to the province of the theologian.

A few years of political union renewed the desire for a still closer approximation. The South German pastors pled for an interview with Luther and a discussion of the theological situation. The meeting-place was to be Eisenach, but Luther was too ill to leave home when the time of conference arose. All the delegates came on to Wittenberg. After some little talk, it was found that all were in agreement save on one point in the doctrine of the Sacrament of the Supper. It was the old story of the corporeal and local (the last being the test word) presence of the body of Christ in the bread in the Lord's Supper. This was a point to which Luther clung with all the tenacity of his nature, and that simply because he thought that the words of Scripture required him to do so. The theory of the local bodily presence had no connection in his mind with any sort of priestly miracle or sacrificial theory of the Supper. He explained the possibility of such a local presence by a scholastic theory of corporeal presence, but he did not cling to his theory. All that he would not give up was the thought that the body of Christ was actually in the mouth of the partakers. He always maintained in its integrity the thought of the spiritual priesthood of all believers, and expressly applied the idea to the partaking in the Lord's Supper. 'There,' he says, 'our priest or minister stands before the altar, having been duly and publicly called to his priestly function, he repeats publicly and distinctly Christ's words of the Institution, he takes the bread and the wine, and distributes it according to Christ's words, and we all kneel beside him and around him, men and women, young and old, master and servant, mistress and maid, all holy priests together, sanctified by the blood of Christ. And we are there in our priestly dignity... We do not let the priest proclaim for himself the ordinance of Christ, but he is the mouthpiece of us all, and we all say with him in our hearts, and with true faith in the Lamb of God, who feeds us with His body and blood.'

The South Germans were able to content Luther so far that they agreed to differ on the one very small point of doctrine that remained over. This cheered Luther immensely. He preached to the little company of theologians a sermon of wonderful power and sweetness. The delegates all partook of the Holy Communion together, and then separated to their distant towns and districts.

These peaceful conferences and the strength they manifested led some of the more spiritually minded Roman Catholic divines to ask whether it was not possible for *all* to come together; and conferences were held at various places with this aim. The most interesting was at Ratisbon, and one has only to read the conclusions come to to see how very nearly the best and deepest theology of the medieval Church approaches the Evangelical. The one thing which really separated the theologians of the two Confessions was the medieval theory of the priesthood and of the miraculous powers which were believed to be conferred on priests in ordination.

Year by year Luther was growing weaker, his attacks of illness became more frequent, and his bodily pains more severe and more continuous. One bit of work remained for him to do, and do it he would at all risks. The Counts of Mansfeld had quarrelled over the division of the properties which they had inherited. It was the division of the small things that had brought about the quarrel – some trifling revenues and the patronage of some churches. They had agreed to accept the mediation of Luther, and he gladly responded. 'I would cheerfully lay down my bones in the grave if I could only reconcile my dear lords,' he said.

He left Wittenberg on the 23rd of January, 1546, in bitterly cold weather. His wife and the Elector would fain have kept him at home. He was very weak and ill. Only six days before he started he described himself as 'old, spent, worn, weary, and cold, with but one eye to see with'. His two sons, Martin and Paul, went with him, to see the old place where their father had been born. He travelled by slow stages, and was detained at Halle for three days, for thaw setting in had burst the ice on the river Saal, and great floods hindered any crossing. His poor wife was very anxious about him, and he wrote to her five times in the fourteen days – whimsical letters for the most part, but always telling her what he had to eat and drink – probably in obedience to some wifely command. She must have scolded him for attempting the crossing before the river was low enough; for he writes: 'Thou must needs takes the cares of God upon thee, as if He were not Almighty, and could not create ten Dr Martins if one old Dr Martin were drowned in the Saal,' which pious reflection was not likely to bring much consolation to poor Catherine.

When he reached Eisleben and Mansfeld, he found the work harder than he had hoped, his chief difficulties being with the lawyers of the respective brothers. But at last all was amicably settled, and Luther accepted the fees of arbiter in the shape of endowments for village schools in the Mansfeld region. The young Counts made much of him, and on the 14th of February he wrote his last letter to his wife. On the outside is: 'To my dear kind housewife, Katharin Luther von Bora, at Wittenberg'; and inside: 'Grace and peace in the Lord, dear Kaethe! We hope to come home again this week, if God will... The young men are all in the best spirits, and make sleigh rides every day with fools' bells on their horses; and the young ladies also; and amuse themselves together... I send thee some trout which the Countess Albrecht has presented to me... Thy sons are still at Mansfeld. Jacob Luther will take good care of them... I have no ailments' – a letter which must have cheered the anxious wife not a little.

But he was never to see his Kaethe again. He had preached in Eisleben in the Church of St Andrew on the 14th with great power and fervour, when suddenly he said quietly, 'This and much more is to be said about the gospel; but I am too weak, and *we will close here*.' These were his last words in the pulpit. On the 16th and 17th the deeds of the reconciliation were duly signed, and Luther's work was done. He was living in the house of the town-clerk of Eisleben – a house whose front windows looked across the street to the church in which he had been baptized sixty-three years ago. The end came somewhat suddenly. He was very ill on the 17th; all his friends waited on him that night – his two boys, Justus Jonas, his host and hostess, and the Count and Countess Albrecht of Mansfeld. His sufferings were great, he uttered many ejaculations, and prayed aloud a short, beautiful prayer. Jonas said early in the morning, stooping down to the ear of the dying man, 'Reverend Father, wilt thou stand by Christ and the doctrine thou hast preached?' Luther roused himself to say 'Yes'. It was his last word. Twenty minutes later he passed away with a deep sigh; poor wife Kaethe doubtless fast asleep at Wittenberg, far away, and dreaming of her husband's safe return, for he had promised her to be home that week. He died on Thursday, 18th February, between two and three in the morning, not a hundred yards from the place where he first saw the light so many years ago.

The Elector, John Frederic, was resolved that his lifelong hero and friend should be laid in the grave at Wittenberg, and Catherine wished that also. So the Eisleben people had a service in the Church of St Andrew, which lasted two days. On the 20th the funeral procession began its long march. The Counts of Mansfeld, with their wives, followed as far as the gates of Eisleben, with the magistrates and the whole population of the town. A troop of fifty light-armed horse, commanded by the sons of the Counts of Mansfeld, rode in front, and escorted the procession all the way to Wittenberg. Delegates from the Elector met the procession when it crossed the boundaries between Mansfeld and Electoral Saxony. The bells tolled in every village church steeple on the route and at all the cross-roads were groups of weeping peasants.

They laid him to rest in the Castle Church of Wittenberg, near the door, where he had nailed up the theses which had kindled such a conflagration.

Luther is a man of his epoch – but what man can ever adequately represent an epoch? The age is always richer than the greatest individual belonging to it, and brings into the world more than any man of the time can see, understand, or make his own. His epoch had elements of culture which Luther either deliberately rejected or was unable to appropriate. There were indestructible elements in the culture of men like Erasmus and Sir Thomas More which Luther could not appreciate. His age was fertile in economic suggestions which were a sealed book to Luther. He might have learned much even from such fanatics as Münzer or the leaders in the Peasants' War. His inability to see the promise and potency of life which lay in the rude strivings of the 'common man' marred his reforming work and still paralyses the European portions of the Church which bears his name. These and other defects may have nevertheless aided him in doing what he did accomplish. He was not too far before his contemporaries to prevent them seeing his footprints and following in his steps. Yet, as Harnack has remarked: 'What an inexhaustible richness his personality included! How it possessed in heroic shape all that the time most lacked – a wealth of original intuition which outweighed all the elements of culture in which it was defective; a certainty and boldness of vision which was of more value than any insistence on free investigation; a power to lay hold on what was true and to conserve what would stand the test of time compared with which the merely critical faculty is pointless and feeble; above all a wonderful ability to give expression to strong feeling and true thought, to be a *seer* and a *speaker*, to persuade by the written and spoken word as the prophet must do.'

His conduct towards Zwingli and the Swiss, as also the strong language which he used towards opponents, reveals to later generations a fund of intolerance which is not what one expects from such a great man; but it is manifest that his contemporaries did not and could not pass the same judgment. While he lived, he held the Protestant forces together in a manner that only a man of broad, wise tolerance could have done. His sincerity, his wise patience, his power of separating what was essential from what was accidental are apparent when we think of what occurred after his death, when he was no longer there to hold in check the petty orthodoxies of the Amsdorfs and Osianders among his followers. It is the fate of most of the authors of revolutions to be devoured by the movement which they have called into being. Luther occasioned the greatest revolution which Western Europe has ever seen, and he ruled it till his death. History shows no other man with such kingly power.

This king among men was also the most human. He had his fits of brooding melancholy, his times of jovial abandonment when one can hear his great jolly laugh and his rich sonorous voice carolling forth songs, his moods of the softest tenderness with wife and children, and his abiding sense of companionship with the Eternal. What is especially Luther-like in this last is that he carries this Holy of Holies about with him, and that it makes him companionable and not solitary. It makes him sympathise with beast and bird and tree and plant – with the hares in the woods about the Wartburg, with the little bird in his garden, with the rooks who built their nests far below his window in the Coburg Castle, with the rose and the flax and the pine trees. The God, who is his closest companion, made them all.

Luther, we may add, is the type of the best German manhood, in his patient industry, his enjoyment of quiet home-life among wife and bairns, his love of music, and his power to kindle when occasion arises into that slow-burning fire which consumes opposition. Dead these long centuries ago, he is still living in the German nation. For, as even Döllinger admits, 'he has stamped the imperishable seal of his soul alike upon the German language and the German mind,' so that 'even those Germans, who abhor him most as the powerful heretic and the seducer of the nation, cannot escape; they must discourse with his words, they must think with his thoughts.'

CHRONOLOGICAL SUMMARY OF
THE HISTORY OF THE REFORMATION

Contemporary Events	Lutheran Church	Reformed Church
1493-1519 - Jan 12, Maximilian I Emperor. At his death the Elector Frederick the Wise of Saxony (1480-1525), viceroy. 1499-1535 - Elector Joachim I (Nestor) of Brandenburg. 1500-1539 - Duke George of Saxony. 1509-1547 - Henry VIII of England. 1515-1547 - Francis I of France	1517 - Oct 31, Martin Luther (b 1483, Nov 10, at Eisleben; 1497, at Latin School at Magdeburg; 1498, at Eisenach (Frau Cotta, d 1511); 1501, at Erfurt; 1505, Master of Arts; July 17, entered the Augustinian Cloister at Erfurt; 1508, Professor at Wittenburg; 1511, at Rome; 1512, Oct 19, Dr of Theology) nailed 95 theses against the abuse of indulgences on the door of the Castle Church at Wittenberg. Counter-theses of John Tetzel, composed by Conrad Wimpina.	Ulrich Zwingli: b 1484, Jan 1, at Wildhaus, in Canton of St Gallen; scholar of Henry Wölflin (Lupulus) at Berne; of Thomas Wyttenbach at Basel; 1499, student of Joachim Vadianus at Vienna; 1506, MA; 1506-16, pastor at Glarus; 1516-18, preacher at St Mary's, Einsiedeln.
1518-1567 - Philip the Magnanimous of Hesse (b 1504).	1518 - Silvester Mazzolini of Prierio: *Dialogus in præsumptuosas M L conclusiones de potestate Papæ*; Luther's *Resp ad Silv Prier*. April 26, Luther at Heidelberg Disputation. Aug: Cited to appear at Rome. Aug 25, Melanchthon at Witttenberg. Oct 12-15, Luther at Augsburg before Card Thomas Vio de Gaeta; appeals *a papa male informato ad melius informandum*.	1518 - Zwingli against the indulgence preached by Bernardin Sampson (Guardian of the Franciscan Cloister at Milan). Dec: Zwingli pastor in the Minster at Zurich.

CHRONOLOGICAL SUMMARY

Revolutionary Movements	Roman Catholic Church	Protestant Theology
	1513, Mar 11-1521, Dec 1 - Leo X. 1517 - The Lateran Council grant to the Pope the tithes of all church property. Indulgence (the fifth between 1500 and 1517) for the building of St Peter's and for the Pope's private needs. Three indulgence commissions granted for Germany, one farmed by Elector Archbishop of Mainz (consec 1514), the Dominican John Tetzel (d 1519) his commissioner. Thomas Vio de Gaeta (Card Cajetan): 'The Catholic Church is the bond-slave of the Pope'; asserts papal infallibility in the widest sense.	PHILIP MELANCHTHON (b 1497, Feb 16, at Bretten; 1509-12, at Heidelberg; 1512-14, at Tübingen; 1514, MA, 1514-18, teaches in Tübingen; 1518, Prof of Greek at Wittenberg; Aug 29, Introductory Lecture, *De Cor-rigendis adolescentiæ studiis*; 1519, Sept 19, Bach of Theology; d 1560, April 19). **Loci communes rerum Theologicarum, seu hypotyposes Theoligicæ,** 1521; three editions in 1521; edition of 1525 modifies absolute predestination; edition of 1535 reconstructs his theology; edition of 1543, Synergism.

CHRONOLOGICAL SUMMARY

Contemporary Events	Lutheran Church	Reformed Church
	Nov: Luther, *On the Sacrament of Penance*.	
1519 - June, *Charles V (since 1516 King of Spain)* - 1556, Aug 27, *Emperor of Germany* (d 1558).	1519 - Jan: Luther's interview with Charles of Miltitz, papal chamberlain at Altenburg; Truce.	1519 - Jan 1, Zwingli delivers his first sermon in Zurich; sermons on St Matthew's Gospel, Acts, and the Pauline Epistles; Reformation sermons, pointing out a clear distinction between Biblical and Romanist Christianity; Humanist study of Scripture (Pauline Epistles).
1519-1566 - Suliman I, Sultan.	June 27-July 8, DISPUTATION AT LEIPZIG: (1) between Eck and Carlstadt, on the Doctrine of Free Will; and (2) between Eck and Luther, *De primatu Papæ*.	
1519-1521 - Fernando Cortez discovers and conquers Mexico.	The controversy is no longer one about a point in scholastic theology; it involves the whole round of ecclesiastical principles.	
	Break with the Roman Christendom.	
	The doctrine of the Priesthood of all Believers.	...
	Christian freedom and the right of private judgment.	
	Luther's sermons on the Sacraments of Repentance and Baptism, and on Excommunication.	
	Demand for the celebration of the Lord's Supper under both kinds.	
1520 - Magellan sails round the world.	1520 - April: Ulrich v Hutten (b 1488, April 21; d 1523, Aug 29); Dialogue: Vadiscus or the Roman Trinity; June 15, Bull of Excommunication against 41 propositions of Luther.	

CHRONOLOGICAL SUMMARY

Revolutionary Movements	Roman Catholic Church	Protestant Theology
	1519 - The Cortes of Aragon ask three Briefs (never sent) from Leo X to restrain the Inquisition. Similarly fruitless applications made by the Estates of Aragon, Castile, and Catalonia to Charles V in 1516.	ZWINGLI: *Commentarius de vera et falsa religione*, 1525; *Fidei ratio ad Carolum Imperatorem*, 1530, July 3; *Sermonis de providentia Dei Anamnema*, 1530; *Christianæ Fidei expositio*, 1531.
	Romanist Theologians in the first period of the Reformation. John Eck, Prof of Theology at Ingolstadt since 1510; b 1486, in the Swabian village of Eck; d 1543.	(a) *Lutheran Theologians*
		George Spalatin: b 1484 at Spalt, in the bishopric at Eichstädt; 1514, court chaplain to Frederick the Wise; 1525, Superintendent at Altenburg; d 1545.
	Jerome Emser, court preacher to Duke George of Saxony; d 1527.	Justus Jonas: b 1493, at Nordhausen; 1521, Provost and Prof at Wittenberg; 1541-46, at Halle; 1551, Superintendent at Eisfeld; d 1555.
	John Cochlæus (Dobeneck), Dean at Frankfort-on-the-Maine, Canonicus in Mainz and Breslau; d 1552; *Commentaria de actis et scriptis M Lutheri* (1517-46); 1549, *Historiæ Hussitarum*.	Nicholas of Amsdorf: b 1483; since 1504 at Wittenberg; 1524, at Magdeburg; 1528, at Goslar; 1542-46, Bishop of Naumburg.

CHRONOLOGICAL SUMMARY

Contemporary Events	Lutheran Church	Reformed Church
	60 days for recantation; Aug: Luther, 'To the Christian Nobles of the German Nation, on the Bettering of the Christian Estate'; Oct: *De Captivitate Eccles Babylonic*; *De libertate Christiana* (of the freedom of a Christian man); Dec 10, Papal Bull burnt.	
1521-26 - First war between Charles V and Francis I. 1525 - Battle of Pavia. 1526 - Peace of Madrid.	1521 - April 17, 18, **Luther at the Diet of Worms**; April 26, leaves Mar 3, 1522. [In Dec begins translation of NT; Tracts: *On Penance, Against Private Masses, Against Clerical and Cloister Vows, The German Postille*.]	IN FRANCE, spread and preaching of Reformed doctrines through William Briçonnet, Bishop of Meaux from 1521. With him Le Fèvre and Farel.
...	May 26, Edict of Worms falsely antedated May 8. May 28, Imperial decree against Luther. June: Carlstadt against celibacy. Oct: The Mass abolished at Wittenberg by the Augustinian monks (Gabriel Didymus). Dec: Carlstadt's innovations. Dec 25, Lord's Supper in both kinds. Dec 27, The Prophets in Wittenberg.	1521- Cornelius Hoën, Dutch jurist, writes *De Eucharistia* (The Lord's Supper purely symbolical); the doctrine brought to Wittenberg and Zurich by John Rhodius, President of the Brother House at Utrecht.
...	1522 - Feb: Riots in Wittenberg against images and pictures.	1522 - April 16, Zwingli: *Von Erkiesen und Fryheit der Spysen*;

CHRONOLOGICAL SUMMARY

Revolutionary Movements	Roman Catholic Church	Protestant Theology
	John Faber, 1518, Vicar-General at Constance; 1549, Provost at Ofen; 1530, Bishop of Vienna; d 1561; 1523, *Malleus hæreticorum*.	after 1550, at Eisenach; d 1565. John Bugenhagen: b 1485; from 1521 in Wittenberg; 1522, pastor; 1536, General Superintendent there. Casper Cruciger: 1528-48, when he died, Prof at Wittenberg.
1521 - The (Zwickau) Prophets in Wittenberg, Nicholas Storch, Marcus Thomæ Stübner, Martin Cellarius.	1521 - Henry VIII of England: *Assertatio vii Sacramentorum contra Lutherum* (Defender of the Faith). April 15, Decree of the Sorbonne condemning Luther's doctrines.	Fredk Myconius, Franciscan at Annaberg, then Pastor in Weimar; 1524, Court preacher at Gotha; d 1546.
Andrew Bodenstein of Carlstadt: 1504, Prof in Wittenberg; 1520 at Copenhagen; 1522, riots about images and vestments; 1523-24, in Orlamünde; then excommunicated in South Germany, East Friesland, Switzerland; d Basel, 1541. ...	May 8, Edict of Charles V (founded on Edict of Worms) against the spread of Reformation doctrines in the Netherlands. [1522, the Augustinian cloister at Antwerp closed for heresy.] 1522-23 - Sept 14, Pope Hadrian VI (tutor to Charles V, Bishop of Utrecht), learned in the old learning; aspiration after a reform of the clergy through	Paul Speratus: 1521, at Vienna, then at Iglau; 1523, at Wittenberg (1524, 'Salvation has come to us'); 1524, in Königsberg; 1529-51, when he died, Bishop of Pomerania in Marienwerder. John Brenz, b 1499: 1520, Romanist preacher at Heidelberg; 1522-46, Lutheran preacher at Hall in Swabia; from 1563, provost at Stuttgart; d 1570, Sept 11.

CHRONOLOGICAL SUMMARY

Contemporary Events	Lutheran Church	Reformed Church
	Mar 7, Luther back in Wittenberg. Mar 9-16, Sermons against fanaticism. July: Contra Henricum regem Angliæ. Sept: Translation of NT finished (whole Bible in 1534). Dec: Diet at Nürnberg; The Hundred Grievances of the German Estates, in answer to Hadrian VI's Brief of Nov 25.	Aug: *Apolo-geticus Archeteles*, to the Bishop of Constance. The Zwinglian theology gradually becomes the more powerful in the Netherlands.
	1522-23 - The Reformation conquers in Pomerania, Livonia, Silesia, Prussia, Mecklenburg; in East Friesland from 1519; 1523, in Frankfort-on-the-Maine, in Hall in Swabia; 1524, Ulm, Strasburg, Bremen, Nürnberg.	1523 - Jan 29, Disputation in Zurich between Zwingli and John Faber, the Bishop's Vicar-General; Zwingli's 67 theses. Oct 26, Disputation at Zurich about image-worship and the Mass.
1523-33 - Frederick I of Denmark 1523-60 - Gustavus Vasa of Sweden	1523 - July 1, Henry Voes and John Esch (Augustinians) burnt at Brussels; the first martyrs. Gustavus Vasa establishes the Reformation in Sweden (Olaf and Lorenz Petersen, Lorenz Andersen). May 7, Sickingen slain; revolt of nobles quelled by the princes. Luther: **Of the Order of Public Worship**; Dec: *Formula Missæ* (Lord's Supper *sub utraque*).	Nov 17, Instruction of Zurich Council to pastors and preachers. 1524 - Thorough reform of church at Zurich; pictures taken down; Friars' convents closed. Victory of the Reformation in Berne (Berchtholdt Haller,

CHRONOLOGICAL SUMMARY

Revolutionary Movements	Roman Catholic Church	Protestant Theology
	the hierarchy. In Spain, from 1520, circulation of Lutheran writings in Spanish translations made at Antwerp.	(b) *Zwinglian Theologians* John Œcolampadius (Heusgen), b 1488; 1515, pastor at Basel; 1519, in Augsburg; 1522, Prof. and preacher at Basel; d 1531, Nov 24.
		Leo Judæus: 1523, curate in St Peter's in Zurich; b 1482; d 1542.
1523 - Conrad Grebel, Felix Manz, and Stumpf in Zurich, against Zwingli's State Church.	1523 - Juan de Avila, 'the Apostle of Andalusia', suffered persecution for Lutheran doctrine.	Oswald Myconius (Geisshüsler): b 1488 at Lucerne; 1532-d 1552, Oct 14, Antistes at Basel.
1524 - Disturbances in Stockholm; Melchior Hoffmann.	1523-34 - Sept 25, Pope Clement VII (Julius Medici, natural son of Julian de Medici).	Conrad Pellican (Kürsner): b 1478; 1493, Franciscan; from 1502, Lector in Franciscan Cloister in Basel; 1527, at Zurich as Prof of Hebrew; d 1556.
	1524 - Cardinal Campeggio, Pope's Legate at the Diet of Nürnberg.	(c) *Intermediate Theologians*
1525 - Thomas Münzer at Mühlhausen; executed May 1525. Tract: *Wider das geistlose sanftlebende Felisch zu Wittenberg*, 1522.	League of South German Roman Catholic States at Regensburg (Ferdinand of Austria, the Dukes of Bavaria, and the South German bishops). Terms: A certain measure of ecclesiastical reform,	Urbanus Rhegius: b 1490, at Argau on the Bodensee; 1512, Prof at Ingolstadt; 1519, Priest at Constance; 1520-22, Preacher in Augsburg; from 1530, Reformer in Brunswick, in the service of Duke Ernest; died at Celle, 1541, May 23.

CHRONOLOGICAL SUMMARY

Contemporary Events	Lutheran Church	Reformed Church
	1524 - *The first German HymnBook*. June- May 1525 THE PEASANTS' WAR; peasants slaughtered at Frankenhausen.	Nic Manuel), Appenzell, Solothurn; Romanist League of the Forest Cantons at Lucerne.
1525 - Albert of Brandenburg (d 1568); last Grand Master of the Teutonic Knights; changed the territory of the Order into the Dukedom of Prussia.	1525 - Jan: Luther: *Against the Heavenly Prophets*. May: Exhorts princes and peasants to keep the peace, with comments on the twelve articles. Then: *Against the robber-murdering Peasants*. June 13, Marries Catherine von Bora. Conservative tendency of Lutheran Reformation; separation from more revolutionary elements.	1525 - The Mass abolished in Zurich; public worship very simple and in German language; Lord's Supper sub utraque. Zwingli's Commentary and first part of Zurich translation of Bible. (First complete edition 1531.)
1525-32 - Elector John the Constant of Saxony (brother of Frederick the Wise).	1525 - Dec: Luther, *De Servo Arbitrio* against Erasmus, Διατριβη *de libero arbitrio*, Sept 1524.	Zwingli's distinctive confessional statement of his doctrine of the Lord's Supper. [Carlstadt publishes his theory of the Lord's Supper in South Germany; δειχτιχϖζ: This My Body, is the Body, etc.]
1526 - Aug 29: Lewis, king of Hungary and Bohemia, falls fighting at Mohacz against the Turks.	1526 - May 4: League at Torgau between Philip of Hesse and John the Constant, joined in June at Magdeburg by other evangelical princes.	
His successor, Ferdinand of Austria (Oct, chosen king of Bohemia), has to make good his claims to Hungary against the Turks.	June 26, League of North German Roman Catholic princes at Dessau.	Zwingli to Matth. Alber at Reutlingen, 1524, Nov 16, *Manducatio spiritualis*; then in his commentary.

CHRONOLOGICAL SUMMARY

Revolutionary Movements	Roman Catholic Church	Protestant Theology
Jan: Rise of the Anabaptists; Jürg Blaurock, a monk from Chur.	and alliance with the civil power; but no further spread of the new doctrines.	Ambrose Blaurer: b 1492, at Constance; 1534-38, Reformer of Würtemberg; to 1548, at Constance; d at Winterthur, 1564. (1534, *Stuttgart Concord*.)
Severe persecution of the Anabaptists (Manz drowned at Zurich, 1527; Balth Hubmaier, burnt at Vienna, 1528; Hetzer beheaded at Constance, 1529).		Martin Bucer: b 1491, at Schlettstadt; 1505, Dominican; from 1524, pastor in Strasburg; 1549, under Edward VI in England, and Prof at Cambridge; d 1551, Feb 28.
	1524 - Peter Caraffa. Bishop of Theate [Pope Paul IV] instituted the Order of the Theatini to stay the spread of the Reformation.	Wolfgang Fabricius Capito: b 1478; 1515 in Basel; 1520, in Mainz: 1523-d 1541, Dec, Provost of St Thomas, Strasburg.
		(d) *Zwinglian Confessions*.
		1523 - Jan 29, Zwingli's 67 Articles.
Melchior Hoffmann: b at Hall, in Swabia; 1523, in Livonia; 1527, in Holstein; 1529, at Strasburg; thence to Friesland, where he joined the Baptists; then in the Netherlands; 1533, in Strasburg; d 1540. (Ordinanz Gottes): a strict millenarian of the more spiritual kind;	1526 - May 29: League at Cognac against Charles V (the Pope, Francis I, Venice, and Milan).	Nov 17, Instructions to the Council of Zurich.
		1530 - July 3, *Fidei Ratio ad Carolum V* (Zwingli, assented to by Œcolampadius and other Reformers).
		1530 - *Confessio Tetrapolitana* (Strasburg, Constance, Lindau, Memmingen); Bucer,

CHRONOLOGICAL SUMMARY

Contemporary Events	Lutheran Church	Reformed Church
	June and July: DIET AT SPEIER. '*In matters of religion each State shall live, govern, and behave itself, as it shall answer to God and His Imperial Majesty.*'	*Against* Zwingli: Bugenhagen. *For* Zwingli: Œcolampadius.
	Oct 20, Synod at Homberg; Hessian Church Order by Francis Lambert (b 1487, at Avignon; Franciscan; fled 1522 to Switzerland; 1527 Prof in Marburg; d 1530); independence of the Christian community, and strictest church discipline.	The Syngramma Suevicum, 1525 (at Hall), by Brenz, Schnepf, Griebler, etc, later Calvin. Luther against Zwingli - (1) in his preface to Agricola's translation of the Syngramma Suevicum; (2) in 1527, 'That the words, This is My Body, etc.'
	Luther - German Mass; Order of Public Worship.	Zwingli's ecclesiastical and political church principles; his political reformation of Switzerland; political league of the Roman Catholic Forest Cantons to preserve their supremacy.
1527 - Sack of Rome	Frederick 1 of Denmark adheres to the Lutheran doctrine (John Tausen in Jutland from 1524).	1526 - The Roman Catholic Cantons attacking the Evangelical. May: Disputation at Baden (Eck and Œcolampadius).

Revolutionary Movements	Roman Catholic Church	Protestant Theology
spreads millenarian views among the Baptists.		Capito, Hedio; during the sitting of the Diet of Ausburg.
Caspar Schwenkfeld: b 1490, at Ossing, near Liegnitz; in the service of the Duke of Liegnitz; 1525, believed that he had found an explanation of the words of the institution: 'Quod ipse panis fractus est corpori esurienti, nempe cibus, hoc est corpus meum, cibus videlicet esurientium animarum'; hence his doctrine of Christ, The Inner Word (*De cursu Verbi Dei, origine fidei et ratione justificationis*, 1527); of the Person of Christ (not made man, but begotten by the Divine Nature: His flesh, Divine); 1528, driven from Silesia; in Strasburg, Augsburg, Speier, Ulm, persecuted from 1539 by Lutheran theologians; in many controversies; d 1561 at Ulm; followers in Silesia; since 1730 in Pennsylvania.	1527 - Process of the Sorbonne against Jacques le Fêvre (d 1537, on a journey to Strasburg, under the	1534 - *Confessio Basiliensis* (Myconius) accepted by Mühlhausen in 1537, and called Conf Mühlhusiana. 1536 - *Confessio Helvetica Prior* (Basil II) drawn up at Basel (Jan to March) by delegates from the Evangelical Cantons, and by their theologians, Bullinger, Myconius, Grynæus, Leo Judæus, etc. (e) *Lutheran Confessions.* 1529 - Luther's *Larger* and *Shorter Catechism* in German; appeared simultaneously. 1530 - **Confessio Augustana**; or, Augsburg Confession, framed out of (1) the 15 Marburg Articles; (2) the 17 Schmalkald Articles drawn up by

CHRONOLOGICAL SUMMARY

Contemporary Events	Lutheran Church	Reformed Church
1527-29 - The second war between Charles V and Francis I; Peace of Cambrai, Aug 1529. 1527 - Henry VIII of England seeks divorce from Catherine of Aragon (Charles V's aunt); 1529, Wolsey in disgrace; Thomas More, chancellor.	1527 - The first Visitation of Electoral Saxony; Gustavus Vasa proposes the Reformation to the Diet at Westerås. Frederick I of Denmark, at the Diet of Odensee, gives the reformed religion the same privileges as the Roman Catholic. 1528 - Otto v Pack's statement of a Roman Catholic League formed at Breslau, 1527; the Reformation spreads in Norway.	1528 - The Reformation victorious in St Gallen (Joachim Vadianus, John Kessler); and in Berne.
1529 - Sept-Oct 14, Suliman lays siege to Vienna.	1529 - Feb 26, Diet at Speier; April 12, the decision of Roman Catholic majority of Electors and Princes, 'Whoever has enforced the Edict of Worms is to do so still; the others are to allow no further innovations; no one to be prevented from celebrating Mass'; April 19, agreed to by the cities. PROTEST: April 25, Appeal taken to the Emperor and Council by Saxony, Hesse, Brandenburg, Anhalt, Lüneburg, and fourteen cities.	1529 - Reformation conquers in Basel (Œcolampadius, Capito, Hedio). League of five Forest Cantons with the House of Hapsburg. June 24, Peace of Cappel; the Forest Cantons abandon the Hapsburg League and recognise liberty of conscience.

CHRONOLOGICAL SUMMARY

Revolutionary Movements	Roman Catholic Church	Protestant Theology
	protection of Margaret of Navarre). 1527 - May 6, Charles of Bourbon storms Rome; the Pope shut up in St Angelo till June 6; Charles V master of most of the States of the Church, proposes to limit the temporal power of the Pope; the Pope appeals to England and France; a French army equipped by English money marches to his assistance. 1528 - June 29: Peace between Emperor and Pope at Barcelona; the Pope gets back the States of the Church and Florence; Heresy to be exterminated.	Luther; (3) Torgau Articles, compiled by Luther, Melanchthon, Justus Jonas, Bugenhagen, and presented to the Elector at Torgau in March 1530. The work of Melanchthon assisted by the evangelical theologians assembled at Augsburg, and revised by Luther. Statement of Evangelical Doctrine, 'In qua cerni potest, nihil inesse, quod discrepet a Scripturis vel ab ecclesia catholica vel ab ecclesia Romana, quatenus ex scriptoribus nota est... Sed dissensus est de quibusdam abusibus, qui sine certa auctoritate in ecclesiam irrepserunt.' Philip of Hesse signed with protest against Article X on the Lord's Supper in the *Invariata*, Impossible to fix the exact text of either the German or the Latin editions; Melanchthon's first

CHRONOLOGICAL SUMMARY

Contemporary Events	Lutheran Church	Reformed Church
	Separation between the Lutheran and South German Protestants; Luther objects to armed resistance; Zwingli plans to abolish the Papacy and the Medieval and Papal Empire; Philip of Hesse tries to bring about union.	
	Oct 1-4, Religious conference at Marburg (Luther, Melanchthon, Zwingli, Œcolampadius, Justus Jonas, Osiander, Brenz, etc); on Oct 4, union on fourteen articles, division on fifteenth - Sacrament of Supper. *Zwingli*: 'There are none on earth's round I would more gladly be at one with than the men of Wittenberg.' *Luther*: 'You have another Spirit than we.' Zwingli's hand refused.	
	Oct 16, Luther at the Convent of Schwabach; Nov 30, at Schmalkald; Saxony breaks away from South German cities.	
1530 - Feb 24, Charles V crowned at Bologna by the Pope. No German princes present.	1530 - **Diet at Augsburg**: June 15, entry of Emperor; fruitless negotiations with the Evangelical princes to induce them to join the Corpus-Christi procession; June 20, Diet opened; June 25, Augs. Confess. read and given in (Aug 3, Con-futation read); July 11, Confes. Tetrapolitana read); Confutation, Oct 17) and Zwingli's *Fidei Ratio*; Aug 16-29, Negotiations with Melanchthon, in which he proves too pliable.	The Roman Catholic Cantons do not observe the terms of peace.
	Nov 19 - Decree of Diet. Protestants to get till April 15, 1531, then suppression by force.	
1531 - Ferdinand of Austria, king of the	1531 - Schmalkald League of Protestants - at the head, Hesse and Saxony.	1531 - May 15, at Aarau the Forest

224

CHRONOLOGICAL SUMMARY

Revolutionary Movements	Roman Catholic Church	Protestant Theology
		printed edition, Wittenberg, 1530, in 4to.
	1530 - Reformed congregations in *Spain*. In Seville: Rodrigo de Valero, Joh Egidius, Ponce de la Fuente. In Valladolid, 1555, Augustin Cazalla. Francis Enzinas translates the N T; 1556, new translation by Juan Perez.	The *Variata* (variations specially in Article X) since 1540. *The Apology for the Augsburg Confession* - The *prima delineatio apologiæ* by Melanchthon in Sept 1530 at Ausburg; fully revised, Nov 1530-April 1531; first edition, April 1531; German edition by Justus Jonas, Oct 1531.
1533 - *The Kingdom of Christ* in Münster.	All stamped out by Philip II and the Inquisition.	
Bernhard Rothmann, Evangelical Superintendent in Münster, joins the Anabaptists; Henry Roll and the Wassenberg preachers from Jülich. Summer: Melchiorites in Münster. Nov: Jan Matthiesen.	*Italy* - The German Reformation awakens religious life and Augustinian theology; Contarini, Reginald Pole, Joh de Merone (Archbishop of Modena), *Peter Paul Vergerius* (went over to the Reformation in 1548; d 1565).	*The Schmalkald Articles*, by Luther, for the Protestant Convention at Schmalkald, 1557, and with reference to the proposed General Council at Mantua. [Strictly Lutheran.] *Controversies in the Lutheran Church.*
1534 - Lent: Riot, destruc-	Reformation at Ferrara (Renée married, 1527, to Hercules II); at Venice; at Naples (Juan Valdez, d 1540; and Bernard Ochino); at Lucca (Peter Martyr).	1548-55 - *Adiaphoristic*: Flacius, Wigand, Amsdorf, against Leipzig Interim.

CHRONOLOGICAL SUMMARY

Contemporary Events	Lutheran Church	Reformed Church
Romans; Bavaria and Electoral Saxony oppose.		Cantons are refused provisions, Zwingli objecting.
1532 - Aug - 1547, John Frederick the Magnanimous, Elector of Saxony; d 1554. Henry VIII divorced by Parliament from Catherine of Aragon. Nov: Marries Anne Boleyn.	1532 - Diet of Nürnberg: Toleration till a General Council. Dessau receives the Reformation.	Oct 11, Battle of Cappel; *Zwingli slain*; Second Peace of Cappel. Henry Bullinger, Zwingli's successor.
1534 - Restoration of Duke Ulrich of Würtemberg by Philip of Hesse.	1534 - Lutheran Reformation gains Würtemberg, Anhalt, Augsburg, and Pomerania.	*Reformation in French Switzerland under Calvin.*

CHRONOLOGICAL SUMMARY

Revolutionary Movements	Roman Catholic Church	Protestant Theology
tion of images and cloisters. Easter Eve: Matthiesen overthrown; John of Leyden at the head of the Anabaptists; Theocracy. 1535 - Eve of St John: Münster taken. 1536 - Jan 22, John of L e y d e n , Knipperdolling, and Krechting executed.	1534-49 - Paul III. Pope (Farnese); Vergerius his legate in Germany.	1549-66: *Osiander*: Andrew Osiander (at Nürnberg, 1522-48; at Königsberg, 1549-d 1552); 1550, *De Justificatione*; 1551, *De Unico Mediatore Jesu Christo*; 'Justification is a participation in the righteousness of Christ', *cujus natura divina homini quasi infunditur*. In connection therewith his doctrine of the Divine image in man. In opposition: Francis Stancarus from Mantua (1551-52 in Königsberg, then in the Siebenbürgen and in Poland; d 1574; 1562, *De Trinitate et Mediatore*, 'Christ our righteousness only as regards His human nature.' 1551-62 - Majorist: George Major (d 1574, Prof at Wittenberg); *bona opera necessaria esse ad salutem*. Against him, Amsdorf; *bona opera perniciosa esse ad salutem*.
1534 - David Joris: b 1501		

CHRONOLOGICAL SUMMARY

Contemporary Events	Lutheran Church	Reformed Church
1535 - Joachim II, Elector of Brandenberg.		*William Farel* (b 1489, in Dauphiné; 1530, in Neufchatel; 1532, in Berne; d 1565, in Geneva); and *Peter Viret* (b 1511, at Orbe; 1531-59, at Lausanne; from 1561, at Nismes and Lyons; d 1571); from 1534, Reformation preachers in Geneva.
1536-38 - Third war between Charles V and Francis I.	1536 - Wittenberg Concord; Melanchthon and Bucer; *Lord's Supper* in Lutheran sense only; eating of the unworthy, 'of the unbelieving', avoided; *Baptism*; *Absolution*; came to nothing; difficulties concealed, not explained. Reformation victorious in Denmark.	
		1536 - JOHN CALVIN at Geneva; b 1509, July 10, at Noyon; studied at Orleans and Paris; 1533, joined Reformation in Paris; at Basel; 1536, **Institutio Christianæ Religionis**; then in Ferrara; strict ecclesiastical discipline; Easter, 1538, banished from Geneva, goes to Strasburg; recalled, 1541; d 1564, May 27.
	1537 - Convention at Schmalkald; the Schmalkald Articles.	
1538 - Ten years' truce at Nice.	1538 - Roman Catholic League at Nürnberg.	
	1539 - Reformation victorious in Ducal Saxony and in Electoral Brandenburg.	
	1540 - June; Conference at Hagenau.	
	Nov 25-Jan 14, at Worms (Granvella, Melanchthon, Bucer, Capito, Brenz, Calvin, Eck, Cochlæus).	*Calvin's Ecclesiastical polity in Geneva* - Worship: prayer and preaching. Organisation: Presbyterian.
1541-53 - Duke Maurice of Saxony; made Elector, 1546.	Feb: Regensburg Interim.	1542 - Jan; *Ordonnances ecclésiastiques de l'église de Genève*. Pastors, doctors, elders, dea-
1541 - Diet at Regensburg; Suliman	1541 - April 27 - May 22, Conference at Regensburg (Contarini, Melanchthon, Bucer, Eck), Transubstantiation the difficulty).	

CHRONOLOGICAL SUMMARY

Revolutionary Movements	Roman Catholic Church	Protestant Theology
at Delft; joins the Anabaptists; reforms them; his influence in the Netherlands and East Friesland; 1542, his *Wunderbuch*; 1544, in Basel; a Mystical-spiritualistic speculation with a rationalist tendency.	1536 - Paul III summons the long-promised Council to meet at Mantua; 1537, adjourned; called to meet at Vicenza; again adjourned.	1556-60 - Synergist: Pfeffinger, 1555, *Propos de libero arbitrio* (in Melanchthon's synergistic sense); against him, Amsdorf (1558, *Confutatio*); and Flacius.
The Mennonites.	1542 - Antonio Paleario (burnt 1570); *Del beneficio di Gesu Christo crocifisso verso i Christiani.*	1560 - Disputation at Weimar between Flacius and Strigel. Flacius: Original Sin is of the substance of man. The Lutheran doctrine overcomes. Heshusius: *de servo arbitrio.*
Menno Simonis: b 1492, at Witmarsum; 1524, priest; 1536, resigned his office, disgusted with the perseuction of the Münster Anabaptists; baptized by an apostle of Jan Matthiessen; reformed and organised the Anabaptist communities in Holland and Friesland; d at Oldesloe in 1559; expelled the enthusiastic fanatical elements, and increased the tendency towards Donatism.	1540 - Sept 27, SOCIETAS JESU constituted by Paul III; *Don Inigo (Ignatius) of Loyola*, b 1491, at the Castle Loyola in the Basque Provinces; wounded (1521) at Pamplona; legends of the Saints; studies at Barcelona; from 1528 in Paris. In 1534, with six companions (Francis Xavier, Jac Lainez, Pet Lefevre, etc) he took the three monastic vows and a fourth of absolute obedience to the Pope. Loyola, d 1556; Lainez, d 1564.	1527-40, and renewed 1556 - *Antinomian*: John Agricola, b 1492, at Eisleben; d 1566, Court preacher at Berlin; 1527, against Melanchthon; and 1537, against Luther. Contrition is taught not by the Law but by the Gospel. Recants 1540. From 1556 controversy about 'Tertius usus legis'.
His followers, Mennonites, tolerated in 1572 by William of Orange in the Netherlands; also found in Emden, Hamburg, Danzig, Elbing, in the Palatinate, and in Moravia; moderated the original Anabaptist	'To advance the interests of the Roman Catholic	1567 - *Crypto-Calvinist*: Melanchthon's admissions to Calvinists in doctrines of Lord's

CHRONOLOGICAL SUMMARY

Contemporary Events	Lutheran Church	Reformed Church
conquers the Hungarians.	1542 - Nicolas v Amsdorf Bishop of Naumburg.	cons. Church discipline.
1542-44 - Fourth war of Charles V with Francis I; Peace of Crespi. 1542 - Diet at Speier; union against the Turk. 1544 - Diet at Speier; recognition of the Protestants; peace all round till a General Council.	1543 - Reformation in the Archbishopric of Köln; Herman v Wied, the archbishop, advised by Bucer and Melanchthon; excommunicated, 1546; abdicates, 1547; d 1552.	*Reformation in France 1559-98.* Earlier: *Francis I.* Humanist, careless in religion, treated the Reformation as a politician; his sister Margaret, Queen of Navarre (d 1549) protected the Reformers; severe persecution of French Protestants in spite of alliance with German Protestant princes, and an invitation to Melanchthon to settle in France, 1535.

1545 - *Reformatio Wittenbergensis.*

1546 - Second Religious Conference at Regensburg; Feb 18, Luther dies at Eisleben; the Protestants do not appear at the Diet.

1546-47 - the Schmalkald War; June 19, league between Maurice and the Emperor; July 20, decree against John Frederick and Philip; Oct 27, Maurice made Elector; April 24, Battle of Mühlberg, John Frederick, prisoner; Philip surrenders at Halle; Emperor breaks faith, and keeps the princes in prison.

1547-49 - Henry II of France; spouse, Catherine de Medici, d 1589.

1547-53 - Edward VI of England; b 1537.	1548 - May 15, Augsburg Interim retains Roman Catholic hierarchy, ceremonies, feasts and fasts; marriage of clergy and Lord's Supper *sub utraque* permitted.	Henry II: Anthony of Navarre, and his wife Joan d'Albret, at the head of the Protestants in France. 1559 - May 25-29, First Reformed Synod at Paris, assembled by an Parisian pastor, Anthony Chandieu; Conf Gallica. 1561 - Sept: Religious Conference at Poissy; Theodore Beza.

CHRONOLOGICAL SUMMARY

Revolutionary Movements	Roman Catholic Church	Protestant Theology
spirit; rejected all dogmatic; forbade oaths and war; appealed to the letter of Scripture.	Hierarchy against Protestantism within and without the Romish Church.' Xavier's mission work in East Asia. Society's Morals: casuistry. Its dogmatic: superstition systematised. 1542 - Cardinal Caraffa advises the reconstruction of the Inquisition to crush Protestantism in Italy. 1545 - *Council of Trent* opened; First period, Mar 11, 1547, at Trent; April 21, 1547-Sept 13, 1549, at Bologna. Second period, May 1, 1551-April 28, 1552, at Trent. Third period, Jan 13, 1562-Dec 4, 1563 (25 Sessions). Romanist doctrinal teaching concluded and petrified. 1564 - *Professio Fidei*	Supper, Christology, and Predestination. From these controversies a need for concord in the Lutheran Church; hence various forms of concord, out of all which came the *Formula Concordiæ*. (1) Swabian Concord of Jac Andreas (from 1562 Prof at Tübingen, d 1590) in 1574; 1575, Swabian Concord of Martin Chemnitz; 1576, Malulbronn Formula of Lucas Osiander. (2) Torgau Convention with the Torgau Book. Thence 1577, *Formula Concordiæ*. *The principal Lutheran Theologians.* *Martin Chemnitz*: 1554- d 1586, Superintendent in Brunswick; *Examen Concilii Trid*; 1565-73, *Loci Theologici*. *Matthew Flacius*: b 1520, at Albona in Illyria; 1545, at Wittenberg; 1548, at Magdeburg; 1557-61 at Jena; d at Frankfort-on-the-Maine, 1575, March 11.

CHRONOLOGICAL SUMMARY

Contemporary Events	Lutheran Church	Reformed Church
	1548 - Leipzig Interim (Maurice of Saxony and Melanchthon). 1551 - Vehement desire of the Emperor that the Protestants should submit to the Council of Trent; Secret League of Maurice of Saxony with Henry II of France.	1562 - Jan: Protestants gain right to worship outside the towns; Francis of Guise massacres Protestant congregation at Vassy.
1553-58 - (Bloody) Mary of England.		
1554 - July 9, Maurice slain in battle near Sievershausen, against Albert, Margrave of Brandenburg. Ferdinand beaten by the Turks in Hungary. 1555-98 - Philip II of Spain. 1556-64 - *Ferdinand I, Emperor*. 1558-1603 - Elizabeth of England.	Oct: Würtemburg ambassadors, and Jan 1552, Saxon ambassadors at Trent. 1552 - Mar 20, Maurice breaks loose; May 19, seizes Ehrenberg Castle and Ehrenberg Pass, the keys of the Tyrol; the Council breaks up; July, Treaty of Passau; John Frederick and Philip free. 1555 - Sept 25: *Religious Peace of Augsburg*; the Lutheran Church (Augs Confes) has the same legal rights as the Roman Catholic: *Cujus regio ejus religio*; the *Reservatum ecclesiasticum*; the Reformed Church not recognised.	1562-63 - Huguenot war. Anthony of Navarre d; Francis of Guise shot before Orleans. 1567-68 and 1569-70 - Huguenot wars. 1572 - Aug 24, Paris massacre on eve of St Bartholomew; Coligny and 20,000 Huguenots murdered. 1574-76 - Huguenot war; Holy League of the Guises. 1588 - Henry and Louis of Guise slain.

CHRONOLOGICAL SUMMARY

Anglican Church	Roman Catholic Church	Protestant Theology
England, 1547-1600, under Henry VIII: John Frith, William Tindal. 1534 - Act of Parliament about Royal supremacy; the King 'the only supreme head on earth of the Church of England'; at the head of the Evangelical party, Thomas Cranmer [1533, Archbishop of Canterbury] and Thomas Cromwell; Translation of the Bible, 1538.	*Tridentinæ*: 1566, *Catechismus Romanus* (Leonardo Marini, Egidio Foscarari, Muzio Calini). 1548 - Philip Neri founds the Oratory. 1550-64 - Julius III (del Monte). 1551 - Foundation of Jesuit Collegium Romanum. 1552 - Foundation of C o l l e g i u m Germanicum. 1555-59 - Paul IV (Caraffa) protests against the Peace of Augsburg; Inquisition.	*Catalogus Testium Veritatis*, 1556; *Ecclesi Hist per aliquot... studiosos et pios viros in urbe Magdeburgica* (the Magdeburg Centuries), 13 vols; 1560-74; *Clavis Script Sac*, 1567; *Glossa Compendaria in N T*, 1570, etc. *John Gerhard*: b 1582, at Quedlinburg; 1606, Superintendent at Heldburg; 1615, General Superintendent at Coburg; 1616-d 1637, Prof at Jena. *Loci Theologici*, 1610-25; *Medit Sac*, etc. *Leonhard Hutter*: 1596-d 1616, Prof at Wittenberg; *Compendium Loc Theol*, 1610; *Loci Commun Theolog*, 1619.
1539 - July 28, Transubstantiation; refusal of cup to the laity; celibacy of the clergy; Masses for the dead; auricular confession. The Reformation of Henry VIII, the act of the King, and meant only revolt from the medieval system, with the King in the place of the Pope.	1559-65 - Pius IV (Medici) rules under the influence of his nephew Cardinal Charles Borromeo, Archbishop of Milan, d 1584. 1564 - *Index librorum prohibitorum*. 1566-72 - Pius V, a zealous Dominican.	*The confessional writings of the Reformed Church universally recognised.*

CHRONOLOGICAL SUMMARY

Contemporary Events	Lutheran Church	Reformed Church
1559-60 - Francis II of France (married Mary of Scotland). 1560-74 - Charles IX of France. 1560-78 - Mary, Queen of Scots; executed 1587. 1564-76 - *Maximilian II, Emperor*. 1574-89 - Henry III of France. 1576-1612 - *Rudolph II, Emperor*. 1588-1648 - Christian IV, King of Denmark. 1589-1610 - Henry IV of France; became Roman Catholic, 1593; murdered by Ravaillac, 1610, May 14. 1598-1621 - Philip III of Spain.	1558 - Disputes between old Lutherans (Gnesio-lutherani) and Melanch-thon's followers. 1560 - Death of Melanchthon, April 19. 1586-91 - Crypto-Calvinist troubles in Electoral Saxony; suppression of Calvinism; execution of Krells, 1601. The Lutheran Church loses to: (a) The Roman Catholic Church. 1558 - Bavaria. 1578 - The Austrian Duchy (Rudolph II). 1584 - The Bishoprics of Würzburg, Bamberg, Salzburg, Hildesheim, etc. 1594 - Steiermark, Carinthia (Ferdinand II). 1607 - Donauwerth. (b) The Reformed Church 1560 - The Palatinate; 1563, Heidelberg Catechism. Reformed under Frederick III; Lutheran under Louis VI, 1576-83; Reformed under Frederick IV, 1583-1610. 1568 - Bremen. 1596 - Anhalt (John George, 1587-1603); repeal of Consist Syst and Lutheran Catechism; 1597-1628, Calvinist Articles.	1589 - Henry III murdered by a League fanatic, J Clement, Aug 1. 1593 - Henry IV becomes a Roman Catholic. 1598 - EDICT OF NANTES: liberty of conscience; right of public worship; full civil privileges; cities given to the Huguenots as pledges. 1620-28 - Huguenot revolts. 1629 - La Rochelle taken. Edict of Nismes. *Ecclesiastical* rights guaranteed to the Huguenots. 1552 - *The 42 Articles*. [1554 - Cardinal Reginald Pole, Papal Legate; 1555-58, Bloody persecutions

CHRONOLOGICAL SUMMARY

Anglican Church	Roman Catholic Church	Protestant Theology
	1567 - Bull of excommunication against 79 Augustinian propositions of Michael Baius (d 1589) Chancellor of University of Louvain.	*Catechismus ecclesiæ Genevensis*; 1541, French; 1545, Latin; Calvin.
Isolation of the Church of England; no relation to the Papacy; no relation to the Reformed Churches.	1568 - *Breviarium*. 1570-*Missale Romanum*.	*Consensio in re sacramentaria ministrorum Tigur Eccles et John Calvini.*
1547 - Under Lord Protector Somerset; Peter Martyr Vermigli (b 1500 at Florence; 1542, at Strasburg; d 1562, in Zurich) and Bernard Ochino (b 1487) brought to Oxford; Martin Bucer and Paul Fagius, to Cambridge.	1572-85 - Gregory XIII: congratulatory letter to Charles IX about Massacre of St Bartholomew; *Te Deum* at Rome in honour of event. 1582 - Reform of Calendar. 1582-1610 - Jesuit missions in China.	**The Heidelberg Catechism**: 1563, written at the suggestion of Frederick III of the Palatinate by Zachary Ursinius (from 1561 Prof at Heidelburg; d 1583) and Caspar Olevianus (Prof at Heidelberg; d 1587). *Confessio Helvetica Posterior*: 1566, sent by Bullinger to Frederick III of the Palatinate.
The Book of Homilies. 1548 - The Book of Common Prayer; revised 1552.	1585-90 - Sixtus V: Vatican Library. 1588 - Baronius's *Eccl Annales*. 1590 - Infallible edition of the Vulgate. 1592-1605 - Clement VII. 1592 - New edition of Vulgate (declared to be the edition of Sixtus V).	*The Decrees of the Synod of Dort*: 1619, recognised in the Netherlands, Switzerland, the Palatinate, and in 1620 in France; not universally recognised.

CHRONOLOGICAL SUMMARY

Contemporary Events	Lutheran Church	Anglican Church
	The Lutheran Church loses to the Reformed Church - 1605 - Hesse-Cassel reformed, under Landgrave Maurice (1592-1627).	under Mary; 1556, Mar 21, Cranmer burnt at Oxford]
	1613 - Dec 25, Brandenburg reformed under the Elector John Sigismund; 1614, *Confessio Marchica.*	*Reformation restored under Elizabeth.*
		1559 - June: Act of Uniformity, Matthew Parker, Archbishop of Canterbury.
	———	Book of Common Prayer revised and restored.
	Anti-Trinitarians	1562 - Jan 23, The 39 Articles: Calvinist doctrine of Predestination; Doctrine of Lord's Supper, Calvinist.
	Michael Servetus from Aragon; 1530, in Basel; 1531, *De Trinitatis erroribus*; 1534, in Lyons; 1537, in Paris; 1540, in Vienne; 1553, *Christianismi restitutio*; burnt at Geneva, 1553.	
	Valentinus Gentilis, from Calabria; beheaded at Berne, 1556.	1567 - Puritans against Uniformity [Puritanism; Reformation from within through the Church community; in England strict acceptance of

Reformed Church		Protestant Theology
Scotland	*The Nertherlands*	JOHN CALVIN: **Institutio R e l i g i o n i s Christianæ**, 1535-36. Three editions, each an enlargement, 1535, 1539 (-43-45), 1559; *Commentaries* on O T and N T from 1539; *De æterna Dei predestinatione*, 1552; *Defensio orthodoxæ fidei de S Trinitate*, 1554, against Servetus.
1558 - Lords of the Congregation; Pure Gospel; King Edward's Prayer-Book.	1559 - Margaret of Parma Stadtholder; Granvella, Bp of Arras. Erection of 13 new bishoprics; Inquisition.	
1560 - Meeting of Estates at Edinburgh; *Scotch Confession*; First Book of Discipline; Presbyterian Government by General Assemblies, Synods, and Kirk-Sessions; Superintendents.	1562 - *Confessio Belgica*; Guido de Brès, Adrien de Savaria, H Modetus, G Wingen; revised by Francis Junius, 1571.	
	1566 - Compromise in favour of Protestants. Riots about images and relics.	*Henry Bullinger*, Zwingli's successor in Zurich, b 1504, at Bremgarten, d 1578, Sept 17; Commentaries on the whole N T, 1554; *Compendium relig Christianæ*; *Histoire des persecutions de l'Eglise*.
John Knox: b 1505, at Haddington; from 1546, preacher in St Andrews; 1547-49, in the galleys; 1553-59, at Frankfort and Geneva; 1559 - d 1574, in Edinburgh.	1567-73 - Duke of Alva. Council of Blood; Persecution of Protestants; 18,000 slain; Egmont and Horn in 1568.	*Theodore Beza*: b 1519; 1549, in Lausanne; 1558, Professor and pastor in Geneva; d 1605. N T translation with annotations, 1565; *Histoire Eccles des réformateurs au royaume de France*, 1580.

CHRONOLOGICAL SUMMARY

Contemporary Events	Lutheran Church	Anglican Church
	Laelius Socinus: b 1525, at Siena; 1546, in Venice; 1547, travels in Switzerland, Gemany, and Poland; d 1562 in Zurich.	the spiritual priesthood of all believers, and consequent objection to clerical vestments, cope, and surplice.]
		1570 - Thomas Cartwright expelled from Cambridge.
	Faustus Socinus: b 1539, at Siena; 1559, in Lyons; 1562, in Zurich; at Florence, then Basel, 1574-78; in Poland, 1579-98; d 1604 - De Jesu Christo servatore; De Statu primi hominis ante lapsum, 1578.	1582 - Robert Browne, chaplain to the Duke of Norfolk: no union between Church and State; each congregation an *independent* church. From 1589 in England.
	1605 - Racovian Catechism.	

CHRONOLOGICAL SUMMARY

Reformed Church		Protestant Theology
1572 - Convention of Leith; Bishops, but without episcopal functions; Tulchans.	1572 - Capture of Brill by the Sea-Beggars; William of Orange.	*Rudolph Hospinian*, pastor in Zurich; d 1629; *De origine et progres controv. sacramentariæ*, etc.
1576 - Government by visitors appointed by the Assembly.	1576 - Nov 8, Treaty of Ghent.	
1578 - Second Book of Discipline.	1579 - Jan 23, Utrecht, Union of Northern Provinces; July 26, Declaration of Independence.	*J H Hottinger*, Professor in Heidelburg and Zurich; d 1667; *Hist Eccl NT*.
1580 - Government by Presbyteries.	1584 - July 10, William of Orange murdered; Maurice of Orange succeeds.	*Caspar Suicer*, Professor in Zurich; d 1684; *Thesaurus Ecclesiasticus*.
	Foundation of Universities - Leyden, 1575; Franecker, 1585; Gröningen, 1612; Utrecht, 1638; Harderwyk, 1648.	*J Dallæus*, Prof at Saumur, d at Paris, 1670; *Traité de l'emplois des S Pères*, 1632.